# 40
Ways to Look at
# BRIGHAM
# YOUNG

A New Approach to a Remarkable Man

D1051266

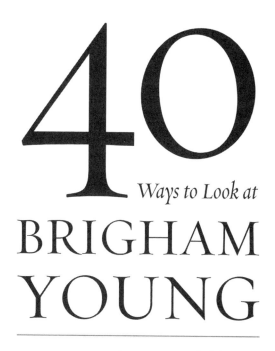

# 40

*Ways to Look at*

# BRIGHAM
# YOUNG

*A New Approach to a Remarkable Man*

## CHAD M. ORTON
### AND WILLIAM W. SLAUGHTER

DESERET
BOOK

Salt Lake City, Utah

Library of Congress Cataloging-in-Publication Data

Orton, Chad M.
  40 ways to look at Brigham Young : a new approach to a remarkable man
  Chad M. Orton and William W. Slaughter.
      p.   cm.
  Includes bibliographical references and index.
  ISBN 978-1-59038-786-3 (paperbound)
  1.   Young, Brigham, 1801-1877.   2.   Church of Jesus Christ of Latter-day
Saints—Presidents—Biography.   3. Mormon Church—Presidents—Biography.
  I. Slaughter, William W., 1952–    II. Title.   III. Title: Forty ways to look at Brigham Young.
  BX8695.Y7O78 2008
  289.3092—dc22
  [B]                                                                              2008012525

Printed in the United States of America
Publishers Printing, Salt Lake City, UT

10   9   8   7   6   5   4   3   2   1

# CONTENTS

# CONTENTS

# ILLUSTRATIONS

Birthplace of Brigham Young, Whitingham, Vermont, 1913, p. 7
Camp Meeting during the Great Awakening, ca. 1829, p. 12
Engraving of Brigham Young, ca. 1855, p. 60
Brigham Young travels through Utah, p. 67
Brigham Young, ca. 1855, p. 75
First view of the Great Salt Lake Valley, p. 82
Indians in front of ZCMI, Main Street, Salt Lake City, 1869, p. 89
Salt Lake City, ca. 1865, p. 96
Mormon pioneers on the plains, 1866, p. 103
Brigham Young's Lion House and Beehive House, Salt Lake City, ca. 1855, p. 118
Brigham and Mary Ann Angell Young with their children, 1845–51, p. 130

*Photo section following page 130:*
  1. Brigham Young, ca. 1846
  2. Brigham Young, 1850
  3. Brigham Young, ca. 1852
  4. Mary Ann Angell Young, ca. 1853, wife of Brigham Young
  5. Brigham Young, ca. 1855
  6. Brigham Young, ca. 1856

# ACKNOWLEDGMENTS

We have been fortunate to be able to stand on the shoulders of previous historians and scholars, whose efforts have allowed us to look at Brigham from a new perspective. Of particular help were works by James B. Allen, Thomas G. Alexander, Leonard J. Arrington, Milton V. Backman, Davis Bitton, Susan Easton Black, Eugene England, Ronald K. Esplin, Susa Young Gates, William G. Hartley, Richard Neitzel Holzapfel, Gordon I. Irving, Dean C. Jessee, Jeffery O. Johnson, Brian and Petrea Kelly, Susan Arrington Madsen, Hugh Nibley, Preston Nibley, Larry Porter, B. H. Roberts, Kristen Rogers, R. Q. Shupe, Clarissa Young Spencer, Ronald W. Walker, and Elden J. Watson. We acknowledge Gretchen Rubin for a great idea on how to write a biography, one that seemed tailor-made for looking at a complex individual such as Brigham Young.

We have also been greatly aided by the support of colleagues, friends, and associates who listened, gave encouragement, and provided needed assistance. This group includes Mark Ashurst-McGee, Ronald O. Barney, Melvin L. Bashore, Christy Best, Jay G. Burrup, Debra Cheney, Heidie Davis,

## ACKNOWLEDGMENTS

W. Randall Dixon, Marie Erickson, Chad O. Foulger, Sharalyn Howcroft, Leigh Hutchingson, Michael N. Landon, Christine Marin, Alison Miles, Pauline Musig, Carl E. Olsen, Ardis Parshall, Ronald Reed, Brian D. Reeves, Kari K. Robinson, Glenn N. Rowe, Jenny St. Clair, Larry Skidmore, Richard E. Turley Jr., Ronald G. Watt, April Williamson, and Fred E. Woods.

We appreciate the assistance of Laurie Cook, Richard Erickson, Tonya Facemyer, Derk Koldewyn, Lisa Mangum, Cory Maxwell, Jay Parry, Anne Sheffield, and Sheryl Dickert Smith of Deseret Book in shepherding the publication of this volume.

We reserve our greatest debt of gratitude for our families. Thanks to Elizabeth, Amy, Laura, Spencer, Taylor, Jane, Louisa, and Bryce Orton, and Sheri, Danielle, and Wes Slaughter for their untiring love and support.

# INTRODUCTION

I f Brigham Young is not the most misunderstood individual on the lists of the 100 greatest and most influential Americans, he likely has been the most maligned. While he is more favorably viewed now than during his lifetime—as evidenced by the fact that he is included in these lists—in many regards he remains as enigmatic and vilified in death as he was in life. Few people have had so much written about them while remaining so little understood.

One reason for the confusion is the many different hats Brigham wore—prophet, colonizer, businessman, governor, superintendent of Indian affairs, and family patriarch, to name a few. Traditional biographies, which largely recount accomplishments and activities in a chronological way, can do as much to hide a man of such complexity as to reveal him. We know the offices and positions he held, but the real face often remains hidden in the shadows of the hats. While we can know something about an individual by his offices and positions, knowing *why* and *how* he did what he did helps us to better understand the *what, when,* and *where*.

Much of what has long been generally believed about Brigham has its origins in newspaper accounts penned by reporters with more or less well-publicized agendas and in deliberately crafted "tell all" works about him. These reporters, newspaper editors, and authors knew that Brigham made "good copy" and were not shy about presenting the Brigham they wanted the public to see. While many who wrote about him were motivated only by money, others were driven by a belief that if they could destroy him, they would end Mormonism and its hated institution of polygamy. As a result, Brigham was the subject of an unfailing river of ridicule and condemnation.

If the stories about Brigham in the national press of the day and in tell-all books are true, no other public figure in U.S. history has so successfully led a double life as Brigham. Either those who personally knew him were duped into believing he was a caring and loving individual, although regularly hard-spoken, or he has been the victim of innuendo, distortion, and half truths rivaling the Salem witch-hunts and McCarthyism. Visitors to Utah who met Brigham regularly noted their shock to discover that he was not the vile, controlling man popularly portrayed.

When it comes to the confusion surrounding Brigham, at times he could be his own worst enemy. Although he was regularly afforded only a sound bite, typically taken out of context, he saw no reason to tone down his frequently fiery rhetoric. He also concluded early on that it would be nearly impossible to change the court of public opinion, given what was being said about him and the Mormons, and determined he would seldom respond to false charges, vindictive distortions, and rumors. He noted in 1855: "I am often made aware of the utter uselessness and folly of seeking to vindicate my character . . . from the simple fact that although the foul aspersions can be bruited far and wide, held to the fluttering breeze by every press and rolled as sweet under every tongue yet when the vile slander is fairly refuted and truth appears in the most incontestible manner it is permitted to lie quietly upon the shelf in slumber the sleep of death or if by chance it should get published in some obscure nook or corner of this great republic be most religiously suppressed as tho in fear that the truth should be known and believed."[1]

While Brigham believed the truth was on his side and time would exonerate him, his approach allowed the one-sided view of him as a less-than-saintly individual to largely spread unchallenged outside Utah. As might be expected, it became the prevailing view during his lifetime. It is not surprising, then, that the American public of his day, largely removed from Brigham by both geography and sympathy, could not fully comprehend such a complex man and would readily believe the stories they were told. What is surprising is that people today, who have greater access to Brigham through both his personal papers and growing historical research, still continue to largely rely upon the hostile nineteenth-century press to understand him. Others have chosen to ignore Brigham in his entirety, treating him as if he were simply a cafeteria from which they were free to choose what food they wanted to digest, such as selecting some of his more blistering oratory to represent the "real" individual.

One of the ironies of trying to understand Brigham is that some scholars have decreed that an "honest" history of Brigham requires a near-unquestioned homage to the oft-told stories of the hostile press, tell-all authors, and cafeteria diners. These people have denounced those who have dared examine the validity of the claims as dishonest historians and branded their scholarship poor. John F. Kennedy could have been talking about this attitude when he stated: "The great enemy of truth is very often not the lie—deliberate, contrived and dishonest—but the myth—persistent, persuasive, and unrealistic. Too often we hold fast to the cliches of our forebears. We subject all facts to a prefabricated set of interpretations. We enjoy the comfort of opinion without the discomfort of thought."[2]

While histories of Brigham have provided valuable insights into the man, they are an uneven, often contradictory mix that have frequently created or preserved stereotypes and myths. The result is an individual whose very name can cause polarization. These histories range from terrifying portrayals of a dictatorial, lecherous tyrant to that of a prominent Western figure where polygamy is barely mentioned. Like the blind men and the elephant, those who read a specific work may think they have hold of the whole animal, but the image they encounter may bear little resemblance to the real Brigham.

The more one looks at him as an individual, the more the incorrect stereotypes melt away. Given the controversy that continues to surround him, the question of who Brigham Young really is requires a new look.

Why "forty ways"? Historically, the number forty was used to represent "a lot," much like "a million" is used today.[3] While forty ways to look at Brigham is "a lot," such a number only begins to scratch the surface of this truly complex and remarkable individual. Others, no doubt, will have different opinions as to what "forty ways" should have been included.

One thing that is clear, however, is that Brigham might be called a late bloomer. For thirty years he was like most of his fellow Americans. He largely thought of himself as having little future outside of eking out a meager existence to support his young family. While his work as a craftsman showed ability—his monuments were well-made furniture, something that he took pride in—he felt that there was something more. Like so many of his contemporaries, he had largely lost hope for the better life he desired. He couldn't fully taste life's sweetness because of a sour taste in his mouth. When he finally encountered the restored gospel, he discovered the better life he sought—and more. "'Mormonism' has done everything for me that ever has been done for me on the earth," he proclaimed. "It has made me happy, it has made me wealthy and comfortable; it has filled me with good feelings, with joy and rejoicing. Whereas before I possessed the spirit of the Gospel, I was troubled with that which I hear others complain of . . . at times, feeling cast down, gloomy and desponding."[4] He also found in Mormonism a key that unleashed the torrent locked inside him. He started to roar like a lion and act like one as well.

To understand Brigham is to understand his religious quest. Although many have attributed other motives to him, his oft-stated desire was to build the kingdom. "Our constant desire, should be to know how to build up the kingdom of God," he wrote.[5] Brigham believed that serving the Lord was a way of life, not just a matter of praying and attending meeting: "We can also serve Him in a life of usefulness, honesty and sobriety, remembering that it should be the object of our existence here that when we leave the world it will be a little better for our presence and our labors."[6] "All of our time, all of our ability and all of our means belong to Him. It is not the privilege of any person to spend his time in a way that does no good to himself nor his neighbours."[7]

Brigham possessed the ability through word and deed to inspire in those who knew him both a faith in God and the courage to be better individuals and to build a kingdom that had not been known before. While tenaciously holding onto revealed principles and practices, he readily adopted new programs and technology to build the kingdom. Given his prophetic call, his unique skills, and his firm conviction in the all-encompassing aspects of the kingdom, it was natural that he was at the center of so much that transpired. His belief that the kingdom encompassed all aspects of life and that everything belonged to the kingdom was not without controversy, however, as some people have long mistakenly believed that he undertook to enrich himself at the expense of his followers.

As an individual, Brigham combined to a remarkable degree practical, spiritual, and aesthetic characteristics seldom found in one man. He was a loving father, husband, and friend. The Saints also viewed him as a father figure, regularly asking his advice on a wide range of problems, and expressed their love in the inclusive term "Brother Brigham." While he was warm and fallible, he never lost sight of the fact that there was an ongoing battle between the Lord's kingdom and that of the devil, and he never forgot that he had the responsibility to raise a warning voice as a prophet of God.

Few people have spoken their minds more frankly and freely. A powerful speaker, he conveyed his feelings on a wide variety of subjects in a vigorous, beautiful, forthright, and often humorous style—without written notes. His sermons were presented in an effective homespun style and show a remarkable range of insight, fluency, and candor. Many have dismissed what he said if they disapproved of it, justifying their position by the popular claim that you could find Brigham taking opposite positions on the same subject. In reality, when his statements are viewed in context, he was very consistent and rational.

While Brigham is often portrayed as a controlling individual, his sermons and actions often suggest otherwise. He used the pulpit primarily to teach the Saints how to be self-governing, not to control them. He once recounted the story of a woman who requested a blessing from a man that Brigham described as "one of those tenacious, ignorant, self-willed, over-righteous Elders." Upon reaching her house, the man "saw a tea-pot on the coals, and supposed that there was tea in it, and immediately turned upon his heels, saying, 'God don't want me to lay hands on those who do not keep the Word of Wisdom.'" Brigham noted that the man did not know what the pot actually contained and "did not wait for any one to tell him. That class of people are ignorant and over-righteous, and they are not in the true line by any means."[8]

Although Brigham had weaknesses, he seldom publicly dwelt on them. He believed that "if you committed sin that no other person on earth knows of, and which harms no other one, you have done a wrong and you have sinned against your God, but keep that within your own bosom, and seek to God and confess there, and get pardon for your sin—confess your sins to whomsoever you have sinned against and let it stop there."[9] Concerning his humanness, he declared: "I am subject to temptation and am as liable to do wrong as any other man. . . . I am never at a loss to know what is right, but sometimes I do not think or I am not guarded against the Tempter."[10]

Brigham had a hard time guarding against two faults—his tongue and temper. "I will say there is not a man in this house who has a more indomitable and unyielding temper than myself," he admitted.[11] "If you find that you cannot keep your tongue still, get some India-rubber and chew it with all your might. . . . When you feel as though you would burst, tell the old boiler to burst, and just laugh at the temptation to speak evil."[12] With troops marching against the Saints during the Utah War, he counseled, "Do not get so angry that you cannot pray; do not get so angry that you cannot feed an enemy—even your worst enemy; if an opportunity should present itself."[13]

While he generally controlled his natural tendency to contend and get angry, he was not always able to adhere to his own advice. Occasionally what he called the "unnatural man" in him came out. "Never in the days of my life, have I hurt a man with the palm of my hand. I never have hurt a person any other way except with this unruly member, my tongue."[14] A number of people, both friends and enemies, knew the sharpness of this "unruly member." Emma Lucy overheard her father dressing down a stable hand for allowing a fine saddle to get trampled in the dirt. She then secretly followed Brigham as he stormed back to the house. Eavesdropping outside his room, she heard him say, "Down on your knees, Brigham! Get down on your knees!"[15] After publicly rebuking bishop Edwin Woolley, Brigham stated, "Now I don't want Brother W[oolley] to apostatise from the Church because I have said what I have." "Don't worry, Brother Brigham," Woolley replied, "this is just as much my Church as it is yours."[16] The response elicited an appropriate laugh from Brigham. Not everyone, however, accepted his rebukes so well.

Brigham was also not immune from either the prejudices or the coarse language of the day. Not everything he tried worked. He made mistakes. Many have concluded that one such error was not taking time away from Church matters after returning to Nauvoo following the martyrdom to pay a timely visit to Emma Smith, the widow of his dear friend Joseph—a fact which may have contributed to her alienation from the main body of the Mormons. Brigham was also unschooled, even by the standards of the day—a fact readily evident in his spelling—but he gained great knowledge by both study and faith.

For a dozen years Brigham was a faithful student and close friend of the Prophet Joseph, who had taught him how to be the leader of the Lord's church. Following Joseph's death, Brigham understood that the keys held by the apostles not only authorized them to preside but demanded that they push forward to carry on the work begun by Joseph. Without Brigham's forceful personality, the Church might not have survived the martyrdom as it did. While long considered an American Moses for leading a unique western exodus, he might also be viewed as an American Joshua since he was able to enter the Saints' promised land and oversaw its settlement for thirty years.

One visitor to Utah concluded after hearing Brigham speak that if the Mormon prophet could indeed elevate "the descendants of his people to the high standards of moral, mental, and physical development which he says they are destined to attain, his posterity may justly associate his name with the most stupendous miracle the world has ever witnessed."[17] Historian Edward Tullidge wrote of Brigham in 1876: "Seldom does it fall to the lot of rulers to sway the scepter so long; still less seldom to keep up in their lives such an unwearied sensation. . . . View the man as we may, Brigham Young is an enduring name."[18] George Q. Cannon believed that "posterity will yet do him justice which those who now live have refused him, and in the annals of the Church his Presidency will be pointed to as a remarkable epoch."[19] That day has not yet fully arrived.

# A LIFE OF QUIET DESPERATION

*The Early Years*

T he mass of men," David Henry Thoreau wrote in his classic *Walden,* "lead lives of quiet desperation. What is called resignation is confirmed desperation."[1] Thoreau's conclusion largely summarizes the first thirty years of one of his contemporaries—Brigham Young—an individual now widely recognized as one of the giants of both the nineteenth century and American history.

Like so many great men of his day, Brigham emerged from humble beginnings. His rise to prominence, however, occurred later in life than was the case with many of his fellow luminaries. Born into poverty, his economic status had improved only slightly three decades later. In spite of having developed locally a reputation as a gifted carpenter and craftsman, he continued to eke out a meager existence. While he was like the majority of Americans of his day in terms of his economic struggles, he differed from most of his contemporaries in the fact that his despair grew not from his daily toil and drudgery but from a gnawing feeling that there was more to life than trying to break the cycle of birth, a hard existence, and death. Summarizing his life he later recalled that he "sought for riches, but in vain; there was something that always kept telling me that happiness originated in higher pursuits."[2] Although raised in a religious home, he found little satisfaction and few meaningful answers in religion. While the woods ultimately provided Thoreau the answer, Brigham, who had a young family to support, was left to simply push forward and hope that someday the fog of desperation that encircled him would evaporate.

The ninth of John and Abigail (Nabby) Howe Young's eleven children, Brigham was born June 1, 1801, at Whitingham, Windham, Vermont, in a modest log cabin built by his father after he had moved his family from Massachusetts earlier in the year. His father, described as a "small, nimble, wiry man," was an orphan when he ran away from abusive guardians at the age of sixteen to join the Continental Army. He served under General George Washington during the last years of the Revolutionary War and participated in three campaigns. Brigham's mother, portrayed as having a "doll-like face, blue eyes, and yellowish brown hair folded in natural waves and ringlets," came from more prosperous circumstances. Her relatives included Eli Howe Jr., who invented the sewing machine, and Julia Ward Howe, who authored "The Battle Hymn of the Republic." Although Nabby's parents thought her foolish to marry "the little orphan" with an uncertain future, on October 31, 1785, John and Nabby were married.[3]

Their life was typical of the average American of the early 1800s. John, an itinerant farmer, frequently moved his family in pursuit of better opportunities, which always seemed to be out of reach. "My father was a poor, honest, hard-working man," Brigham recalled. "His mind seemingly stretched from east to west, from north to south; and to the day of his death he wanted to command worlds; but the Lord would never permit him to get rich."[4] Brigham later remembered that during his early life he regularly lacked food and clothes. He used to work "logging and driving team, summer and winter, not half clad, and with insufficient food until my stomach would ache."[5] On another occasion he reported: "In my youthful days, instead of going to school, I had to chop logs, to sow and plant, to plow in the midst of roots barefooted, and if I had on a pair of pants that would cover me I did pretty well."[6] When he finally obtained a pair of shoes, he used them only on Sundays. To make them last, he walked to his meetings barefoot, put on his shoes for the service, and then removed them before walking home.

Brigham characterized his father and grandfather as "some of the most strict religionists that lived upon the earth."[7] His mother, also religiously devout, had a gentle temperament that was a balance to her husband, whose disciplinary style Brigham described as "a word and a blow, . . . but the blow came first."[8] Concerning his religious training, Brigham noted: "I was brought up so strict, so firm in the faith of the Christian religion by my parents, that if I had said 'Devil,' I believed I had sworn very wickedly. . . . If I used the name of Devil, I should have certainly been chastised, and that severely."[9] He further recalled that his mother "taught her children all the time to honour the name of the Father and the Son, and to reverence the holy Book. She said, Read it, observe its precepts, and apply them to your lives as far as you can: do every thing that is good; do nothing that is evil; and if you see any persons in distress, administer to their wants: never suffer anger to arise in your bosoms; for, if you do, you may be overcome by evil. . . . Never did my mother or father countenance any of their children in anything to wrong their neighbour or fellow-being, even if they were injured by them."[10]

In the three years that the Youngs lived in southern Vermont, struggling to coax an existence out of the rocky New England soil, John tried to establish four farms in the vicinity of Whitingham. Finally, in the spring of 1804, he moved his family west to Sherburne (later renamed Smyrna), Chenango County, New York, where land was reportedly better. Here the family remained until Brigham's thirteenth year. "At an early age I labored with my father, assisting him to clear off new land and cultivate his farm, passing through many hardships and privations incident to settling in a new country."[11] In addition to helping his father clear the family's own land, Brigham, along with his brothers, hired out to help others clear their land in exchange for badly needed products and supplies. "I used to have the privilege of cutting down the hemlock, beech and maple trees . . . and then rolling them together, burning the logs, splitting the rails, and fencing the little fields," he recalled.[12] His endeavors at "picking up brush, chopping down trees, rolling logs, and working amongst the roots" regularly resulted in bruised "shins, feet, and toes."[13]

Because Brigham had little opportunity for formal education—by his own account, only eleven days—his surroundings and responsibilities became his textbooks. He studied these as judiciously as any dedicated student. In addition to his labors in the field, he also helped with the household chores. His mother had contracted tuberculosis before he was born and over time her health wouldn't allow her to perform many of the labors around the home. He frequently braided for himself the straw hats that protected him from the summer sun. He also "learned to make bread, wash the dishes, milk the cows, and make butter. . . . Those are about all the advantages I gained in my youth."[14] Thus, from an early age Brigham learned how to be both independent and self-sufficient.

Brigham's daughter, Susa Young Gates, wrote that her father's childhood was "marked by plain living and high thinking."[15] Nabby Young tried to teach her children culture, manners, and proper behavior. Brigham stated: "Of my mother—she that bore me—I can say, no better woman ever lived in the world than she was. I have the feelings of a son towards her: I should have them—it is right; but I judge the matter pertaining to her from the principles and the spirit of the teachings I received from her. Would she countenance one of her children in the least act that was wrong according to her traditions? No, not in the least degree," he proclaimed.[16]

In the winter of 1813, John Young again moved his family, this time fifty miles to the west. "Shortly after the commencement of the late war with Great Britain," Brigham wrote, "my father and family removed to the town of Genoa, Cayuga County, New York."[17] It was at Genoa, shortly after Brigham's fourteenth birthday, that Nabby's tuberculosis finally took her life. Following her death on June 11, 1815, the family was split apart. Some of Brigham's brothers and sisters were "farmed out" to relatives, while John

Young sought a new location for Brigham and the children who remained with him.

Leaving behind the Genoa farm with its hard-won improvements, John Young moved thirty-five miles west in Steuben County. The area was considered "the Far West" because of its dense wilderness and few settlers. John Young made his living gathering maple syrup, which Brigham would haul on his back to the nearest settlement, reportedly fifteen miles away, to trade for flour. On one occasion when the family was virtually without flour, Brigham killed a robin with his father's musket and made a stew.

In 1817, John Young remarried, further splitting up the family. Brigham reported that "when I was sixteen years of age, my father said to me, 'You can now have your time; go and provide for yourself.'"[18] Moving to the nearby town of Auburn, he initially worked odd jobs for room and board. Eventually he was apprenticed to a cabinetmaker, painter, and chair manufacturer, and a career was launched. Brigham worked hard to become a skilled artisan and developed a reputation as such.

From Auburn, Brigham moved eight miles north to Port Byron, situated on the Erie Canal. There he worked repairing chairs, building boats for use on the canal, and manufacturing wooden pails. After he created a system for mixing paint to be used on the pails, he was promoted from painter to carpenter. He began to produce tables, chairs, settees, cupboards, mantels, and doors. When he learned years later that one of the chairs he had built a half century earlier was going to be put on display, Brigham wrote: "I have no doubt that many other pieces of furniture and other specimens of my handiwork can be found scattered about your section of the Country, for I have believed all my life that, that which was worth doing was worth doing well, and have considered it as much a part of my religion to do honest, reliable work, such as would endure, for those who employed me, as to attend to the services of God's worship on the Sabbath."[19]

While at Port Byron, Brigham met Miriam Angeline Works, described as "a beautiful blonde, with blue eyes, a finely chiselled face and wavy hair. She possessed a gentle, uncomplaining spirit and was in every way most lovable."[20] On October 5, 1824, twenty-three-year-old Brigham and eighteen-year-old Miriam married. The following September the couple's first daughter, Elizabeth, was born.

In 1828 Brigham and Miriam moved to Oswego, New York, on the shores of Lake Ontario, where he helped build a large tannery. The following year they moved to Mendon, situated sixty miles to the southwest, where several of Brigham's brothers and sisters had previously gathered. Concerning the one-room home Brigham established at Mendon, one visitor recalled: "His house and shop stood some 80 rods from the highway, nothing but a footpath led to it. . . . I followed the path which lay along the side of a beautiful little stream of clear water noted for the speckled trout it contained. A dam had been thrown across this stream and a sufficient water power obtained to run a turning lathe in his shop."[21]

On June 1, 1830, Brigham's twenty-ninth birthday, Miriam gave birth to the couple's second daughter, Vilate. In spite of this joyous event, as Brigham entered his thirtieth year the family's future was not particularly bright. Shortly after moving to Mendon, Miriam had contracted tuberculosis, the same debilitating illness that had claimed Brigham's mother's life. Soon Brigham was forced to spend more and more time caring for her and the children. As a result, he spent less and less time making a living and his debts began to accrue. Brigham's friend, Heber C. Kimball, recalled that the Youngs "were in low circumstances and seemed to be an afflicted people in consequence of having a great deal of sickness and sorrow to pass through; and of course were looked down upon—by the flourishing church where we lived."[22]

The great nineteenth-century American poet Oliver Wendell Holmes wrote about those who "die with all their music in them!":

> Nay, grieve not for the dead alone
> Whose song has told their hearts' sad story,—
> Weep for the voiceless, who have known
> The cross without the crown of glory![23]

In the summer of 1830, as Brigham entered his thirtieth year, his future looked bleak. Unless he was able to find the real happiness of "higher pursuits" that he pined for, Holmes seemed to be describing his fate.

*Birthplace of Brigham Young, Whitingham, Vermont, 1913*

## ❧ 2 ❧

# RELIGIOUS SEEKER
# AND CONVERT

lthough the exact date in April 1832 *when* Brigham was baptized a
member of The Church of Jesus Christ of Latter-day Saints is
unclear, there is no question as to *why* he embraced Mormonism.
In a small diary, he recorded "Apriel 9th 1832[.] I was baptized under the hand
of Elezer [Eleazer] Miller."[1] In 1862, however, Brigham stated, "It is thirty
years the 15th day of next April (though it has accidentally been recorded
and printed the fourteenth) since I was baptized into this Church."[2] As far as
his decision to be baptized, he would unequivocally proclaim: "I did not
embrace Mormonism because I hoped it was true, but because I knew it was
that principle that would save all the human family, that would obey it. . . .
Joseph Smith lived and died a prophet."[3] "This I know by the revelations of
Jesus Christ to me, and by the testimony of the Holy Ghost. Had I not so
learned the truth, I should never have been what is called a 'Mormon.'"[4]
Summarizing his life as a religious seeker, Brigham later stated that there
was "more or less of a gloom over my feelings from the earliest days of my

childhood . . . until I heard the everlasting Gospel declared by the servants of God."[5]

While John and Nabby Young taught their children to revere the Bible and to render good for evil, this training was within the confines of a narrow religious upbringing. "I was kept within very strict bounds, and was not allowed to walk more than half-an-hour on Sunday for exercise," Brigham recalled. "The proper and necessary gambols of youth [were] denied me."[6] From his study of the Bible, however, Brigham became convinced that religion should fill people with hope and happiness. Not only was this lacking in his own religious experiences, but he noted that many church-going people carried sad countenances and long faces. Equally troubling was the fact that people who attended church on Sunday seemed to have no problem cheating their neighbors in business dealings during the week. For Brigham, religion was to be an everyday way of life, not simply a set of unused moral values. As a result, he later noted, he spent "many anxious hours" searching for a religion that could fulfill him.[7] "I would have given worlds if I could have known the truth in my childhood," he declared.[8]

As a teenager in western New York, Brigham experienced the same religious upheavals that troubled Joseph Smith. He attended a number of religious meetings, but, like Joseph, he was unsatisfied in his quest for the truth. "I was . . . more or less acquainted with almost every other religious ism," he recalled, but "as I became acquainted with smart, intelligent, literary priests and professors of religion, I thought, Now I can obtain some intelligence from this or from that man; and I would begin to ask questions on certain texts of Scripture; but they would always leave me as they found me, in the dark."[9]

After listening to the renowned Methodist preacher Lorenzo Dow (for whom one of Brigham's brothers was named) lecture for "two or three hours," Brigham found himself asking, "'What have you learned from Lorenzo Dow?' and my answer was, 'Nothing, nothing but morals.'"[10] His growing dissatisfaction with traditional Christianity led him to conclude, "I would as lief [leave] go into a swamp at midnight to learn how to paint a picture, and then define its colors when there is neither moon nor stars visible and profound darkness prevails, as to go to the religious world to learn about God, heaven, hell or the faith of a Christian."[11] He desired to be taught not by a preacher of morals only, but by a prophet who possessed both the knowledge and power of heaven.

Ultimately, his inability to satisfy his intense religious yearnings caused him to feel "cast down, gloomy, and desponding." Everything seemed to wear "a dreary aspect," causing even the most beautiful scenes to be shrouded with "a shade of death."[12] Lacking what others considered an appropriate outward piety, he was labeled a nonbeliever. "Christians called me an infidel," he reported, "because I could not swallow [their doctrines and practices] . . . but I could not if they had been greased over with fresh butter. I did not read the Bible as they read it."[13] Eventually, he unenthusiastically became a Methodist like his parents.

Brigham had heard and read a "great many stories and reports" concerning the Book of Mormon before he was given a copy to look at by his brother Phineas.[14] Given his experiences with religion, it is not surprising that he approached his study of Mormonism without great expectations. "When I undertook to sound the doctrine of 'Mormonism,'" he admitted, "I supposed I could handle it as I could Methodist, Presbyterian, and other creeds of Christendom." His view soon changed. "I found it impossible to take hold of either end of it; I found it was from eternity, passed through time, and into eternity again. When I discovered this, I said, 'It is worthy of the notice of man.'"[15] Nevertheless, Brigham did not want to rush in and make a mistake about something so important to his earthly life and eternal salvation. From the time he received a copy of the Book of Mormon in the summer of 1830 around the time of his twenty-ninth birthday, he spent nearly two years deliberately studying Mormonism, reflecting on it teachings, and comparing its doctrines to the Bible. During this time he wrestled with each question and doubt and looked at it from all sides. Concerning his initial approach to Mormonism, he later noted: "'Wait a little while; what is the doctrine of the book, and of the revelations the Lord has given? Let me apply my heart to them;' and after I had done this, I considered it to be my right to know for myself, as much as any man on earth."[16]

However, it was not his study of the Book of Mormon and Mormon doctrine alone that led to his decision to be baptized. Ultimately, he reported, it was the pure and simple testimony of a common man, whose "testimony was like fire in my bones." He recalled that he "could easily out-talk" "the brethren who came to preach the Gospel to me."[17] But "if all the talent, tact, wisdom, and refinement of the world had been sent to me with the Book of Mormon, and had declared, in the most exalted of earthly eloquence, the truth of it, undertaking to prove it by learning and worldly wisdom, they would have been to me like the smoke which arises only to vanish away." However, it was only after he "saw a man without eloquence, or talents for public speaking, who could only say, 'I know, by the power of the Holy Ghost, that the Book of Mormon is true, that Joseph Smith is a Prophet of the Lord,'" that Brigham determined to be baptized. "The Holy Ghost proceeding from the individual illuminated my understanding, and light, glory, and immortality were before me. I was encircled by them, filled with them, and I knew for myself that the testimony of the man was true."[18] Moved by his testimony, Brigham pushed aside all doubts and planted his feet firmly on a new course.

Prior to his baptism in his own millstream, Brigham pondered what effect his conversion might have on family and friends. He concluded that Mormonism was worth the possible loss of both. While his new religion did indeed cost him friends, it did not cost him his family. "My father and stepmother embraced the plan of salvation as revealed through Joseph the Prophet; and four of my brothers, five sisters, and their children and their children's children, almost without exception, are in this Church; also many of my cousins, uncles, and other classes of what we call relatives or relations, are in this Church." He never asked Miriam her feelings concerning Mormonism, for he felt that she had to make her own decision independent of his. "I did not ask my wife whether she believed the Gospel; I did not ask her whether she would be baptized. Faith, repentance, and baptism are free for all."[19] Nevertheless, three weeks after his baptism, she too was baptized.

Following his baptism, his life took on new meaning. "Since I have embraced the Gospel," he proclaimed, nothing has "worn to me a gloomy aspect."[20] He felt as if he had gone into another world, and that looking back into the old one was "like looking into Hell."[21] Not surprisingly, given his feelings, from the moment of his conversion Mormonism assumed the place of primary importance in his life.

*Camp Meeting during the Great Awakening, ca. 1829*

# 3

# To Thunder and Roar Out the Gospel

## Brigham As Missionary

Following his baptism in April 1832, Brigham could no longer live the simple, relatively uneventful life of a skilled carpenter and jack-of-all-trades. Later, he explained the life-affirming effect his conversion had upon him: "I wanted to thunder and roar out the Gospel to the nations. It burned in my bones like fire pent up, so I . . . [began] to preach the Gospel of life to the people. . . . Nothing would satisfy me but to cry abroad in the world, what the Lord was doing in the latter days. . . . I had to go out and preach, lest my bones should consume within me."[1] Although lacking education and public speaking experience, he called himself on a mission and spent the summer following his baptism "preaching the Gospel in the regions round about, baptizing and raising up churches."[2] "I traveled, toiled, labored and preached continually," he recalled.[3] In the twelve years from his first mission until the 1844 martyrdom of Joseph Smith, Brigham would serve ten additional missions. A look at those twelve years of missionary service reveals a man from whom much was asked and, likewise, by whom much was willingly given. While not all of these missions were traditional proselytizing missions, all were designed to further the kingdom. Drawing upon his own experience as a model, Brigham would later call individuals on similar specialized missions to assist the work.

After the heartbreaking but not unexpected death of his wife Miriam in September 1832, Brigham locked up his carpentry shop. The move marked a complete break with his past life. He now undertook a life completely dedicated to the Lord. "I was worth a little property when I started to preach; but I was something like Bunyan—it was 'life, life, eternal life,' with me, everything else was secondary."4 He placed his two daughters in the care of Vilate Kimball (for whom Brigham's second daughter was named) and traveled from Mendon, New York, to Kirtland, Ohio, in company with his brother Joseph and Heber C. Kimball to meet Joseph Smith. Along the 325-mile journey, they preached the gospel and visited branches of the Church.

Immediately after returning to New York, the two brothers undertook a two-month mission to Canada. Leaving in December 1832, they traveled on foot to Kingston, Ontario, "most of the way through snow and mud from one to two feet deep."5 They returned to Mendon in February 1833, but not before holding forty meetings and baptizing fourteen, including Artemus Millett, who would play a prominent role overseeing the exterior work on the Kirtland Temple.

In late April 1833, Brigham returned to Canada alone and on foot, regularly preaching on the journey as opportunity permitted. On July 1 he left Canada in company with several converts bound for Kirtland. After a brief stay in Ohio, he returned to Mendon, where he spent his last days as a resident of western New York preaching in the surrounding communities before moving to Kirtland.

After the Latter-day Saints had been driven from Jackson County, Missouri, Joseph Smith organized Zion's Camp in 1834 to help return them to their homes. Brigham was part of the expedition that set out from Kirtland in May 1834 on a journey of nearly a thousand miles on foot. Although Zion's Camp failed in its stated purpose, Joseph Smith selected nine of the first apostles, including Brigham, from its ranks, and Brigham later acknowledged the valuable lessons he learned on the journey. During the journey, Brigham and his brother Joseph Young regularly sang for the members of Zion's Camp. Individuals would later recall that "their musical voices cheered many a drooping heart, and encouraged their flagging energies while performing [on] that memorable journey." One member of the company later stated that "the songs of Brigham and Joseph were the sweetest I ever heard in the Camps of Zion."[6]

Shortly after being called to the Quorum of the Twelve Apostles, Brigham and other members of the Twelve served missions to the eastern United States and Canada from May to September 1835, where they both proselytized and organized branches of the Church. During "this season," as he referred to it, he traveled 3,264 miles by foot, wagon, and canal boat. The following summer he was again called by the Prophet, this time to New England. "It has never entered into my heart," he later declared, "from the first day I was called to preach the Gospel to this day, when the Lord said, 'Go and leave your family,' to offer the least objection."[7] On this mission, Brigham experienced his first train trip (from Providence to Boston). He also found himself in situations all too familiar to him as a missionary. One of these was a meeting with a hostile Boston minister that prompted Brigham to write, "We bore testmoney of the book of Mormon and drouned him in his own words and let him goe."[8] Brigham spent March to August 1837 on a third proselytizing mission to the eastern United States.

His next mission, and probably his best known, was to Great Britain, in company with eight other Apostles, and lasted from September 14, 1839, to July 1, 1841. This mission call was the fulfillment of a revelation given to the Prophet Joseph in which the Apostles were instructed "to go over the great waters, and there promulgate my gospel, the fulness therefore, and bear record of my name."[9] Brigham's departure for England came close on the heels of the Saints settling in Commerce (later Nauvoo), Illinois, and its sister city of Montrose, Iowa (where Brigham was living at the time). Having just been driven from Missouri, the Saints were poorer than ever and were exhausted and stricken by chills and fevers caused by the swampy nature of their new home. Brigham's health was so bad that, as he recalled, "I was unable to go thirty rods to the [Mississippi] river without assistance. After I had crossed the river I got Israel Barlow to carry me on his horse, behind him, to Heber C. Kimball's, where I remained sick. . . . I left my wife sick, with a babe only ten days old, and all of my children sick and unable to wait upon each other."[10]

As with previous missions, Joseph had instructed the Twelve to follow the biblical practice of traveling without purse or scrip. Although Brigham would have followed the counsel anyway, on this occasion he had little choice, for he had neither. "We were in the depths of poverty, caused by being driven from Missouri, where we had left all."[11] Brigham's family did not have "a second suit to their backs, for the mob in Missouri had taken all he had," Heber C. Kimball reported.[12] Concerning his own wardrobe, Brigham recounted that it "had not much of a ministerial appearance."[13] His cap was made out of "a pair of old pantaloons" and he took "a small quilt from the trundle bed, and that served for my overcoat."[14]

Upon reaching Nauvoo, his sister Fanny, noticing his situation, said, "Brother Brigham, what necessity is there for you to go to England while you are sick? Why not tarry here until you are well?" Brigham stubbornly objected to her suggestion. "I never felt better in my life." He later noted that he "was determined to go to England or to die trying. My firm resolve was that I would do what I was required to do in the Gospel of life and salvation, or I would die trying to do it."[15] As a deathly ill Brigham and an equally sick Heber C. Kimball pulled away from Heber's home, Brigham joined his friend in feebly standing up in the wagon in which they were riding and, while swinging their hats over their heads three times, gave a cheer to those they were leaving behind: "Hurrah, hurrah, hurrah for Israel!"[16]

After reaching New York City, the challenges continued for Brigham. While trying to jump onto a ferryboat, he fell against an iron ring on the dock, dislocating his shoulder. To help him with the injury, two of the brethren held him down and Parley P. Pratt grabbed Brigham's arm; then, with his foot squarely placed against Brigham's ribs, Parley pulled the limb to the point where Brigham could guide the bone back into the socket with his other hand.

Brigham's first ocean voyage, which began on March 4, 1840, was not a pleasant experience. The stormy trip regularly found him on his knees, both because of sickness and to petition his Heavenly Father. The remainder of his time was largely spent in his berth. "I was very sick in my head and stomach. I felt as though I could not endure many such voyages. Were it not for the power of God and his tender mercy I should despair. But the Lord is my strength."[17] Arriving in Liverpool on April 6, Brigham could not have been more overjoyed: "I gave a loud shout of hosannah."[18] "I felt that the chains were broken, and the bands that were upon me were burst asunder."[19]

Unable to rely upon the Prophet Joseph's daily counsel, the Twelve blossomed as individuals and as a group. As a result of their faith, prayers, sacrifice, and reliance upon the Spirit, they accomplished a great work as they served with their "heart, might, mind and strength."[20] Brigham summarized their experience this way:

> It was with a heart full of thanksgiving and gratitude to God, my heavenly Father, that I reflected upon his dealings with me and my brethren of the Twelve during the past year of my life, which was spent in England. It truly seemed a miracle to look upon the contrast between our landing and departing from Liverpool. We landed in the spring of 1840, as strangers in a strange land and penniless, but through the mercy of God we have gained many [f]riends, established Churches in almost every noted town and city in the kingdom of Great Britain, baptized between seven and eight thousand, printed 5,000 Books of Mormon, 3,000 Hymn Books, 2,500 volumes of the *Millennial Star* [a monthly LDS publication inaugurated under the direction of Brigham and the apostles that would serve the British Saints for 130 years], and 50,000 tracts, and emigrated to Zion 1,000 souls, established a permanent shipping agency, which will be a great blessing to the Saints, and have left sown in the hearts of many thousands the seeds of eternal truth, which will bring forth

fruit to the honor and glory of God, and yet we have lacked nothing to eat, drink or wear: in all these things I acknowledged the hand of God.[21]

Following this mission, Joseph's confidence in Brigham and his dependency upon him increased over time and played an important role in the development of the Quorum of the Twelve as a body equal to that of the First Presidency. While Brigham had ever-increasing responsibilities as president of the Quorum of the Twelve and as a civic leader following his return to Nauvoo, he still served three more missions before the death of the Prophet. From September through November 1842 he visited various towns in Illinois in an effort to counteract anti-Mormon propaganda. From July to October 1843 he once again traveled the eastern states, this time in an effort to raise money for the construction of the Nauvoo House and the Nauvoo Temple. In May 1844 he journeyed back East to campaign for Joseph Smith's bid for the U.S. presidency, where he was when the Prophet was martyred.

During Brigham's twelve years of missionary service, his talents as a leader grew and developed. With each new mission, the future president of the Church increased in faith, grew in wisdom, learned the value of obedience, successfully took on new and greater responsibilities, and gained greater love and understanding of the gospel as he witnessed firsthand in the lives of others an experience that he knew only too well—the power of the gospel to bring positive change, renew a sense of hope, and give purpose to life.

# 4

# BRIGHAM YOUNG CHRONOLOGY

| 1801 | June 1 | Born in Whitingham, Vermont |
| 1804 | | Family moved to New York |
| 1815 | June 11 | Mother died |
| 1823 | | Joined Methodist Reform Church |
| 1824 | October 8 | Married Miriam Works |
| 1829 | | Moved to Mendon, New York |
| 1830 | | Introduced to Book of Mormon |
| 1832 | April | Baptized into The Church of Jesus Christ of Latter-day Saints |
| | Summer | Served preaching mission in Mendon and vicinity |
| | September 8 | Miriam Works Young died, leaving Brigham a widower with two children |
| | November | Met Joseph Smith at Kirtland, Ohio |
| | December | Undertook mission to Canada with his brother Joseph Young |
| 1833 | February | Returned to Mendon |
| | April–August | Served second mission in Canada |
| | September | Moved his family to Kirtland |

| 1834 | February 18 | Married Mary Ann Angell |
| | May–July | Served as member of Zion's Camp |
| 1835 | February 14 | Began service as member of Quorum of Twelve Apostles |
| | May–September | Fulfilled mission to eastern states with other members of the Twelve |
| | Fall | Attended Hebrew School |
| 1836 | March 27 | Participated in dedication of Kirtland Temple |
| | Summer | Undertook business mission to eastern states with Willard Richards |
| 1837 | March–June | Fulfilled mission to New York and Massachusetts |
| | Fall | Kirtland Bank failed; Brigham defended Joseph Smith |
| | December | Fled Kirtland for his own safety |
| 1838 | March 14 | Reached Far West, Missouri |
| | Fall | Experienced the "Missouri Persecutions" |
| 1839 | February | Led family and poor Latter-day Saints from Missouri to Quincy, Illinois |
| | April | Returned to Far West to fulfill Joseph Smith prophecy |
| | May | Moved family to Montrose, Iowa |
| | September 14 | Departed for mission to England although very ill |
| 1840 | March 9 | Sailed from New York City for England |
| | April 6 | Arrived in England with other members of Twelve |
| 1841 | January 19 | Appointed president of the Twelve |
| | April 21 | Left England along with Saints bound for Nauvoo |
| | July 1 | Returned to Nauvoo, Illinois |
| | September 4 | Elected to Nauvoo City Council |
| 1842 | | Joseph Smith began teaching temple ordinances; Joseph Smith taught principle of plural marriage; Brigham took first plural wife |
| 1843 | July–September | Served mission to eastern states to collect funds for temple and Nauvoo house |

| 1844 | Spring | Along with other members of Twelve met regularly with Joseph and was taught and received keys |
| | May 22 | Served mission to eastern United States in support of Joseph Smith's presidential candidacy |
| | June 27 | Joseph and Hyrum Smith martyred |
| | July 16 | Recognized that the Twelve hold the necessary keys |
| | August 8 | Church members at Nauvoo voted to sustain the Twelve |
| 1845 | | Began preparations for Latter-day Saints to leave Nauvoo |
| | December | Initiated ordinance work in the Nauvoo Temple |
| 1846 | February 15 | Left Nauvoo to lead Mormon exodus west Established Winter Quarters on Missouri River and other way stations in Iowa |
| 1847 | January 14 | Received "Word and Will of the Lord" (D&C 136) |
| | April 14 | Left Winter Quarters at head of vanguard pioneer company |
| | July 24 | Entered Salt Lake Valley |
| | August 18 | Began return journey to Winter Quarters |
| | December 5 | Ordained president of the Church at Kanesville |
| 1848 | May 26 | Left Winter Quarters for Salt Lake Valley with more than 1,200 Saints |
| | September 20 | Arrived at Salt Lake Valley |
| 1849 | March 12 | Provisional State of Deseret was established; Brigham elected governor |
| | Fall | Initiated Perpetual Emigration Fund |
| 1850 | February | Helped establish University of Deseret |
| | September 20 | Appointed governor of newly created Utah Territory |
| 1851 | | Began annual visits to outlying settlements |
| | July 21 | Established three Indian agencies for Utah |
| | August 8 | Divided Utah into three judicial districts |

| | August | Perry Brocchus and other non-Mormon territorial officials arrived in Utah |
|---|---|---|
| | October 29 | Selected Fillmore as Utah's territorial capital |
| 1852 | August | Made public announcement of practice of plural marriage |
| 1853 | February 14 | Broke ground for Salt Lake Temple |
| | July 18 | Walker Indian War commenced in Utah |
| | October 26 | John W. Gunnison and party of U.S. topographical engineers were killed by Indians near Sevier River |
| 1854 | May | Signed peace treaty with Ute chief, ending Walker Indian War |
| | August 2 | Recommended that emigrants from England sail to northern port rather than New Orleans |
| 1855 | | Utah experienced drought and cricket infestation |
| 1856 | | Held first 24th of July celebration at Brighton |
| | Fall | Mormon Reformation began |
| | October 5 | Initiated rescue effort of handcart and wagon companies |
| 1857 | May | First learned of an army having been ordered to Utah |
| | July 24 | Celebrated tenth anniversary of arrival of Saints in Utah |
| | September 11 | Mountain Meadows Massacre occurred |
| | September 15 | Declared martial law in Utah |
| 1858 | March 21 | Ordered abandonment of northern Utah communities to avoid clash with approaching army |
| | April 12 | Welcomed Alfred Cumming, his successor as governor, to Utah |
| | June 11 | Met with peace commissioners; official end of Utah War |
| | June 26 | U.S. army passed through Salt Lake City en route to Cedar Valley |
| | July | Young family returned to Salt Lake City, along with other inhabitants of territory |

| 1860 | | Contracted to construct 500 miles of overland telegraph line |
| 1861 | Spring | "Down and back" companies began to gather emigrants |
| 1862 | March 6 | Dedicated Salt Lake Theater |
| 1863 | March 10 | Arrested on charges of bigamy under 1862 antibigamy law |
| 1865 | April | Black Hawk Indian war began |
| 1867 | March 21 | Deseret Telegraph Company was established, with Brigham Young as president |
| | | Salt Lake Tabernacle was completed |
| | Fall | Reorganized Women's Relief Society |
| | December | Organized the School of the Prophets |
| 1868 | May 21 | Contracted to grade 150 miles of Union Pacific Railroad through Utah |
| | October | Elected president of Zion's Cooperative Mercantile Institution |
| 1869 | May 10 | Transcontinental railroad was completed |
| | May 17 | Broke ground for Utah Central Railroad |
| | June 1 | Provo Woolen Mills was organized, with Brigham Young as president |
| | November | Organized Young Ladies Retrenchment Association |
| 1870 | January 10 | Drove last spike in Utah Central Railroad at Salt Lake City |
| | November | Began spending winters in St. George |
| 1871 | October 2 | Arrested on charge of cohabitation and confined to his home |
| | October 9 | Admitted to bail |
| | October 24 | Left for St. George, Utah; accused of fleeing from justice |
| | November 9 | Dedicated St. George Temple site |
| | December 26 | Case was called to trial; returned to Salt Lake City |

| 1872 | January 2 | Appeared in Third District Court; case continued until March; bail refused; guarded in his own home |
| | April 25 | Released from custody on writ of habeas corpus |
| | December | Traveled to St. George with Thomas L. and Elizabeth Kane |
| 1873 | April 6 | Called five additional counselors in First Presidency; resigned as Church trustee-in-trust |
| | Fall | Began organizing united orders in southern Utah settlements |
| 1874 | May | Organized united orders in Salt Lake City |
| 1875 | February | Ann Eliza Webb Young divorced Brigham |
| | Spring | Organized Young Men's Mutual Improvement Association |
| | | Organized Brigham Young Academy in Provo, Utah |
| | | Defined seniority in Quorum of the Twelve by length of service, not age |
| 1876 | | Directed establishment of first colonies along Little Colorado in Arizona |
| 1877 | January 1 | Attended initial dedicatory session of St. George Temple |
| | March 23 | John D. Lee executed for role in Mountain Meadows Massacre |
| | April 6 | Attended final dedicatory session of St. George Temple |
| | April | Undertook reorganization of wards and stakes |
| | April 25 | Dedicated Manti Temple site |
| | May 15 | Dedicated Logan Temple site |
| | July 11 | Issued circular letter regarding priesthood |
| | August 29 | Died at his residence in Salt Lake City |

## ❧ 5 ❧

# FAITHFUL FRIEND AND DEVOTED DISCIPLE

## *Brigham and Joseph*

From the moment the Spirit testified of the truthfulness of the restored gospel, Brigham began a lifelong devotion to the Prophet Joseph Smith. Brigham's loyalty to Joseph was without bounds because Joseph had provided the way by which Brigham's life was transformed from gloom and despair to hope and peace. Joseph's teachings, along with his efforts as a mentor, role model, and friend, helped transform Brigham from a common man into an uncommon leader. Brigham loved Joseph as a friend, but more importantly, he revered him as a prophet of God. Brigham frequently and admiringly spoke of Joseph and the personal debt he owed him. Because of Joseph, the hopelessness that had haunted Brigham since his youth "vanished, and has not since troubled me for a moment."[1] Given this fact, it is not surprising that Brigham would devote his life to learning from, supporting, and teaching about "our Moses that the Lord has given us."[2]

Theirs was a symbiotic relationship. While Joseph helped mold Brigham into a strong and inspired leader, Brigham became Joseph's most faithful disciple and was an ardent defender and protector of Joseph and the truths he taught. Brigham was drawn to Joseph and Joseph to Brigham because for both men the kingdom was what was important. Joseph provided the vision while Brigham, as the quintessential disciple, provided the implementation and organizational structure.

The bond between them continued after Joseph's death. Brigham enthusiastically and unwaveringly sought to build on what the Prophet Joseph had begun. He tried to copy Joseph's personal qualities and consciously and faithfully embraced his teachings. Brigham regularly testified that he taught and did what he had learned from the Prophet. Brigham's sermons and writings reveal how one prophet prepared another.

Brigham always sought to "learn principle and wisdom from the mouth of the Prophet."[3] He noted: "I never did let an opportunity pass of getting with the Prophet Joseph and of hearing him speak in public or in private, so that I might draw understanding from the fountain from which he spoke, that I might have it and bring it forth when it was needed. . . . Such moments were more precious to me than all the wealth of the world."[4] On another occasion he stated: "From the first time I saw the Prophet Joseph I never lost a word that came from him concerning the kingdom. And this is the key of knowledge that I have to-day, that I did hearken to the words of Joseph, and treasured them up in my heart, laid them away, asking my Father in the name of his Son Jesus to bring them to my mind when needed."[5] While Brigham spoke with his own voice, he remained true to what he had learned, and his sermons provide insight into Joseph's teachings and life. "I do not think that a man lives on the earth that knew him any better than I did," Brigham proclaimed. "I am his witness."[6]

Brigham's message was simple: Joseph lived and died a prophet and laid the foundation for the work in the last days. Brigham had an unshakable conviction in Joseph's divine calling as a prophet who received and taught the revelations of Jesus Christ. Brigham made it clear that he did not "serve" the man Joseph Smith but rather the doctrines that "the Lord has revealed through him."[7] "It was my duty to throw [my] influence around Joseph,"

Brigham later recalled. "Yes I tied the people to Joseph Smith the Prophet. Every cord I could get hold of I hooked it to Joseph."[8]

Brigham also loved and cherished Joseph for the greatness of his character. If people spoke against Joseph, "they spoke against as good a man as ever lived."[9] He further testified that "no man ever honored his mission more," except for the Savior.[10]

Prior to his baptism, Brigham found that to talk to the religious ministers of the day "was more unsatisfactory" than "to talk with lawyers."[11] He felt "that if I could see the face of a Prophet, such as had lived on the earth in former times, a man that had revelations, to whom the heavens were opened, who knew God and His character, I would freely circumscribe the earth on my hands and knees."[12] It is not surprising that after being convinced that there was such a man on the earth, Brigham took advantage of the first opportunity to meet him.

Upon reaching Kirtland in company with his brother Joseph and Heber C. Kimball, they were directed to the nearby woods where they "found the Prophet, and two or three of his brothers, chopping and hauling wood." Brigham recalled, "Here my joy was full at the privilege of shaking the hand of the Prophet of God, and received the sure testimony, by the Spirit of prophecy, that he was all that any man could believe him to be, as a true Prophet."[13]

Later Brigham reported, "When I first saw Joseph, . . . I had but one prayer," and that was "to hear Joseph speak on doctrine, and see his mind reach out untramelled to grasp the deep [things] of God."[14] In this regard, Brigham was not disappointed. "He took heaven, figuratively speaking, and brought it down to earth; and he took the earth, brought it up, and opened up, in plainness and simplicity, the things of God."[15]

Joseph made only brief note of his initial meeting with Brigham: "About the 8th of November [1832] I received a visit from Elders Joseph Young, Brigham Young, and Heber C. Kimball of Mendon, Monroe county, New York. They spent four or five days at Kirtland during which we had many interesting moments."[16] One of those interesting moments was when

Brigham spoke in tongues, the first recorded incident among the Latter-day Saints (Joseph stated that Brigham had spoken in the pure Adamic language). Levi Hancock later claimed that as Brigham first approached Joseph, the Prophet turned to Levi and proclaimed, "There is the greatest man that ever lived to teach redem[p]tion to the world and will yet lead this People."[17]

During a second visit in 1833 to "sit at the feet of Joseph," Brigham responded to Joseph's call to gather to Kirtland and help build up Zion. "In 1833 I moved to Ohio where I became acquainted with Joseph Smith, Jr., and remained familiarly acquainted with him in private councils, and in his public walk and acts until the day of his death, and I can truly say, that I invariably found him to be all that any people could require a true prophet to be, and that a better man could not be, though he had his weaknesses; and what man has ever lived upon this earth who had none?"[18]

Among the things that drew Brigham to Joseph and verified that he was a true prophet was the absence of the stiff piety that largely characterized most religious leaders of the day. Brigham found in Joseph an individual who believed in moderation in all good things and who was able to keep things in perspective. Indeed, Joseph was equally at home chopping wood and working the fields as he was at the pulpit and on his knees in prayer. Though Joseph was completely earnest about his mission, he nevertheless loved playing games with the children, engaging in tests of strength such as stick-pulling, socials, and music. Joseph's example of a well-rounded, balanced man of God served as an example that Brigham would emulate. Joseph provided a perfect counterpoint to Brigham's rigid upbringing.

Like Brigham, Joseph was uneducated by the standards of the day, but he likewise confidently faced his mission straight on. Brigham learned from Joseph that the Lord relied on men of faith, courage, and integrity, and that He would bless them with all they needed to succeed. When an individual commented to Brigham shortly before his death that a picture of Joseph "did not show any great amount of strength, intelligence, or culture," Brigham responded that Joseph "was not a man of education, but received such enlightenment from the Holy Spirit that he needed nothing more to fit him for his work as a leader. 'And this is my own case also. . . . All that I have acquired is by my own exertions and by the grace of God, who sometimes chooses the weak things of earth to manifest His glory.'"[19]

Joseph's human frailties little bothered Brigham. "Though I admitted in my feelings and knew all the time that Joseph was a human being and subject to err, still it was none of my business to look after his faults." Brigham would not listen to criticism, for he believed that Joseph "was superior to them all, and held keys of salvation over them."[20]

During the dark days at Kirtland, Brigham "stood close by Joseph, and, with all the wisdom and power God bestowed on me, put forth my utmost energies to sustain the servant of God."[21] Brigham's loyalty was noted by Joseph, who lamented that only Brigham and Heber C. Kimball among the original Twelve Apostles never "lifted their heel against me."[22]

Brigham did not believe it was his prerogative to question what Joseph did. "He was God's servant, and not mine." Nevertheless, there was a brief time, Brigham would later confess, when he privately wavered in his support of Joseph, "not concerning religious matters—it was not about his revelations—but it was in relation to his financeiring."[23] For a brief moment during the Kirtland period, Brigham was privately influenced by some of "the first Elders of this Church" who had "decided that Joseph did not understand temporal matters." But Brigham quickly regained perspective.[24] After that, when he found himself tempted to question Joseph, he "repented" of his "unbelief, and that too, very suddenly."[25] He concluded that "when a revelation came to Joseph for the people to perform any labor or duty . . . the Prophet knew more than I knew, that the Lord spoke through him, and that He could do as He pleased about speaking to me."[26]

Brigham readily acknowledged that the secret to his success in leading the Church was because he was a devoted student of Joseph. "I never let an opportunity pass of learning what the Prophet had to impart. This is the secret of the success of your humble servant."[27] Upon returning to Nauvoo following the martyrdom, Brigham assured the grieving Saints that he had "spared no pains" to learn from Joseph.[28] "An angel never watched him closer than I did," he later recalled. As a result of his constant observation, Brigham learned from Joseph "doctrine and principle beyond that which he expressed."[29]

Veterans of Zion's Camp recalled that Joseph did not lead "as a haughty chieftain." They spoke about "how kind and modest he was" and "how determined and resolute in carrying out the will of the Lord," characteristics that Brigham would try to emulate.[30] To the grumblers on the journey, Brigham stated that he found the spiritual benefits outweighing any hardship and despair and that to be able spend night and day with the Prophet for three months was a treasure beyond compare. "I told those brethren that I was well paid—paid with heavy interest—yea that my measure was filled to overflowing with the knowledge that I had received by travelling with the Prophet."[31]

Like the Saints generally, the martyrdom also hit Brigham hard. In 1849 he noted: "All disappointments, losses, and crosses never bring a tear. Bringing it [the martyrdom] to mind brings tears."[32]

With the passage of time he would joyfully proclaim: "I feel like shouting hallelujah, all the time, when I think that I ever knew Joseph Smith, the Prophet whom the Lord raised up and ordained, and to whom He gave keys and power to build up the kingdom of God on earth and sustain it. These keys are committed to this people, and we have power to continue the work that Joseph commenced, until everything is prepared for the coming of the Son of Man. This is the business of the Latter-day Saints, and it is all the business that we have on hand."[33]

Brigham's daughter Zina noted that shortly before he died, "he seemed to partially revive, and opening his eyes, he gazed upward."[34] "Joseph, Joseph, Joseph, Joseph," were the last audible words that Brigham uttered.[35]

# 6

# THE LION OF
# THE LORD

I n January 1845, W. W. Phelps published a list of titles that he felt best
described the members of the Twelve Apostles. "I know the Twelve,
and they know me," he wrote. While many may have wondered at the
meaning of titles given to some members of the Twelve, the title fittingly
bestowed upon Brigham was largely self-evident: "The lion of the Lord."[1]

By his own admission, Mormonism transformed Brigham and produced
in him the heart of a lion with a roar to match. It was a cause for which he
would readily express himself and was willing to give his all. Almost
overnight he was transformed from an uneducated carpenter and joiner toil-
ing away in western New York into an individual who would be widely recognized as one of the most influential Americans of all time. Someone
succinctly summarized the attitude that earned Brigham his nickname in
January 1847: "Our President doesn't stick [balk] at anything that tends to
advance the gathering of Israel, or promote the cause of Zion in these last
days; he sleeps with one eye open and one foot out of bed."[2]

Once in Utah he declared that the gospel still "invigorates, buoys up, strengthens, and fills every power of my capacity with unspeakable joy."[3] He would also proclaim: "Excuse me if I speak loud. Were I to speak as I feel [about Mormonism], I should speak like a Methodist for a little while, and cry, 'Hallelujah!—praise ye the Lord.'"[4] Although he had been forced to abandon several homes and spent extended periods away from his family as a missionary, Brigham scoffed at the idea that Mormonism had required a sacrifice of him. "I hear people talk about their troubles, their sore privations, and the great sacrifices they have made for the Gospel's sake. It never was a sacrifice to me. Anything I can do or suffer in the cause of the Gospel, is only like dropping a pin into the sea."[5]

From the moment he received the gift of the Holy Ghost, Brigham felt the need to express his feelings. A week after his baptism, he preached his first sermon. "I was but a child, so far as public speaking and a knowledge of the world was concerned," he recalled, "but the Spirit of the Lord was upon me, and I felt as though my bones would consume within me unless I spoke to the people and told them what I had seen, heard and learned—what I had experienced and rejoiced in." His first sermon lasted more than an hour. "I opened my mouth and the Lord filled it."[6] Concerning, his early preaching, he later recalled his desire to roar: "I could not satisfy my own feelings without talking with a loud voice."[7]

"When I first commenced preaching," he noted, "I made up my mind to declare the things that I understood, fearless of friends and threats, and regardless of caresses. They were nothing to me, for if it was my duty to rise before a congregation of strangers and say that the Lord lives, that He has revealed Himself in this our day, that He has given to us a Prophet, and brought forth the new and everlasting covenant for the restoration of Israel, and if that was all I could say, I must be just as satisfied as though I could get up and talk for hours. If I could only say that I was a monument of the Lord's work upon the earth, that was sufficient."[8]

Brigham initially felt that he needed a "stool in order to reach high Enough to tie the shoes" of some of the original members of the Twelve.[9] That view was not shared by Joseph, who recognized the heart of a lion behind Brigham's rough exterior. Soon Brigham's courage was unmatched by any other individual as he demonstrated his loyalty to Joseph and his devotion to the kingdom during the dark days of Kirtland.

When some people began to lose faith in Joseph and began to criticize him and talked about appointing someone else as prophet, Brigham forcefully defended Joseph in deed and word. "What I have received from the Lord, I have received by Joseph Smith," he proclaimed. "He was the instrument made use of. If I drop him, I must drop these principles: they have not been revealed, declared, or explained by any other man since the days of the Apostles."[10]

During the construction of the Kirtland Temple, the threats against Joseph were so constant that Brigham slept "upon the floor scores and scores of nights ready to receive the mob who sought his life."[11] On one occasion, after hearing rumors of a possible assassination attempt, Brigham went out to meet the stagecoach in which the Prophet was traveling and escorted him the final miles into Kirtland.[12]

When some members questioned whether it was Joseph's prerogative to deal with temporal topics, Brigham asked them to draw a line between spiritual and temporal. He asked them to give an example of when a prophet had not given practical, everyday advice. "I went into the Temple and just challenged them [the Brethren] to show wherein the Lord ever conferred upon any man in the world the power to dictate in spiritual affairs, that he did not in temporal affairs," he recalled. "They could not do it. I told them they could not draw the line between the spiritual and the temporal."[13] Brigham then proclaimed: "He was called of God; God dictated him, and if He had a mind to leave him to himself and let him [the Prophet] commit an error, that was no business of mine. And it was not for me to question it, if the Lord was disposed to let Joseph lead the people astray, for He had called him and instructed him to gather Israel and restore the Priesthood and kingdom to them. . . . If He should suffer him to lead the people astray, it would be because they ought to be led astray."[14]

During this time when some desired to appoint David Whitmer as prophet in Joseph's stead, Brigham "stood close by Joseph, and, with all the wisdom and power God" gave him used his "utmost energies to sustain the servant of God and unite the Quorums of the Church." He told the mur-murers that he knew Joseph was a prophet and while "they might rail and slander him as much as they pleased, they could not destroy the appointment of the Prophet of God, they could only destroy their own authority, cut the thread that bound them to the Prophet and to God and sink themselves to hell."[15]

On another occasion when a man walked the streets of Kirtland late one night proclaiming that Joseph was a fallen prophet, Brigham went out to confront the man. He told the individual "that if he did not stop his noise and let the people enjoy their sleep without interruption" that he "would cow-hide him on the spot, for we had the Lord's Prophet right here, and we did not want the Devil's prophet yelling round the streets."[16]

Concerning these dark days in Kirtland, Heber C. Kimball recalled that "a man's life was in danger the moment he spoke in defense of the Prophet of God."[17] Since no one was a more visible defender of Joseph during this time than Brigham, it is not surprising that he eventually was forced to flee Kirtland to preserve his own life.

After the Saints had been driven from Missouri, Brigham insisted that the Twelve return to the state to fulfill a revelation given to Joseph stating that they were to depart from the temple site at Far West on April 26, 1839, for a mission to England.[18] Enemies of the Church had declared that this rev-elation would never be fulfilled, proof that Joseph was not a prophet. While there were those who argued that under the circumstances the Lord would take the "will for the deed," Brigham worried that their failure to accomplish the revelation might provide their enemies ammunition against Joseph. Under Brigham's leadership, and with the threat of death or imprisonment facing them, the apostles gathered at the temple site during the predawn hours in accordance with the revelation. Certain that no effort would be made to fulfill the revelation, mob leaders had left no guard.

Once in England, Brigham evidenced the same determination. In

September 1840 he wrote to Joseph: "Our motto is *go ahead*. Go ahead—& *ahead* we are determined to go—till we have conquered every foe. So come life or death we'll go ahead, but tell us if we are going wrong & we will right it."[19]

In July 1841, shortly after Brigham returned from his mission to England, Joseph Smith received the following revelation: "Dear and well-beloved brother, Brigham Young, verily thus saith the Lord unto you: My servant Brigham, it is no more required at your hand to leave your family as in times past, for your offering is acceptable to me. I have seen your labor and toil in journeyings for my name. I therefore command you to send my word abroad, and take especial care of your family from this time, henceforth and forever. Amen."[20] Although there was a marked difference in the length and frequency of his missions following this revelation, Brigham nevertheless continued to give of his time and energy to the kingdom. Six months after this revelation, he poignantly wrote in his journal on January 18, 1842: "This evening I am with my wife a lone by my fireside for the first time for years. We injoi [enjoy] it and feele [feel] to prase [praise] the Lord."[21]

At Nauvoo, when opposition was raised against the Prophet Joseph by some of the leading men, the Prophet asked Brigham to respond to their criticisms. Much as he was at Kirtland, Brigham found himself "pretty well charged with plenty of powder and ball" until he felt "like a thousand lions." Grabbing the scriptures, he declared that he "would not give the ashes of a rye straw" for them without the accompanying teachings of "the living oracles of God." Without the living prophets, he declared, the restored Church of Jesus Christ was "no better than" any other church.[22]

In spite of growing persecution in the aftermath of the martyrdom, the lion in Brigham pushed hard to finish the temple at Nauvoo. "We want to build the Temple in this place," he proclaimed, "if we have to build it as the Jews built the walls of the Temple in Jerusalem, with a sword in one hand and the trowel in the other."[23]

In Utah, Brigham continued to roar, much to the dismay of non-Mormon territorial officials and travelers through the territory. One notable incident involved Judge Perry Brocchus, one of the first non-Mormon territorial officials, who shortly after arriving in Utah in August 1851 made some public comments that were widely viewed as defaming the virtue of Mormon women. Daniel W. Jones, who had arrived in Utah only days before the meeting, sat in dismay. Jones found himself losing respect for Brigham, "who sat perfectly still with his mouth twisted a little to one side," and Jones told the man sitting next to him that he would not allow such talk if he had a wife or mother present, but would kick Brocchus off the stand. The individual, who had seen the Lion of the Lord in action before, told Jones to just wait. When Brigham arose to answer Brocchus, Jones "understood why nothing had been said to interfere with his speech. Brochus was given full liberty to 'empty himself.' Then he got his dose."[24] In his remarks Brigham defended the Saints and sharply criticized the judge as "either profoundly ignorant or wilfully wicked." Brigham noted that if he allowed such talk in the future from Brocchus, there would "be either pulling of hair or cutting of throats."[25] Brigham's roar frightened Brocchus so badly that he and other territorial officials quickly left the territory. Brocchus's exaggerated reports of what happened have widely become viewed as an attempt to justify his own cowardly behavior.

In August 1873, Brigham expressed frustration that pioneers sent to Arizona had not found a suitable location to establish a settlement. Referring to Brigham's comments, George Q. Cannon stated that he was thankful "there was no disposition" on Brigham's part "to let up, or to say, 'I am in years now [seventy-two years old], and I will lay back and take my ease and leave the burden of this work to younger men, who ought to step forward and shoulder it.' He has the spirit of the pioneer in him as much to-day, probably, as he ever had." Cannon further noted that he believed "it was a true remark" when Brigham proclaimed "that if he had been in Arizona, there would have been good places found for settlement."[26] It would be easy to dismiss this claim as egotistical, but those who were familiar with the "Lion of the Lord" realized he probably spoke the truth. He had long exhibited that type of courage and determination.

## ᴄᴏ 7 ᴄᴏ

# FAITH

### *His Dominant Characteristic*

I
n May 1858, shortly after he and other residents of Salt Lake abandoned their homes in the face of an approaching army during the Utah
War—and at a time when the outcome of the conflict was less than
assured, and it seemed possible that the Saints would have to leave their
mountain home—Brigham wrote to missionaries returning to Utah: "The
Lord is at the helm of the old ship Zion, and she sails well."[1] Given what was
transpiring, it would be easy to characterize his statement as a Pollyanna
attempt to put the best spin on a bad situation. In reality, his statement is
simply evidence of his most dominant characteristic—faith. A look at his life
reveals that he had taken to heart the proverb that says: "Trust in the Lord
will all thine heart; and lean not unto thine own understanding. In all thy
ways acknowledge him, and he shall direct thy paths."[2]

Time and time again Brigham proclaimed his belief that a loving
Heavenly Father was watching over the Latter-day Saints individually and
collectively and would direct their efforts to accomplish His purposes if they
trusted in Him. Brigham's great faith made him certain of both his direction

and his destination and allowed him to push unhesitatingly forward. His approach to both his life and his leadership was straightforward: "My religion is to know the will of God and do it."[3] He further instructed the Saints to "learn to be in the hands of God as clay in the hands of the potter."[4] After settling in Utah, Brigham wrote: "We are in the hands of our heavenly father, the God of Abraham, and Joseph who guided us to this land. He is our Father and our protector; we live in his light, are guided by his wisdom, protected by his shadow, and upheld by his strength."[5] Later he told the Saints, "Let us do the will of God and there is no fear from any quarter."[6]

Regarding his move to Kirtland, Ohio, in the fall of 1833 with his two young daughters, he later recalled: "If any man that ever did gather with the Saints was any poorer than I was—it was because he had nothing."[7] He reached Kirtland with borrowed boots and pants and an old homemade coat inadequate for cold weather. As winter approached, many Saints also experiencing tough times anticipated leaving the city to obtain work to ensure their survival. The Prophet Joseph, however, advised the Saints to remain at Kirtland and build it up rather than use their labor to build up non-Latter-day Saint communities. While many left, Brigham followed counsel. "I made up my mind that I would stay in Kirtland," he noted, "and work if I never got a farthing for it."[8] Throughout the winter he found his faith rewarded. "I would gather a little here and a little there, and a day would not pass without its having sufficient food."[9]

Recounting the story years later, he reported that while he didn't get rich, "the Lord opened the way most astonishingly" because he heeded the words of a prophet.[10] Brigham recalled that "Joseph would often ask me how I lived. I told him I did not know—that I did my best, and the Lord did the rest."[11]

During these early years, Brigham demonstrated on at least two occasions that he had faith enough to control the elements. While he was sailing Lake Erie in November 1839 en route to England, an unfavorable wind arose in the middle of the night. "I went up on deck and I felt impres[sed] in spirit to pray to the Father in name of Jesus for a forgiveness of all my sins," he wrote in his journal, "and then I fe[l]t to command the winds to sees [cease] and let ous goe safe on our Jorney the winds abated and Glory & ouner [honor] & prase be to that God that rules all things."[12]

During the subsequent ocean voyage to England he suffered greatly with seasickness, but on the return voyage in 1841 he had an experience similar to what occurred on Lake Erie. Two weeks into the journey, the wind ceased and the boat became "be calmed on the Banks of new found Land. I was verry sick & destressed in my head & stomick. . . . ware it not for the power of god & his tendere mercy I should despare." At this point Brigham and other members of the Twelve "a gread to humble them selves before the Lord and ask him to . . . give us a fair wind, we did so & the wind emeditly changed and from that time to this it has blone in our favor."[13]

When he left Nauvoo and "crossed the Mississippi river" for the west-ward journey in 1846, he did not know at the time "whither we were going," but he "firmly" believed that "the Lord had in reserve for us a good place in the mountains, and that He would lead us directly to it."[14] The following year Brigham's one formally canonized revelation—received in early 1847 at Winter Quarters and known as the "Word and Will of the Lord"—addressed the subject of faith:

> Go thy way and do as I have told you, and fear not thine ene-mies; for they shall not have power to stop my work. Zion shall be redeemed in mine own due time. . . . Fear not thine enemies, for they are in mine hands and I will do my pleasure with them. My people must be tried in all things, that they be prepared to receive the glory that I have for them, even the glory of Zion; and he that will not bear chastisement is not worthy of my kingdom. . . .
>
> . . . Ye can not yet bear my glory; but ye shall behold it if ye are faithful in keeping all my words that I have given you. . . . Be diligent in keeping all my commandments, lest judgments come upon you, and your faith fail you, and your enemies triumph over you.[15]

While the Saints were en route to the Salt Lake Valley, Jim Bridger told Brigham that he "considered it imprudent to bring a large population into the Great Basin until it was ascertained that grain could be raised; he said he would give one thousand dollars for a bushel of corn raised in that Basin."[16] Brigham's reply was characteristic of his faith. "I told him if he would wait a year or two we would show him what could be done."[17]

Brigham believed that since God had directed them to the valley, He would open the way. Upon reaching the valley he told the Saints: "We have been kicked out of the frying-pan into the fire, out of the fire into the middle of the floor, and here we are and here we will stay. God . . . will temper the elements for the good of His Saints; He will rebuke the frost and the sterility of the soil, and the land shall become fruitful. . . . God will temper the climate, and we shall build a city and a temple to the Most High God in this place. We will extend our settlements to the east and west, to the north and to the south, and we will build towns and cities by the hundreds, and thousands of the Saints will gather in from the nations of the earth. This will become the great highway of the nations. Kings and emperors and the noble and wise of the earth will visit us here."[18]

He further proclaimed: "We have been driven from Nauvoo here, but the hand of the Lord is in it,—visible as the sun shining this morning; it is visible to my natural eyes; it's all right: and I expect when we see the result of all we pass through in this probationary state, we will discover the hand of the Lord in it all, and shout Amen—it's all right!"[19]

Brigham regularly preached that faith without works was dead. Individuals should not depend upon miracles until they were needed. In 1853 he proclaimed, "While we have a rich soil in this valley, and seed to put in the ground, we need not ask God to feed us, nor follow us round with a loaf of bread begging of us to eat it. He will not do it, neither would I, were I the Lord. We can feed ourselves here; and if we are ever placed in circumstances where we cannot, it will then be time enough for the Lord to work a miracle to sustain us."[20]

When grasshoppers threatened to destroy the crops in 1855, Brigham counseled the Saints "not to fret their gizzards about the failure of the crops or anything else. The Lord would take care of his people . . . *if they did their duty.*"[21]

Brigham also had faith that adversity, both individually and as a group, could further the work, depending upon how people responded: "Marvel not that we have what are called troubles: marvel not that our enemies seek to destroy us and the kingdom of God from the earth. These persecutions are to prepare the humble and faithful to dwell in the presence of God the Father and his Son."[22] He declared that no one could expect to go through life "without losses and crosses": "If you had no opposition, never was afflicted with sickness, never experienced poverty and want, where would be the trial of your faith?"[23]

He noted that while his enemies took shots at him from "sunrise to sun-down," his faith was "that they would never see to take a good sight, for they would shoot a little higher or on one side, unless my work was fully accomplished. . . . Joseph Smith escaped many conspiracies against his life. He lived just as long as the Lord let him live. But the Lord said—'Now let my servant seal up his testimony with his blood.'"[24] He reminded the Saints that although "the Government of the United States and all the kings of the world may go to war with us, . . . God will preserve a portion of the meek and humble of this people to bear off the Kingdom to the inhabitants of the earth . . . and He will not suffer the Priesthood to be again driven from the earth."[25]

Ten years after reaching the valley, Brigham's faith was both tested and manifest during the Utah War. Two days after the Saints held their tenth anniversary celebration of the settling of the valley, on July 26, 1857, Brigham stated concerning the army that had been ordered to march on Utah:

> Have they been trying to destroy "Mormonism?" Yes. Did they destroy it when they took the life of Joseph? No. "Mormonism" is here, the priesthood is here, the keys of the kingdom are here on the earth. . . . If the wicked should succeed in taking my life, the keys of the kingdom will remain with the Church. But my faith is that they will not succeed in taking my life. . . . If they kill me, it is all right; but

they will not until the time comes; and I think that I shall die a natural death; at least I expect to.[26]

The experience of the Latter-day Saints at both Missouri and Nauvoo caused him to be initially cautious in predicting the outcome of the Utah War, but he was confident that if the Saints did all in their power, the Lord's will would be done. "We have to trust in God for the results," he declared. "We shall do what we can, and leave the work in his hands."[27] He mobilized the territorial militia to employ methods short of bloodshed to slow the advancing troops. Grasslands and supply wagons were burned, provisions and cattle were confiscated, and the advanced troops were harassed. Finally, heavy snows forced the army to camp for the winter at Fort Bridger, a hundred miles from Salt Lake City.

Thomas Kane, who went to Utah in 1858 to negotiate a peaceful end to the war, suggested a policy for Brigham to pursue. Brigham "told him I should not turn to the right nor the left, only as god dictated."[28] Likewise, when newly arrived Governor Alfred Cumming cautioned Brigham to avoid actions that could create another Utah War, he replied: "With all due respect to your Excellency, I do not calculate to take the advice of any man that lives in relation to my affairs." Brigham's faith was in the arm of God, not of man. Brigham said he would "follow the councils of my heavenly Father, and I have faith to follow it, and risk the consequences." He told Cumming, "You may think strange of it, but you will yet see that I am right."[29]

When the Mormons returned to the homes they had abandoned during the "Move South," the same soldiers who had been unable to enter the Salt Lake Valley the year before viewed them as a defeated and broken foe. Within three years, however, with the outbreak of the Civil War, these soldiers left the territory. The Mormons had come off victorious and were even able to turn the very soldiers hoping to destroy Mormonism to their benefit as they purchased surplus army goods at a fraction of their cost.

With the army still camped in the territory, Brigham told the Saints: "I feel as calm and serene as the autumn sun. . . . [God] guides the ship, and will bring us safely to port. All we have to care about is to take care of ourselves and see that we do right."[30] Later, when anti-Mormon feelings picked up in the 1870s, he stated: "When they blow out the sun and stop the moon from shining and the earth from revolving on its axis, they may talk about 'wiping out' the 'Mormons' or the Gospel, but not until then. This is the way I feel. I am as unconcerned and just as happy as a man can be. It is no matter if the whole world is against us, God is for us."[31] On another occasion he further declared: "There is not the least reason for fear. . . . 'But' some say, 'cannot they kill us?' Yes, they can kill you and me, if the Lord permits; but if He does not, I reckon they cannot. . . . Look back, members of this Church, for thirty-nine years! Has the Lord fought our battles? He has. Has He protected and fed and clothed us? Certainly He has."[32]

"We will continue to grow, to increase and spread abroad," Brigham proclaimed. "The Lord Almighty has said [to our enemies], Thus far thou shalt go and no farther, and hence we are spared to carry on his work. . . . The hearts of all living are in his hands."[33]

Shortly before his death, Brigham acknowledged what was then obvious—that he had learned "to trust in God. This is His work, and He will take care of it. If He does not, we cannot."[34] Charles L. Walker noted that in 1876 Brigham "took my hand in both of his and said, God bless you, Br Charley, and God has blessed you hasn't He?" Walker reported that "in an instant all the blessings I had ever recei[v]ed were before Me. My emotion was too much to answer him." When Walker was finally able to speak, his answer must have pleased Brigham: "I have learned to trust in the Lord."[35]

## ∞ 8 ∞

# IN THE CONTEXT OF HIS TIME

### United States Presidents

Thomas Jefferson, 1801–9

James Madison, 1809–17

James Monroe, 1817–25

John Quincy Adams, 1825–29

Andrew Jackson, 1829–37

Martin Van Buren, 1837–41

William Henry Harrison, 1841

John Tyler, 1841–45

James K. Polk, 1845–49

Zachary Taylor, 1849–50

Millard Fillmore, 1850–53

Franklin Pierce, 1853–57

James Buchanan, 1857–61

Abraham Lincoln, 1861–65

Andrew Johnson, 1865–69

Ulysses S. Grant, 1869–77

Rutherford B. Hayes, 1877–81

### United States Population

1810: 7,239,881

1820: 9,638,453

1830: 12,866,020

1840: 17,069,453

1850: 23,191,876

1860: 31,443,321

1870: 39,818,449

1880: 50,155,783

## States of the Union

1801: 16 States (Delaware, Pennsylvania, New Jersey, Georgia, Connecticut, Massachusetts, Maryland, South Carolina, New Hampshire, Virginia, New York, North Carolina, Rhode Island, Vermont, Kentucky, Tennessee)

1877: 38 States (Ohio, 1803; Louisiana, 1812; Indiana, 1816; Mississippi, 1817; Illinois, 1818; Alabama, 1819; Maine, 1820; Missouri, 1821; Arkansas, 1836; Michigan, 1837; Florida and Texas, 1845; Iowa, 1846; Wisconsin, 1848; California, 1850; Minnesota, 1858; Oregon, 1859; Kansas, 1861; West Virginia, 1863; Nevada, 1864; Nebraska, 1867; Colorado, 1876)

## World Leaders

### ENGLISH MONARCHS

George III, 1760–1820
George IV, 1820–30

William IV, 1830–37
Victoria, 1837–1901

### FRANCE

*First Republic/First Empire*

Napoleon Bonaparte, 1799–1815 (became Emperor Napoleon I, 1804)

*Second Republic/Second Empire*

Louis Napoleon Bonaparte, 1848–70 (became Emperor Napoleon III, 1852)

*Bourbon Restoration*

Louis XVIII, 1814–24
Charles X, 1824–30
Louis-Philippe ("Citizen King"), 1830–48

*Third Republic*

Louis Adolphe Thiers, 1871–73
Marie E. P. M. De MacMahon, House of Bourbon-Orleans 1873–79

## RUSSIAN TSARS

1801–25 Alexander I

1825–55 Nicholas I

1855–81 Alexander II

## CATHOLIC POPES

1800–1823 Pius VII

1823–29 Leo XII

1829–30 Pius VIII

1831–46 Gregory XVI

1846–78 Blessed Pius IX

## ARCHBISHOPS OF CANTERBURY (CHURCH OF ENGLAND)

1783–1805 John Moore

1805–28 Charles Manners-Sutton

1828–48 William Howley

1848–62 John Bird Sumner

1862–68 Charles Thomas Longley

1868–82 Archibald Campbell

## Governors of Utah Territory

Brigham Young, 1850–58

Alfred Cumming, 1858–61

John W. Dawson, 1861

Stephen Harding, 1862–63

James D. Doty, 1863–65

Charles Durkee, 1865–69

John Shaffer, 1870

Vernon Vaughan, 1870–71

George Woods, 1871–75

Samuel Axtell, 1875

George W. Emery, 1875–80

## First Presidency, 1847–77

### FIRST COUNSELORS

Heber C. Kimball, 1847–68

George A. Smith, 1868–75

John W. Young, 1876–77

### SECOND COUNSELORS

Willard Richards, 1847–54

Jedediah M. Grant, 1854–56

Daniel H. Wells, 1857–77

## OTHER COUNSELORS

Joseph F. Smith, 1866–77
(Counselor to the First
Presidency)

Lorenzo Snow, 1873–77
(Counselor to President
Young)

Brigham Young Jr., 1873–77
(Counselor to President
Young)

Albert Carrington, 1873–77
(Counselor to President
Young)

John W. Young, 1873–77
(Counselor to President
Young)

## *Members of the Quorum of the Twelve Apostles*

Thomas B. Marsh, 1835–39

David W. Patten, 1835–38

Brigham Young, 1835–77

Heber C. Kimball, 1835–68

Orson Hyde, 1835–78

William E. McLellin, 1835–38

Parley P. Pratt, 1835–57

Luke Johnson, 1835–38

William B. Smith, 1835–45

Orson Pratt, 1835–81

John F. Boynton, 1835–37

Lyman E. Johnson, 1835–38

John E. Page, 1838–46

John Taylor, 1838–87

Wilford Woodruff, 1839–98

George A. Smith, 1839–75

Willard Richards, 1840–54

Lyman Wight, 1841–48

Amasa Lyman, 1842–67

Ezra T. Benson, 1846–69

Charles C. Rich, 1849–83

Lorenzo Snow, 1849–1901

Erastus Snow, 1849–88

Franklin D. Richards, 1849–99

George Q. Cannon, 1860–1901

Joseph F. Smith, 1867–1918

Brigham Young Jr., 1868–1903

Albert Carrington, 1870–85

## 9

# THE PETERBOROUGH EXPERIENCE

### *Brigham's Defining Moment*

At the time Joseph and Hyrum Smith were martyred on June 27, 1844, Brigham and Wilford Woodruff were at a railway station in Boston, Massachusetts. "While sitting in the depot," Brigham later recalled, "I felt a heavy depression of Spirit, and [became] so melancholy I could not converse with any degree of pleasure. Not knowing anything concerning the tragedy enacting at this time in Carthage Jail, I could not assign any reasons for my peculiar feeling."[1] It was not until July 16 at Peterborough, New Hampshire, after he heard a letter from Nauvoo read recounting the murders, that he understood the feeling that overcame him three weeks earlier: "I felt then as I never felt in my life. . . . My head felt so distressed I felt as though it would crack. It come to me Joseph and Hyrum are gone, is the Priesthood taken from the Earth[?] . . . The organization of the Kingdom and Church passed before me. It came like a clap. It came to me like Revelation—the keys of the Kingdom are here and [I] was satisfied it was all right."[2] Orson Pratt was sitting to Brigham's left. "We were both leaning back on our chairs," Brigham reported. "Bringing my hand down on my knee, I said the keys of the kingdom are right here with the Church."[3]

That moment, when he understood that the Quorum of the Twelve had the keys necessary to carry on the work, defined Brigham Young as the appointed successor to Joseph Smith. Many see Brigham marked as Joseph's inspired replacement in what transpired at Nauvoo in the aftermath of the martyrdom, or in Brigham's success as an American Moses, or in his work overseeing the settlement of the Intermountain West. But these are only manifestations of the reality of the inspiration he received at Peterborough.

Some, then and now, viewed the church that Joseph organized as facing a succession crisis following the martyrdom. For Brigham, the crisis passed the moment the inspiration came. In spite of natural feelings of inadequacy and concerns about facing a new situation, Brigham knew that because the Twelve held the keys God had restored to the earth through Joseph, the work would go forward under their direction. So sure was Brigham of that fact that upon returning to Nauvoo he told the Saints, "If you do want any other man or men to lead you [besides the Twelve Apostles], take them and we will go our way to build up the kingdom in all the world."[4]

The day after Brigham's Peterborough experience, he returned to Boston, where he was reunited with Wilford Woodruff. "We reached out our hands, but neither of us was able to speak a word," Woodruff recalled. After arriving at the home of Sister Vose, they gave vent to their grief, their faces "soon bathed in a flood of tears." Following this time to weep, Brigham comforted his friend with this assurance, "Thank God, the keys of the kingdom are here."[5]

In the months leading up to the martyrdom, Joseph, moved by the Spirit, met with the Twelve "almost every day for weeks."[6] During this time he conferred upon them "all the ordinances, keys, covenants, endowments, and sealing ordinances of the priesthood."[7] According to Orson Hyde, after Joseph "conducted [the Twelve] through every ordinance of the holy priesthood, . . . he rejoiced very much, and [said], now if they kill me you have got all the keys, and all the ordinances and you can confer them upon others, and the hosts of Satan will not be able to tear down the kingdom."[8] Wilford Woodruff later recalled that Joseph told the Twelve that "you have to round up your shoulders to bear up the kingdom. No matter what becomes of me. . . . You are called upon to bear off this kingdom."[9]

Elder Woodruff reported that while Joseph's language was "plain enough," at the time they "did not understand it any more than the disciples of Jesus when he told them he was going away, and that if he went not the Comforter would not come."[10] Like Peter and the ancient apostles before them, Brigham and the Twelve understood that they now had both the responsibility and the authority to carry out "all things pertaining to the kingdom, ordinances, and government of God."[11]

On August 6, Brigham and the other members of the Twelve who had been in the eastern United States at the time of the martyrdom returned to Nauvoo. There they found the Saints largely uncertain of their future. "They felt like sheep without a shepherd," Elder Woodruff wrote.[12] In their absence would-be leaders had come forth, the most notable of which was Sidney Rigdon, who had reached Nauvoo three days previous. A counselor to Joseph Smith in the First Presidency, Rigdon had become disenchanted with the Prophet and was at Pittsburgh, Pennsylvania, at the time of the martyrdom. More significantly, he had not been present in Nauvoo when Joseph conferred the keys upon the Twelve in the spring of 1844.

Upon reaching Nauvoo, Rigdon told the Saints that he had received a revelation appointing him "guardian" of the Church. He then called for a meeting on August 8 for the Saints to vote on the matter. The day after Brigham and other members of the Twelve returned to Nauvoo, which was the day prior to the scheduled meeting, Brigham and the Twelve met with Rigdon and other priesthood leaders to discuss succession. According to the meeting minutes, Brigham's response to Rigdon's claim that he had been "commanded to speak" for Joseph and that "the martyred Prophet is still the head of this church" was direct:

"I do not care who leads the church, even though it were Ann Lee [founder of the Shakers]; but one thing I must know, and that is what God says about it. I have the keys and the means of obtaining the mind of God on the subject. . . .

"Joseph conferred upon our heads all the keys and powers belonging to the Apostleship which he himself held before he was taken away, and no man or set of men can get between Joseph and the Twelve in this world or in the world to come."[13]

Brigham's journal entry was more to the point: "I followed him and showed the brethren the errors and follies which brother Rigdon manifested."[14]

For many who attended the 10:00 A.M. August 8 meeting, the foremost question was who would lead the Church. The uncertainty in Brigham's mind was not who would lead, but whether the Saints understood the significance of the Twelve holding the keys.

Rigdon spoke first, and for an hour and a half put forth his claim as to why he should be appointed guardian; his discourse covered a wide range of topics and seemed to reveal his ambitions more than his piety and sincerity. After Rigdon spoke, Brigham, as President of the Quorum of the Twelve, arose and briefly addressed the congregation, telling them that he would prefer to be spending his time mourning Joseph and Hyrum rather than dealing with the issue of who would lead the Church. "My hart was swolen with compasion to[w]ards them and by the power of the Holy Gost even the spirit of the Prophets, I was enabled to comfort the harts of the Saints," he wrote.[15]

Though it was unknown to Brigham at the time, the question of succession was instantly settled for many while he spoke. Some proclaimed that he was briefly transfigured into Joseph before their eyes, while others stated that they heard Joseph's voice. For many, this singular event was divine confirmation of the authority of the Twelve. While it served as a defining moment for many, Brigham did not make note of it.

In the afternoon meeting, Brigham spoke for two hours in an "open, frank and plain" fashion about Rigdon's claim and the imperative need for the Saints to build upon the foundation established by Joseph. Although

Brigham was willing to go it alone if necessary, his remarks evidenced his love for his fellow Saints and his sincere desire that they enjoy all the blessings to which they were entitled. He began by plainly proclaiming that he was acting in his office as one of the "Apostles whom God has called by revelation through the Prophet Joseph, who are ordained and anointed to bear off the keys of the kingdom of God in all the world." Succinctly addressing the succession question, he outlined what he had clearly realized at Peterborough:

> For the first time in my life, for the first time in your lives, for the first time in the kingdom of God in the 19th century, without a Prophet at our head, do I step forth to act in my calling in connection with the Quorum of the Twelve. . . .
>
> Heretofore you have had a Prophet as the mouth of the Lord to speak to you, but he has sealed his testimony with his blood, and now, for the first time, are you called to walk by faith, not by sight. . . .
>
> If any man thinks he has influence among this people to lead away a party, let him try it, and he will find out that there is power with the Apostles which will carry them off victorious through all the world, and build up and defend the church and kingdom of God. . . .
>
> You cannot fill the office of a prophet, seer and revelator: God must do this. . . .
>
> Does this church want it as God organized it? Or do you want to clip the power of the priesthood, and let those who have the keys of the priesthood go and build up the kingdom in all the world, wherever the people will hear them? . . .
>
> Now, if you want Sidney Rigdon or William Law to lead you, or anybody else, you are welcome to them; but I tell you, in the name of the Lord that no man can put another between the Twelve and the Prophet Joseph. Why? Because Joseph . . . committed into their hands the keys of the kingdom in this last dispensation. . . .
>
> . . . We have a head, and that head is the Apostleship, the spirit and power of Joseph, and we can now begin to see the necessity of that Apostleship.

Brother Rigdon was at his side—not above. No man has a right to counsel the Twelve but Joseph Smith. Think of these things. You cannot appoint a prophet; but if you let the Twelve remain and act in their place, the keys of the kingdom are with them and they can manage the affairs of the church and direct all things aright.[16]

According to Wilford Woodruff's summary, Brigham emphasized that the First Presidency was dissolved with the death of the Prophet and that the Quorum of the Twelve have "the keys of the Kingdom of God in all the world" and would have to ordain any man unto the office of prophet.[17] This teaching was consistent with what the Lord proclaimed in D&C 107:24 that the Twelve Apostles "form a quorum, equal in authority and power to the three presidents."

When a vote was put to the congregation as to whom they would follow, it was reportedly unanimous in favor of the Quorum of the Twelve. Concerning the day's events, Brigham simply noted, "We organized and set in order the Church as far as was necessary for the furtherance and prosperity of the kingdom."[18] Three days later he wrote to his daughter that because of "the great anxiety of the church, there was a conference held. . . . The power of the Priesthood was explained and the order thereof, on which the whole church lifted up their voices and hands for the twelve to move forward and organize the church and lead it as Joseph lead it. Which is our indispensable duty. . . . The brethren feel well to think the Lord is still mindful to us as a people."[19]

Rigdon continued to proclaim that his position was superior to that of the Twelve, prompting Brigham to note that while Joseph's one-time counselor claimed "all things [had been] shown to him" yet "he did not tell what the saints should do to save themselves."[20] For his part, Brigham went to work both teaching and showing the Saints what they must do to participate in their own salvation. In this regard, Brigham literally became like Joseph Smith and caused one Latter-day Saint to unabashedly write in October 1844: "Who cant see that the mantle of the prophet . . . has fallen on President Young and the Twelve? Who cant see that the same spirit which inspired our beloved brother Joseph Smith, now inspires President Young?"[21]

## ∽ 10 ∽

# BRIGHAM AS LEADER

When Brigham's accomplishments are considered in light of the obstacles that both man and nature put in his way, his place as one of the greatest Americans seems assured. Others have done great things for a few years in the face of great obstacles—Abraham Lincoln and Franklin D. Roosevelt led the nation through devastating wars, for instance—but few Americans have played such a major role for such a long time. Even critics acknowledge he was a great leader—they only wish his efforts hadn't been misdirected on Mormonism.

After meeting Brigham, French visitor Jules Remy wrote that few men "possess in so high a degree as he does, the qualities which constitute the eminent politician and the able administrator. All who have had an opportunity of seeing him at his work, friends or enemies, are unanimous on this point."[1] Fitz Hugh Ludlow described Brigham as enjoying the "great American talent of *un-cornerableness*" to a degree that he had "never seen surpassed in any great man in any nation." By this Ludlow meant that Brigham was never "put into a position where he [was] at the end of his resources."[2]

Brigham believed his accomplishments were not the result of his natural talents and abilities as a leader but because he was a devoted and steadfast follower. "What I know concerning God, concerning the earth, concerning government, I have received from the heavens, not alone through my natural ability, and I give God the glory and the praise. Men talk about what has been accomplished under my direction, and attribute it to my wisdom and ability; but it is all by the power of God, and by intelligence received from him."[3] On another occasion he stated: "What do you suppose I think when I hear people say, 'O, see what the Mormons have done in the mountains. It is Brigham Young. What a head he has got! What power he has got! How well he controls the people!' These people are ignorant of our true character. It is the Lord that has done this. It is not any one man or set of men; only as we are led and guided by the spirit of truth. It is the oneness, wisdom, power, knowledge and providences of God; and all that we can say is, we are his servants and handmaids."[4]

"With us, it is the kingdom of God, or nothing," Brigham proclaimed in a statement that succinctly characterized him as a leader and summarized the secret of his success.[5] Everything he did, everything he tried to get his followers to do, was with the kingdom in mind. At the August 8, 1844, meeting at which the Saints voted to follow the Twelve, Brigham declared: "Brother Joseph, the Prophet, has laid the foundation for a great work. . . . We can build a kingdom such as there never was in the world."[6] In spite of critics' claims that Brigham was trying to establish an earthly empire, he viewed the settling of the Great Basin as simply a means to an end. "The Kingdom of God is all that is of real worth," he taught. "All else is not worth possessing, either here or hereafter."[7]

For more than thirty years Brigham kept this vision of the kingdom before the Saints. Unlike leaders who only emphasized getting the job done, Brigham desired that the Saints understood *why* they did what they did. In some cases it took longer to accomplish the task because of the time spent teaching people, but he knew in the long run the end result would be better. His life's work was to create Saints, true followers of the Savior Jesus Christ, who understood they were children of a personal God and had the potential to become like Him. He also taught that the happiest life came as people devoted their time and energy to making God's interests their own.

As a result of Brigham's emphasis as a leader, he likely would prefer his legacy to be the devotion and spiritual strength that still characterizes the Latter-day Saints rather than the many settlements they founded, and that people focus less on *what* the Saints accomplished and more on *why* they accomplished it. Brigham's belief in the kingdom gave him confidence and courage to push on in spite of obstacles and opposition. "Daniel saw that in the latter days the God of heaven was going to set up his kingdom upon this his earth. He has set that kingdom up, as you who are here this day are witnesses. . . . The God of heaven showed Nebuchadnezzar that this kingdom would never be destroyed; and that is my testimony," he assured the Saints at the beginning of the Utah War.[8]

Because the Latter-day Saints shared Brigham's vision, they did not see themselves as simply eking out an existence or establishing settlements. Because they were building God's kingdom on earth, even the smallest task had a spiritual component and eternal consequences. Like their leader, this view helped the Saints as a body maintain their focus in spite of trials. Thus, there should be no marveling at the discipline, devotion, courage, and ingenuity that they employed to establish their desert commonwealth.

Brigham was a practical leader who demonstrated versatility, good judgment, and common sense. He believed that people needed to be led "with the even steady hand of mercy and justice."[9] While pragmatic and flexible— he displayed a willingness to adapt, abandon, and innovate to "carry out all the measures of Joseph"—he maintained a stubborn adherence to policies and practices received by revelation.[10] While a number of enterprises did not succeed as hoped, and while there were times when his patience was tried, his absolute faith in the final outcome allowed him to be optimistic and to view setbacks in proper perspective.

The Church was small enough to be an extended family, and in many regards Brigham is best understood as leader in terms of a loving father who was required to teach, instruct, and correct. For many this relationship started upon his return to Nauvoo following the martyrdom: "The Brethren ware over joyed to see us come home, for they ware little children with out a Father."[11] As he prepared to leave Winter Quarters for the West he noted that he felt "like a father with a great family of children around me."[12] As a father figure he employed a forthright speaking style that included abrasive, public chastising that largely worked in the close-knit community that was Utah, for his listeners knew firsthand that he spoke from experience and that there was a genuine concern behind his strong and harsh words.

As a leader Brigham had an ability, it might even be said a compulsion, to organize and to do. Under his direction, the Saints did as much in eighteen months toward completing the Nauvoo Temple as they had in the previous three years. Brigham also fixed things. If others wouldn't do it, he would. He found jobs for new emigrants, took care of the widows, and definitively advocated "prudence and economy" to help the Saints survive famines and droughts.

To become the leader the Lord needed, Brigham had to harness his natural tendency to hurry and get things done. During the whirl of activities leading up to the Mormon exodus from Nauvoo, he had a dream that profoundly influenced him: "This morning I dreamed I saw brother Joseph Smith and . . . he says brother Brigham don't be in a hurry—this was repeated the second and third time, when it came in a degree of sharpness."[13] The counsel was received. When prompted by the Spirit he acted quickly; otherwise he approached things slowly and consistently and was deliberate in his decision making. He characterized his life as "an even continuation," and denied being "subject to excitement in my feelings."[14] "You are in too much of a hurry," he told the Saints. "You do not go to meeting enough, you do not pray enough, you do not read the Scriptures enough, you do not meditate enough, you are all the time on the wing, and in such a hurry that you do not know what to do first."[15]

Brigham's confidence in the ultimate outcome allowed him to proceed without undue haste, fear, or anxiety. His belief that God was guiding the work also allowed him to act decisively, which made him appear stubborn and domineering to some followers and most outsiders. Remy observed that Brigham was "calm, cool, prudent in council, he decides slowly," but when "the time of action arrived," Brigham would work "with an energy which stops only at success."[16]

One of his strengths as a leader was his ability to put things into context. His was a steady and encouraging voice in the midst of persecution, plague, and pestilence. He continually tried to keep the big picture before people who might otherwise have focused on the challenges: "We talk about our trials and troubles here in this life: but suppose that you could see yourselves thousands and millions of years after you have proved faithful to your religion during the few short years in this time, and have obtained eternal salvation and a crown of glory in the presence of God; then look back upon your lives here, and see the losses, crosses, and disappointments, the sorrows . . . , you would be constrained to exclaim, 'But what of all that? Those things were but for a moment, and we are now here. We have been faithful during a few moments in our mortality, and now we enjoy eternal life and glory.'"[17]

The idea that Brigham seemingly held all power in Utah was troubling to non-Mormons. He was "the only absolute monarch in America," Mark Twain wrote, indicating the prevailing attitude.[18] Many federal officials went to Utah as the territory's savior but were shocked to find that the Saints overwhelmingly rejected their efforts to introduce laissez-faire capitalism and encourage individualism. What outsiders failed to understand was that Brigham's power had not been forced upon the Saints but had been freely given to him. Rather than being dupes or fools, Latter-day Saints believed that Brigham had empowered them by giving them control over their own lives.

While the ideal was never reached, Brigham longed for the day when Utah would become a theocracy. "I believe in the one-man power," he proclaimed. What the critics failed to understand is who he believed should hold the power. "Who is that man? Our Father in heaven, God, the eternal Father."[19]

For Brigham, revelation was the key to leadership. "I have no counsel for a man, unless I have the testimony of Jesus on the subject."[20] "I want to say for the consolation of the Elders of Israel . . . , you need have no trouble with regard to the building up of this kingdom, only do your duty in the sphere to which you are assigned. I think there is more responsibility on myself than any other one man on this earth pertaining to the salvation of the human family; yet my path is a pleasant path to walk in, my labors are very agreeable. . . . I trouble not myself with regard to my duties. All I have to do is to live . . . and keep my spirit, feelings and conscience like a sheet of blank paper, and let the Spirit and power of God write upon it what he pleases. When he writes I will read; but if I read before he writes, I am very likely to do wrong. If you will take the same course you will not have the least trouble."[21]

Brigham rejected the idea that leaders were to be followed blindly. "How easy it would be for your leaders to lead you to destruction, unless you actually know the mind and will of the Spirit yourselves."[22] "Do you know whether I am leading you right or not? . . . Do you know whether the wisdom and the mind of the Lord are dispensed to you correctly or not? . . . I have a request to make of each and every Latter-day Saint . . . to so live that the Spirit of the Lord will whisper to them and teach them the truth. . . . In this there is safety; without this there is danger."[23] "Now let me ask you, if you trust to my faith, to my word and teachings, counsel and advise [sic], and do not seek after the Lord to have His Spirit to guide and direct you, can I not deceive you, can I not lead you into error? Look at this and see to what mischief it would lead, and what an amount of evil could be done to a people if they did not live so that the Spirit of the Lord would dwell with them that they might know these things for themselves."[24]

"I have had some people ask me how I manage and control the people," Brigham noted. His response, "I do it by telling them the truth and letting them do just as they have a mind to"—a response similar to Joseph Smith's answer to the same question.[25] Brigham further declared: "The Lord has revealed certain principles from the heavens by which we are to live. . . . The principles which He has revealed I have taught to the people and . . . they control themselves. . . . This is the great secret now in controlling this people. It is thought that I control them, but it is not so."[26] Brigham believed that "one of the simplest things in the world is to control a people. Is there any particular art in making this people obedient? There is just one. If you Elders of Israel can get the art of preaching the Holy Ghost into the hearts of the people, you will have an obedient people. This is the only art required. Teach the people truth, teach them correct principles; show them what is for their greatest good and don't you think they will follow in that path?"[27] Brigham found they would.

*Engraving of Brigham Young, ca. 1855*

## ∽ 11 ∽

# BROTHER BRIGHAM

n 1860 visit to Salt Lake City prompted a *New York Herald* reporter to write, "Strange world, strange folks!" His conclusion was based not so much upon doctrine but upon what he observed at a local dance—Brigham casually intermingling with ordinary Latter-day Saints. In most cases, the amazed reporter noted, "such familiarity" between a leader and his followers would "be fatal to great claims."[1]

Throughout history men have risen to power by force and largely maintained their control by keeping themselves aloof from those over whom they held sway to ensure a certain mystique and air of superiority. While it was widely proclaimed that Brigham was a ruthless despot who ruled through intimidation and fear, what the reporter observed flew in the face of both conventional wisdom and popular perception. Brigham's power, the reporter discovered, resulted from the fact that the Latter-day Saints loved, not feared, him. "There can be no question that Brigham Young is both revered and beloved by the mass of the people," Charles Marshall likewise observed a decade later.[2] Like Joseph Smith, Brigham did not claim to be greater than his followers, but simply a fellow servant of God.

61

John Hyde concluded that "the whole secret of Brigham's influence lies in his *real sincerity*. Brigham may be a great man, greatly deceived, but he is not a hypocrite. . . . For the sake of his religion, he has over and over again left his family, confronted the world, endured hunger, come back poor, made wealth, and given it to the Church. . . . No holiday friend, nor summer Prophet, he has shared their trials, as well as their prosperity."[3] As with Joseph, the Saints honored Brigham with a unique combination of familiarity and obedience reflected in the way they lovingly referred to him: "Brother Brigham."

This warm relation was in spite of Brigham's frequent and harsh rebukes. Few people have dared to publicly speak to and about others as he did. "Although I may get up here and cuff them [the Latter-day Saints] about, chastising them for their forgetfulness, their weaknesses and follies, yet I have not seen a moment when they did not love me. The reason is," he proclaimed in 1852, "because I love them so well."[4]

For Brigham, his rebukes were evidence he hadn't given up on them and they shouldn't give up on themselves. While he reproved with sharpness, he also afterwards regularly showed forth an increase of love as the scriptures commands.[5] "There is not a soul that I chasten but what I feel as though I could take them and put them in my bosom and carry them with me day by day."[6] On one occasion he noted, "Though I may sometimes chastise my brethren, and speak to them in the language of reproof, there is not a father who feels more tenderly towards his offspring, and loves them better than I love this people."[7]

The kind side claimed by Brigham was noted by a newspaper reporter in 1876: "President Brigham Young addressed the assembled concourse in a kind, fatherly and instructive manner, his words and the feeling that prompted them going direct to the hearts of his hearers. At the conclusion of his brief discourse he blessed the people, every one in his place and station, in the name of Jesus Christ, and by the authority of the priesthood he holds, according to his right and privilege."[8]

The Saints were willing to make the heavy sacrifices he asked of them, for they knew he understood the "cost of discipleship." The Saints knew that

Brigham had "been there, done that" and that he was personally aware of the struggles and the sacrifices that the kingdom required. When Brigham proclaimed in September 1844 that he had "travelled these many years in the midst of poverty and tribulation, and that too with blood in my shoes, month after month, to sustain and preach this gospel and build up this kingdom," they knew he was telling the truth.[9] He likewise knew the price involved with the gathering of the Saints and having to start over more than once. "I have left my home five times, and a good handsome property each time," he told them.[10] They responded to his varied calls, from planting sugar beets to going on foreign missions, because of his example. "I ask not that of my brethren but what I am willing to give myself," he proclaimed, "and what I do as your leader, or president you should be willing to do the same."[11]

Brigham believed that "example is the best method of preaching."[12] The Saints knew him as a walking sermon who practiced what he preached. His attitude was "Come, boys," not "Go, boys."[13] When he stated, "I expect that if I should see a wagon in the mud, my shoulder would be first to the wheel to lift it out," the Saints knew he meant it.[14] When a ferry was needed during the journey of the 1847 vanguard company to Utah, "President Young stript himself and went to work with all his strength" and assisted in making "a first rate White Pine and White Cotton Wood Raft."[15] The following year, on his second journey to Utah, Brigham crossed and recrossed the North Platte to make certain that all were safely across.[16] During an 1864 journey, Brigham and his party came across "an old gentleman with a heavier load than his team could pull over a bad place on the road." Upon seeing him, Brigham "stepped out of the carriage, and with a wave of his hand cried out, 'Come on, boys, let's help this good old farmer out of his troubles.'"[17]

The Saints were accustomed to seeing Brigham undertake things most leaders left to others, but outsiders were amazed at what they saw. A stranger approached Brigham while he was on the steps of his carriage loading his luggage. "Is Governor Young in this carriage?" he asked. "No, sir," Brigham replied, "but he is on the steps of it."[18]

Elizabeth Kane noted that during a journey she and her husband made with Brigham that he personally inspected "every wheel, axle, horse and mule, and suit of harness belonging to the party" to make sure they were in good condition.[19] When the reporter for the *New York Herald* attended an annual Twenty-fourth of July celebration in the mountains, he was amazed to observe that after almost everyone had started for home, a solitary figure went from campfire to campfire to make certain "all fires were extinguished."[20] It was Brigham, practicing what he preached about being a good steward.

Brigham showed great concern for the Saints as individuals. At Winter Quarters he reminded the Saints that their temple covenants had application to the poor who had not yet reached that location. "Let the fire of the covenant which you made in the House of the Lord, burn in your hearts, like flame unquenchable, till you . . . [can] go straightway, and bring a load of the poor from Nauvoo . . . [for] this is a day of action."[21] Later, during the rescue of the stranded 1856 emigrant companies, he stated, "Were I to answer my own feelings, I should do so by undertaking to do what the conference voted I should not do, that is, I should be with them now in the snow."[22] In the aftermath of the tragedy, he took into his home many of those who needed the most care and visited others who had gone through the ordeal. Thirteen-year-old Mary Goble Pay, a member of the Hunt wagon company, lost her mother and two sisters on the journey and suffered from a bad case of frostbite that would require the amputation of her toes. The day after reaching Salt Lake, Brigham visited the family. Mary reported that "he shook hands with all of us. When he saw our condition—our feet frozen and our mother dead—tears rolled down his cheeks."[23]

During the early days in the valley, a correspondent reported that Brigham could be seen all day, every day, chopping wood, working in his garden, building houses, and so forth. The story is told that Jedediah M. Grant sought Brigham out on a public matter and found the President of the Church (and governor of the territory) shingling a roof. Brigham told him to come back in the evening. Grant replied: "Now, Brother Brigham, don't you think it is time you quit pounding nails and spending your time in work like this? We have many carpenters but only one Governor and one President of the Church. The people need you more than they need a good carpenter." Brigham reportedly came down off the roof and seldom thereafter spent his days in manual labor. Instead he "travelled and counselled, projected industry, watched over emigration, considered the claims of the people and gave himself heart and soul to the ministration to which he had been called and appointed. But he loved the honest labour of hand as well as brain and always honoured those who toiled to make life a joyous reality."[24]

Each year Brigham made a visit to the outlying settlements, which allowed him to strengthen the Saints and to see what had been done and what needed to be done. The visits were necessary for efficient planning, evaluation, and communication; they also provided a means to bless and counsel the Saints and to build the spiritual unity necessary to build the kingdom. They also provided him grassroots contact with those whom he called upon to make great sacrifices. He did not wish either distance or changing circumstances to separate him from the Saints. One reporter concluded that "without these visits the people might become narrowed up in their feelings and sectional."[25] The reporter further noted that "a visit from the Presidency and Twelve is refreshing to the officers and people. They partake of the spirit which prevails at head-quarters, and can better keep pace with their brethren who reside there."[26]

Brigham's journey through the settlements required great strength and effort, regularly taking a month or more to complete. In each town he was greeted by banners and parades, feasts and dances. Concerning one of his early trips, he wrote that he spent his time "instructing, comforting, and blessing the Saints, selecting new locations, forming acquaintances with and striving to promote peace among the different bands of Indians; and, by the blessing of heaven, accomplished all we could reasonably anticipate."[27] Eighteen years later, his report was slightly self-effacing: "Our visit & travels have proved of great mutual advantage. . . . [The time was spent] teaching, counselling & exhorting the Saints in the various settlements, doing all the good, & the very least portion of harm we possibly could"—counsel he frequently gave local leaders.[28] When he returned to Salt Lake, people gathered in the street to welcome him back.

In addition to formal meetings, Brigham also held an "open house" in each settlement for any who wished to meet with him. Elizabeth Kane reported that "at these informal audiences, reports, complaints, and petitions were made; and I think I gathered more of the actual working of Mormonism by listening to them than from any other source. They talked away to Brigham Young about every conceivable matter, from the fluxing of an ore to the advantages of a Navajo bit, and expected him to remember every child in every cotter's family. And he really seemed to do so, and to be at home, and be rightfully deemed infallible on every subject. I think he must make fewer mistakes than most popes, from his being in such constant intercourse with his people. I noticed that he never seemed uninterested, but gave an unforced attention to the person addressing him, which suggested a mind free from care. I used to fancy that he wasted a great deal of power in this way; but I soon saw that he was accumulating it."[29]

Brigham gave special attention to children. He answered their questions, listened to their stories, and gave them small gifts, such as marbles. His concern for the children even prompted him to ask the bishops to see that there was "a swing in each ward for the benefit of the children."[30]

On one of Brigham's journeys, one of Erastus Snow's young daughters spied Brigham cleaning his dentures. After he quickly replaced his teeth, the young girl excitedly pleaded, "Oh, Brother Brigham, show me your teeth! Show me your teeth, Brother Brigham!" He responded to her curiosity by taking them out so she could examine them.[31] On another occasion Brigham held one of Anson Call's young daughters on his knee during a visit to her family home. "During a lull in the conversation, . . . [Brigham] started to tell her how pretty she was, when [the child] blurted out, 'Your eyes look just like our sow's!' . . . [Taking] the child by the hand," Brigham stated: "'Take me to the pig pen. I want to see this pig that has eyes just like mine.'" When the story was later retold, Brigham laughed as much as anyone.[32]

Another thing that endeared Brigham was his lack of pretension. Shortly after Daniel W. Jones reached Salt Lake City, Edmund Ellsworth wanted to take him to visit Brigham: "I asked him to wait until I changed my clothes. This he would not allow, but insisted I should go as I was, adding that Brother Brigham did not judge a man by his dress. I went and can say I was completely won by President Young's manner. He asked me a great many questions, and I was satisfied that he did not doubt my sincerity."[33]

Elizabeth Kane was "amused" at Brigham's "odd appearance" on one of his annual journeys to the outlying settlements when he wore "a great surtout, reaching almost to his feet, of dark-green cloth . . . lined with fur, a fur collar, cap, and pair of sealskin boots with the undyed fur outward" and "a hideous pair of green goggles."[34]

"What made me love Joseph so?" Brigham once asked. Answering his own question, he noted that Joseph had "never spared any pains to do me good. I knew when my hand met his that he would lay down his life for me."[35] The Latter-day Saints loved "Brother Brigham" for much the same reason.

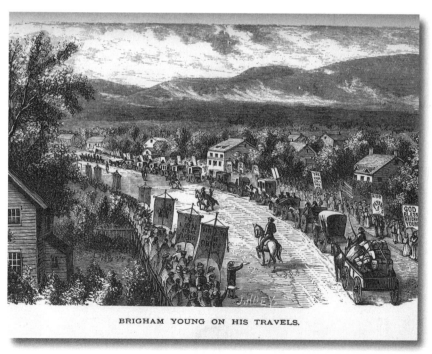

BRIGHAM YOUNG ON HIS TRAVELS.

*Brigham Young travels through Utah.*

## 12

# BRIGHAM ON BRIGHAM

One biographer wrote that "the key to understanding" Brigham was "not in the Rocky Mountains" but in "the files of . . . great Eastern newspapers prosperous and wise enough to . . . [have sent] their best reporters to Salt Lake City."[1] While it is true that the Eastern press and most non-Mormon newspapers from coast to coast largely presented a fairly consistent view of Brigham during his lifetime, it is a portrayal at odds with the one found in his sermons and in the comments of those closely associated with him. In many regards, the contrast between the "Wasatch Front" Brigham and the "Eastern" Brigham couldn't be more dramatic—Dr. Jekyll or Mr. Hyde, depending upon which author you read. In one location he was primarily portrayed as a gentle spiritual leader while in the other his image is largely less-than-saintly.

After a few months in Utah in 1858, Elizabeth Cumming, whose husband replaced Brigham as governor, commented on the discrepancy between what she observed and what she read in recently arrived Eastern newspapers. Marveling at "the *quantity* of news about Utah," she concluded that "it is strange that *not one single truth* should be told—yet such is the fact. . . . The chief peculiarity of all these stories lies in the fact that there is not even a *foundation* for any of them."[2] Mark Twain also weighed in on the press. After two days in Salt Lake, his party left "hearty and well fed . . . but not so very much wiser, as regards the 'Mormon question.' . . . We had a deal more 'information' than we had before . . . [but] all our 'information' had three sides to it, and so I gave up the idea that I could settle the 'Mormon question' in two days. Still," he sarcastically added, "I have seen newspaper correspondents do it in one."[3]

During his extended visit to Utah, Jules Remy concluded: "Of those who have written on the Mormons, by far the greater number have derived their information from sources little to be relied upon. The historians and travellers who have been their guides, have either never inspected the facts on the spot, or have looked at them from the point of view of their own foregone opinions, and too often of their passions."[4] Remy, however, was not immune to the problem he noted, incorrectly reporting that Brigham "had nine [children] born to him in one week."[5]

Outsiders were not the only ones to get things wrong. In 1853 Brigham tried to correct a frequently mistold story concerning himself and then informed his primarily Latter-day Saint audience: "I wished to lay it before you as it was, in consequence of the different statements which have been made, that vary considerably from the truth, after passing through a few hands. After relating the simple facts as they existed, you may regard them as you please; but when you tell them over again to your neighbors, tell them as they were, or not at all."[6]

Brigham is largely an open book because he frequently waxed autobiographical in his letters and sermons. Proponents of the "Eastern" Brigham, however, have long been reluctant to systematically and honestly mine these treasure troves, while advocates of the "Wasatch" Brigham have frequently used his words to create their own stereotype. Brigham believed that "no man can hide [himself] if he is allowed to talk; he will be sure to manifest his true feelings."[7]

Brigham found the lessons of his youth "perfectly astonishing" and nearly "impossible . . . to get rid of."[8] For example, he reported that he knew "how to economize, for my father had to do it."[9] He further noted that he had been from "boyhood a person of observation."[10]

Early on he evidenced a fierce independent streak and cherished both his freedom and his agency. "My independence is sacred to me," he declared.[11] "I do not know how to do without the liberty that my father fought for."[12] "I am naturally opposed to being crowded, and am opposed to any person who undertakes to force me to do this, or not do that."[13] Although a temperance advocate, he refused to sign the pledge. "'If I sign the temperance pledge I feel that I am bound, and I wish to do just right, without being bound to it; I want my liberty,'" he explained. "I have conceived from my youth up that I could have my liberty and independence just as much in doing right as I could in doing wrong."[14] "I want to live perfectly above the law, and make it my servant, instead of its being my master."[15]

He was troubled by those who professed one thing and did another. "I had seen and heard enough to make me well acquainted with the people in their acts and dealings one towards another, the result of which was to make me sick, tired, and disgusted with the world; and had it been possible, I would have withdrawn from all people, except a few, who, like myself, would leave the vain, foolish, wicked, and unsatisfying customs and practices of the world."[16] When an early professional endeavor required him to "either to be dishonest or quit," he quit.[17]

"When I think of myself, I think just this—I have the grit in me, and I will do my duty," he proclaimed.[18] Recognizing that someone needed to "stand on guard" after the martyrdom of Joseph Smith, he came forward. "Had it not been for that, I could not have stepped forth as I did at Nauvoo," he admitted.[19] "When duty prompts me I mean to do it," he declared a few years later, "let consequences be what they may."[20]

Initially the responsibility of leading the Church pressed down upon him like a "twenty-five ton weight."[21] Over time, the anxiety faded. "I am full of peace by day and by night," he noted.[22] As he came to fully trust the prophetic mantle, he instantaneously fell asleep upon retiring and then rested as "soundly as a healthy child in the lap of its mother."[23] He acknowledged that it took time for him to have the confidence to deal with prominent individuals. "I used to think, until I was forty-five years of age, that I had not knowledge, sense, or ability enough to enable me to associate with the men of the world." Things changed when he understood that "the inhabitants of the earth were groveling in darkness and ignorance, and that their professed knowledge contained but few correct principles."[24]

Rather than a dictator, he advocated tolerance. "I am not a stereotyped Latter-day Saint, and do not believe in the doctrine. . . . Away with stereotyped 'Mormons.'"[25] Referencing the Greek myth of the Bed of Procrustes, he stated: "Every man, and more particularly my immediate associates who are with me daily, know how I regret the ignorance of this people—how it floods my heart with sorrow to see so many Elders of Israel who wish everybody to come to their standard and be measured by their measure. Every man must be just so long, to fit their iron bedstead, or be cut off to the right length: if too short, he must be stretched, to fill the requirement."[26]

Contrary to the image of Brigham as a bloodthirsty individual that is often portrayed by his critics, he consistently denied a desire to take human life or exact revenge. "I wish to meet all men at the judgment Bar of God without any to fear me or accuse me of a wrong action," he declared.[27] "I feel happy; I feel at peace with all the inhabitants of the earth; I love my friends, and as for my enemies, I pray for them daily."[28] While some members of Zion's Camp were angered that they did not have the opportunity to use their weapons to redeem Zion, "so far as I was concerned," Brigham recalled, "I did not wish to fight."[29] In Utah, he noted that the Saints "could wipe the few enemies now in our borders out of existence in a very short time, if I would give the word to do so. . . . If it were left to me solely, under the guidance of the spirit pertaining to man, probably I should have had them in eternity before now. But the Lord dictates, governs, and controls: I do not, neither do I wish to."[30] Instead, he "fervently" prayed that he would "never be brought into circumstances to be obliged to shed human blood."[31] "I wish to save life, and have no desire to destroy life. If I had my wish, I should entirely stop the shedding of human blood. The people abroad do not generally understand this," he declared with understatement.[32]

What would Brigham do "if the wicked, the ungodly, and those who have persecuted and driven us from our homes, and have consented to the death of the Prophets and the innocent" settled among the Saints? "I would do, I think, about as the Lord does; He lets them alone to take their own course."[33]

Brigham also denied the commonly told story that he was motivated by money. "There are those in this congregation who are so short-sighted, and so destitute of eternal wisdom and knowledge, that they believe that brother Brigham is after property—after the things of this world. That is a false feeling, a false view, and a false faith."[34] "I own property, and I employ the best men I can find to look after it," but as far as "letting my own mind dwell upon the affairs of this world, I will not do it."[35] "I have been robbed several times of my all in this life, and my property has gone into the hands of my enemies, but as to property, I care no more about it than about the dirt in the streets, only to use it as God wishes."[36] "I have not the slightest feeling in my heart that I own a single thing. What I am in possession of, the Lord has merely made me a steward over."[37] "I am a public hand, and myself and all I possess belong to the Lord."[38] After six years in Utah he was personally owed more than thirty thousand dollars, but noted he had never "distressed a man" for repayment "or crowded any person in the least."[39]

He acknowledged that he had petitioned God for relief when poverty threatened his family but believed that people who pray for "more than this are off more or less from the track that leads to life eternal."[40] To a man who had recently lost his fortune, Brigham wrote: "I have ben poor and it is good for a man to be poor that we may lern humility and also to serve the Lord, in poverty as well as in welth."[41]

Brigham was largely philosophical about statements directed towards him, even treating them with humor. Once he introduced himself to some California-bound emigrants as "the notorious Brigham Young."[42] "Were I to renounce my religion I could . . . be honored, I could go abroad in the world and be respected, but I love my religion above all things else," he declared.[43] "Facing the storm of villification, slander, abuse, and persecution of the most vile and cruel character, [since becoming a Latter-day Saint] until this moment, is very strong proof that I do not trim my sails to catch the popular breezes of the world's cliques and circles," he wrote a childhood friend.[44] "I tremble not, I fear not, neither do I care for the insults of the world, for the Lord is my bulwark, my shield and my deliverer."[45] "I am accused of a thousand evils," he noted, "but I have never feared but one thing with regard to myself—and that is, that I should be left to do an evil that people may truly blame me; while they cannot speak evil of me and tell the truth, it never harms me."[46] He further stated: "I neither count the favors, nor fear the frowns of man, knowing full well that the cause in which I am enlisted will ride triumphant over all opposition."[47]

Brigham reported: "I have been asked, 'Brother Brigham, are you going to bear this? Do you not know that such and such persons are scandalizing your character?' Said I, 'I do not know that I have any character, I have never stopped to inquire whether I have one or not. It is for me to pursue a course that will build up the kingdom of God on the earth, and you may take my character to be what you please, I care not what you do with it, so you but keep your hands off from me.'"[48] He told the Saints concerning negative comments about him in the Eastern press: "I care nothing about my character in the world. I do not care what men say about me; I want my character to stand fair in the eyes of my Heavenly Father."[49] "I will say that if men will do the will of God and keep his commandments and do good, they may say what they please about me."[50]

In a public self-interview, Brigham declared: "'Have you not committed wrong?' I may have committed a great many wrongs for want of judgment or wisdom—a little here and a little there. 'But have you not done great wrongs?' I have not."[51]

A powerful speaker, he admitted that "although I have been a public speaker for thirty-seven years, it is seldom that I rise before a congregation without feeling a child-like timidity; if I live to the age of Methuselah, I do not know that I shall outgrow it."[52] He further stated, "Had it not been that I clearly saw and understood that the Lord Almighty would take the weak things of this world to confound the mighty, the wise, and the talented, there was nothing that could have induced me, or persuaded me to have ever become a public speaker."[53]

While his sermons contained warnings and admonishments, he preferred to accentuate the positive. "From the day I commenced preaching the Gospel to this present moment, I never had a feeling in my heart to occupy much time in preaching hell to the people, or telling them much about being damned. . . . There are more beauty, glory, excellency, knowledge, power, and heavenly things than I have time to talk about."[54]

"I have a great many reflections, especially when alone," he noted. "I converse with myself upon these eternal things, things which the frivolous, the vain, and those who are engaged only with the things of this world, never think of."[55] He reported that "I sometimes feel that I have not a pound of strength left, just from sitting and thinking."[56] He tried "to live so as to know my business and understand my duty, and to do it at the moment without long study."[57]

In 1873, Brigham made a rare public pronouncement regarding his spiritual experiences: "I have had many revelations; I have seen and heard for myself, and know these things are true."[58] Like Joseph, he too was taught by heavenly messengers. "I like some of God's messengers, who travel about, to visit me. I am fond of their society."[59] These messengers included Jesus Christ, Michael, Elijah, Moses, and the ancient Apostles.[60]

Looking back over his life, Brigham declared, "I have learned enough to be happy, when I am in the enjoyment of the blessings of the Lord. That is a great lesson for a man to learn."[61]

He acknowledged that he had "done the best I know how."[62] He also confessed: "I do not know that I could do better than I have done since I have been in this kingdom if I were to live my life over again. I should be afraid to try it, lest I might make the matter worse instead of better."[63]

When Horace Greeley suggested that Brigham seemed in no hurry to get to heaven, he responded: "I wish to stay here and fight the Devil until he is bound, and all wickedness is cleansed from the earth, and it is made ready for Christ to come."[64] Shortly before his death he declared, "I know not how soon the messenger will call for me, but I calculate to die in the harness."[65] Concerning his death he stated, "I do not wish any of you to cry and feel badly." Instead, he desired people to follow his example and continue "to fight the devils."[66]

*Brigham Young, ca. 1855*

## ∽ 13 ∽

# BRIGHAM AS
# AMERICAN MOSES

For more than sixty years following the "opening" of the West by Lewis and Clark until the completion of the transcontinental railroad, an estimated five hundred thousand pioneers set out on America's overland trails for various westward locations. Within this general migration is the unique story of some seventy thousand Mormon pioneers who were led by a modern Moses to their own "promised land." Concerning his role as "American Moses," Brigham later stated: "I did not devise the great scheme of the Lord's opening the way to send this people to these mountains. Joseph contemplated the move for years before it took place. . . . It was the power of God that wrought out salvation for this people. I never could have devised such a plan."[1] Be that as it may, by the time Brigham had the responsibility of leading the monumental emigration of Latter-day Saints into the American West, he had already proven himself to be an able and inspiring leader.

Beginning with the Saints' expulsion from Nauvoo, Illinois, in 1846, and for the succeeding twenty-two years, the Mormon migration was a unique saga in the settlement of the American West. Unlike most emigrants, who usually traveled by themselves or in small groups, the Mormons traveled together in large numbers. While most emigrants who went west were largely motivated by economic reasons—seeking fertile farmland or gold, or following the promise of work or business opportunities throughout the West—the Mormons journeyed specifically to one location, which they called "Zion," where they gathered with the hopes of serving God free from persecution. Most extraordinary among those who left behind all they knew—sometimes even never-to-be-seen-again family and friends—for the hope of a better life was the fact that throughout the years the Latter-day Saints were led by one imposing, devout, and pragmatic man. Under his direction an 1847 vanguard company of religious refugees cut a trail into the vast frontier beyond the Missouri River that would subsequently be used by tens of thousands of others.

On August 6, 1842, the Prophet Joseph had prophesied that "some of you will live to . . . see the Saints become a mighty people in the midst of the Rocky Mountains."[2] To prepare and plan the move west, Brigham studied the most current maps, read John C. Fremont's 1845 *Report of the Exploring Expedition to the Rocky Mountains,* and even consulted Lansford W. Hasting's *The Emigrant's Guide to Oregon and California.* Later he wrote Joseph A. Stratton, who presided over the Saints in St. Louis, to bring him "one half dozen of Mitchell's new map of Texas Oregon & California and the regions adjoining." He then added, "If there is any thing later or better than Mitchell's, I want the best."[3]

Brigham's preparation for leading the Saints west, however, began more than a decade earlier at the feet of the Prophet Joseph during the 1834 march of Zion's Camp. "I have travelled with Joseph a thousand miles. He has led the camp of Israel: I have watched him and observed every thing he said or did. . . . This was the starting point of my knowing how to lead Israel."[4] During this time Brigham had his first lesson in directing large groups as Joseph organized the company into effective groups of tens, fifties, and hundreds. The mental notes he made later proved valuable in first evacuating the

Saints from Missouri, then in organizing the exodus to the Salt Lake Valley, and finally in gathering Church members from Europe and the eastern United States.

During the dark and bitter winter of Joseph Smith's imprisonment in Liberty Jail and the Saints' expulsion from Missouri, Brigham put the lessons into action as he led the Saints across Missouri under the most adverse of conditions. Under his direction, more than ten thousand Saints left Missouri beginning in January 1839. His personal effort was remarkable as he frequently traveled as much as twenty miles across frozen Missouri landscape, established temporary shelter for his family, and then retraced his steps to lead poor and destitute Saints who had been forced to remain behind because of their circumstances. In this way he led the Saints across the state to the safety of the compassionate residents of Quincy, Illinois. The events of Missouri, although horrid, gave Brigham some experience to implement an even greater exodus from Nauvoo seven years later, once again in the dead of winter.

From the beginning, the move west from Nauvoo was a huge undertaking. The *Sangamo Journal* of Springfield, Illinois, reported that "the whole number of souls now on the road may be set down in round numbers at twelve thousand. . . . about eight hundred or less still remain in Illinois. This comprises the entire Mormon population that once flourished in Hancock [County]."[5]

Although the Mormons were pressured to leave their beloved City of Joseph, Brigham viewed his "exodus" with an eye to the future possibilities. Three weeks after leaving Nauvoo in February 1846, he wrote his brother Joseph Young: "Do not think . . . I hate to leve my house and home. no! far from that I am so free from bondedge at this time that Nauvoo looks like a prison to me, it looks plesent ahead but dark to look back."[6]

The 1846 journey across Iowa consumed more time and resources than the Saints anticipated as they encountered what has been described as "a continuous mud hole."[7] While the Iowa experience exhausted Brigham both physically and emotionally—Brigham lost so much weight that his clothes no longer fit—it served as a valuable reminder of the Saints' dependence upon God's help, much like the Red Sea served a similar purpose for ancient Israel.

On January 14, 1847, as the Saints were making preparations at Winter Quarters in anticipation of resuming their journey west, Brigham received the "Word and Will of the Lord" (D&C 136). In this revelation the Lord drew a comparison between the exoduses of the ancient Israelites and the modern Saints with references to "covenants," "commandments," "statutes," and "ordinances." He also made reference to the lesson Brigham had been taught by Joseph during Zion's Camp on how to organize the camps of modern Israel. The following month, Brigham had a dream in which Joseph appeared to him and, after embracing Brigham, looked at him "with his usual earnest, expressive & pleasing countenance, [and] replied 'It is all right.'"[8] Both the "Word and Will of the Lord" and the vision of Joseph helped renew Brigham's confidence as he anticipated leaving for the place that God had prepared for the Saints.

Brigham did not want a repeat of Iowa on the journey west, where many had left Nauvoo unprepared for the journey, contrary to counsel. Throughout the fall of 1846 and into the spring of 1847, Brigham continued to admonish the Saints to prepare for the move west by building and repairing wagons, procuring strong oxen and horses, and obtaining supplies needed to start their new home. As people continued to ignore his counsel and example, a frustrated Brigham declared in March 1847 that if the leaders of emigrating companies could not report that those planning to leave that year were properly outfitted with the supplies they would need once they reached Utah, he would "rub your ears for you—worse than I have done tonight."[9]

Interestingly, when it came to food Brigham instructed these modern religious refugees that one hundred pounds of provisions per person would be sufficient on their journey to their promised land. Brigham believed that it could rain manna on the plains of America as easily as in Arabia and told the Saints that "he wanted all to stay here [Winter Quarters], who had not faith to go with that amount."[10]

By early April 1847, the vanguard pioneer company was ready to leave Winter Quarters for the journey west. Because they were the "Camp of Israel," Brigham purposefully chose 144 men for the journey—twelve men representing each of the twelve tribes of Israel. Ultimately, the final makeup of the company varied a bit from the 144—there were 143 men, 3 women, and 2 children.[11] One member of the company wrote: "It was hard for me to leave my little family sick among howling wolves and the roaming savages of the West but the servants of the Lord said go and I felt as ever to leave all for the benefit of the Gospel or the salvation of the people."[12]

On April 16 one of the most atypical pioneering companies ever to cross the plains resolutely began the long journey toward an uncertain location in the West under the confident leadership of a man who resolutely trusted in the word and guidance of the Lord. When asked how he would know when they had reached their promised land, Brigham confidently responded: "Oh, I will know it when I see it. We shall continue to travel the way the Spirit of the Lord directs us. The Lord has reserved for us a good place in the mountains and he will lead us directly to it."[13] He later noted that while at Nauvoo he had experienced "a vision of Joseph Smith" in which he was shown the Saints' new home.[14]

In addition to implementing the company's organization, Brigham specified "the order for travelling and camping." At 5:00 A.M. the bugle would call "every man to arise and attend prayers before he leaves his wagon." At 7:00 A.M. the company was to be ready to move out. At night, the wagons were to be brought into a circle, with "the horses and stock tied inside the circle. At 8½ P.M. the bugles to be sounded again at which time all to have prayers in their wagons and to retire to rest by 9 o'clock."[15]

The journey revealed that Brigham remained a frontiersman at heart. What Patty Bartlett Sessions wrote of Brigham in 1846—"Br. Brigham came up with his company driving his team in the rain and mud to his knees as happy as a king"—applied equally to 1847.[16] As a "dynamic, hands-on leader," he personally scouted out the route, selected camp sites, stood guard, hunted food, dealt with traders and mountaineers and Indians, built rafts, waded rivers, jumped into mud to help pull a rope when needed, set a broken leg, fixed a broken wagon axle, and traveled at the back of the train where he "ate trail dust."[17]

Later, he painted this tribute to the Mormon vanguard pioneers:

> We made and broke the road from Nauvoo to this place. Some of the time we followed Indian trails; some of the time we ran by the compass; when we left the Missouri river we followed the Platte. . . . [We] made roads and built bridges till our backs ached. . . . We carried every particle of provision we had when we arrived here. . . . If we had not brought our goods in this manner we should not have had them, for there was nothing here. You may say this is a burlesque [exaggeration]. Well, I mean it as such, for we, comparatively speaking, really came here naked and barefoot.[18]

The three-month journey came to an end in late July 1847. Members of the company had already begun to settle the Salt Lake Valley two days before Brigham reached the summit of Big Mountain. On July 24, Wilford Woodruff recorded that after a six-mile journey, "we came in full view of the great valley or Bason [of] the Salt Lake and land of promise held in reserve by the hand of GOD for a resting place for the Saints upon which A portion of the Zion of GOD will be built." Brigham, who was traveling in the back of Woodruff's carriage in a sickbed, instructed Woodruff to turn the carriage so that he could have a better view of the Saints' promised land. Woodruff wrote in his journal that "President Young expressed his full satisfaction in the Appearance of the valley as A resting place for the Saints & was Amply repayed for his Journey."[19] Later, Woodruff reported that Brigham "was enwrapped in vision for several minutes. He had seen the valley before in vision, and upon this occasion he saw the future glory of Zion and of Israel, as they would be."[20] Woodruff further reported that after Brigham had gazed for a time upon the scene he declared, "It is enough. This is the right place. Drive on." Brigham subsequently noted that "the spirit of light rested upon me and hovered over the valley, and I felt that there the Saints would find protection and safety."[21]

A month after reaching their promised land, Brigham and others began the long return journey east to Winter Quarters to gather their families for a westward journey they would undertake the following year. This return journey brought joyful reunions with other companies still on the trail. Brigham's countenance no doubt reflected both his joy at finding the promised land and his gratification that others had the faith to follow him into the wilderness.

The experience and successes of the vanguard company proved the Mormon Trail to be a trail of hope. The trail's end brought them to a place prepared for them by God—a retreat from the tribulations of the past and a place to advance into the future. Although the initial Mormon emigrants were pushed out of Nauvoo and into the West, subsequent groups were pulled to join them in Zion. Long after again returning to the valley in 1848, Brigham continued to serve as a Moses by directing the gathering of tens of thousands of additional Saints.

FIRST VIEW OF GREAT SALT LAKE VALLEY, FROM A MOUNTAIN PASS.

*First view of the Great Salt Lake Valley*

## ∞ 14 ∞

# BRIGHAM HOLDS BACK
# THE WORLD

Four days after proclaiming Salt Lake Valley the "right place," Brigham
told the few Saints gathered there that he desired them to "live free
& independent, untrammeled by any of their [gentile] detestable
customs & practices. You don't know how I detest & despise them."[1] For the
next thirty years, Brigham battled both those within and without the Church
to try to accomplish this ideal. Among the former, many never caught his
vision. Among the latter, the issue was control of the territory and assimila-
tion, since Brigham's economic policies were outside the mainstream. For
Brigham, the issue was not simply a matter of control. His desire to hold back
the world was more far-reaching. "I have had visions and revelations
instructing me how to organize this people so that they can live like the family of heaven," he proclaimed in 1863, "but I cannot do it while so much selfishness and wickedness reign in the Elders of Israel."[2] His hope was that the
Saints would become "one family, each seeking to do his neighbour good."[3]

Given his views, it is not surprising that he chose the beehive to serve as
the symbol and model of what he was trying to accomplish. (*Deseret* is a Book

of Mormon term for honeybee.) He wanted the Saints to be unified, orderly, and cooperative, and to work for the well-being of the group rather than following the worldly pattern of each individual primarily seeking his or her own interests. Because his views were contrary to the trends of the time, especially in terms of economic policies, government officials and business interests united to oppose them. Ironically, some of the very practices he advocated—central direction, cooperation, and long-term planning—are now embraced by both business and government.

Many have mistakenly viewed Brigham as an isolationist when in reality he was a selective adopter of practices and policies. Brigham had no illusions of the Saints becoming isolated. Rather his ultimate goal was to have the Saints adopt a lifestyle based upon higher, celestial laws, which resulted in a unified and cooperative community equal to the task that lay before them of establishing the foundation of God's kingdom on earth.

Brigham's economic policies were both systematic and pragmatic, given what he was trying to accomplish. While the focus in neighboring territories was largely upon mineral wealth, he encouraged the Saints to first focus upon agricultural pursuits so that they could become as self-sufficient as possible. "If a man wants food or clothing, a little gold is very useful," he proclaimed. "Suppose we were all to leave our harvest and dig gold, and have no food, . . . our gold would be a curse to us."[4] Rather than the Saints seeking gold and silver, he encouraged mining for industrial, "civilizing" metals such as iron and the harvesting of minerals such as salt and coal. He also advocated a wide variety of commercial and manufacturing enterprises designed to benefit the community. Not only did he understand the problems that came with an economy dependent on others, but he desired money to remain in the territory in Mormon hands where it could be used for other important endeavors, such as gathering the Saints.

From their beginnings in Utah, the Latter-day Saints had to deal with outside influences that threatened the goal of self-sufficiency. Starting in 1849, miners bound for the California gold fields began passing through Salt Lake by the hundreds. When a Latter-day Saint desired to take his family to the gold mines to make a better living so that he could pay more tithing, Brigham reminded him that the love of money was the root of all evil. Brigham believed that money in and of itself was not a cure-all but was an indifferent object that had limitations. While the Lord expected the Saints to contribute financially to the building of the kingdom, Brigham informed his son that "the devil cannot work without money, whereas the Lord can."[5]

Brigham hoped those whose primary focus was acquiring wealth would not lose sight of that fact. "Gold is a good servant, but a miserable, blind, and helpless god, and at last will have to be purified by fire, with all its followers."[6] He wryly recounted that during the gold rush a man bound for the California gold fields met him on the street: "He asked me if I knew where hell was. I told him I thought that he was on the road to that very place; and when he crossed over the Sierra Nevada mountains into the gold diggings in California, if he discovered that he had not found hell, to come back and let me know. As I have not since heard from him, I presume he found it."[7]

There was a need for gold, Brigham recognized, but the need was limited. To meet the demand, he called gold missionaries to undertake a special mission to acquire gold needed to mint money and meet other expenses. For the rest of the Saints, however, he encouraged them to focus upon "iron and coal, good hard work, plenty to eat, good schools and good doctrine."[8]

For Brigham, economy and frugality were more important than acquiring money. Every cent "luxuriously expended" was money unavailable to build the kingdom, particularly for gathering the poor. He counseled his sons to observe the poor, learn how they could live on next to nothing, and then to implement those practices in their own lives.[9]

After the Saints had survived gold fever, Brigham in the mid-1850s tried to implement on a wide scale what had become a key component of his own life—the "Law of Consecration and Stewardship." In so doing, he was a faithful follower of Joseph Smith, who had received the law by revelation in 1831. When Joseph tried to implement it at Kirtland, the Saints were not yet ready to live it. In Utah it fared little better. Brigham understood that only voluntary involvement would allow the system to operate as intended. "I want to have you consecrate your property if you wish to. If not do as you please with it," he stated.[10]

Less than half the Saints chose to consecrate their property, prompting Orson Pratt to conclude that "the Saints were still devoted to 'the Gentile god of property' . . . 'because of the hardness of our hearts, and the blindness of our minds, and our covetousness.'"[11]

With the approach of the railroad a decade later, Brigham again made a concerted effort to hold back the world by establishing a cooperative movement. In 1867 he established Zion's Cooperative Mercantile Institution (ZCMI), a wholesale trading establishment designed to continue the economic interdependency and self-sufficiency that had allowed the community of Saints to grow and prosper.

In an additional effort to check the negative influences associated with the railroad, that same year he reestablished both the School of the Prophets for men and the Relief Society for women. Rather than devoted entirely to learning, the School of the Prophets primarily considered issues of civil government and economic planning and then carried out the specific policies agreed upon. To prevent an influx of unruly railroad workers and camp followers and non-Mormon merchants catering to them, the School of the Prophets obtained the contract to build the last section of the Union Pacific line from Echo Canyon to Promontory Summit. Brigham "acknowledged the hand of the Lord in giving this [people] the privilege of performing the work; thus keeping away from our midst the swarms of scalliwags that the construction of the railway would bring here."[12]

In reemphasizing the Relief Society, Brigham also adapted and adopted the program to fit current needs. Under the direction of Eliza R. Snow, the basic mission of the Relief Society was expanded from solely providing help for the poor and needy to bettering the lives of Latter-day Saint women and their families. Emphasis was placed upon food storage, and the sisters were trained in the domestic arts and home industries and encouraged to "dress themselves beautifully in the workmanship of their own hands."[13] In a pragmatic response to a growing taste for finer things, Brigham encouraged the production of silk. During the 1870s, nearly every Relief Society cultivated silk worms on their own mulberry trees and spun and wove their own thread.

Because Brigham desired the Latter-day Saints to be different from the world in fashion as well as finance, in November 1869 he called his daughters together and organized them into a Retrenchment Society. He instructed them on economy and modest living, and the girls pledged to avoid extravagant practices and to retrench, or cut back, excesses in dress, diet, and speech. The Young Ladies Retrenchment Association, later renamed the Young Women's Mutual Improvement Association, was subsequently implemented throughout the settlements. In 1875, the Young Men's Mutual Improvement Association was organized for a similar purpose.

In a further attempt to hold back the world, Brigham publicly decried what he called the "everlasting ding-dong about fashions."[14] "In my feelings they are positively ridiculous, they are so useless and unbecoming. Do you recollect a fashion there was a few years ago . . . when a woman could not walk through the streets without holding her clothes two feet in front of her if her arm was long enough? . . . Now it is on the other side, and I do not know but they will get two humps on their backs, they have one now, and if they get to be dromedaries it will be no wonder."[15] He mused that some women's dresses might conceal a six-horse team with "a dozen dogs under the wagon."[16] In a further overstatement to make his point, he publicly threatened to divorce his wives who couldn't get over their fashion fixation.[17]

In 1873, Brigham pushed his last major effort to hold back the world by introducing the United Order of Enoch among the Saints. The cooperative movement, Brigham informed the Saints, had only been "a stepping stone to what is called the Order of Enoch, but which is in reality the Order of Heaven."[18] Eventually more than 150 united orders were established throughout the territory. These united orders operated in a variety of ways, as Brigham recognized that they needed to be flexible enough to accommodate a diversity of Saints and communities. As with the law of consecration, he did not see it as "part of this Order to take away the property of one man and give it to another, neither to equally divide what we possessed." Rather, it was to allow all "the opportunity of enriching themselves through their diligence" and freeing surplus property for the task of "carrying on the work of God generally."[19]

In April 1877, Brigham reminded the Saints that "we have no business here other than to build up and establish the Zion of God. It must be done according to the will and law of God, after that pattern and order by which Enoch built up and perfected the former-day Zion."[20] The best known of the united orders was the "Orderville" model where everyone shared everything in common. It lasted the longest and came closest to reaching the ideal. Brigham's nephew John R. Young later wrote of the demise of the united orders: "President Brigham Young was the pilot, the guiding star. When he died the master mind was gone."[21] Most united orders were short lived and all "failed" in the sense that the Saints reverted back to less cooperative economies. They "succeeded" in contributing to the fundamental goal by directing the Saints' focus upon the kingdom.

Brigham was not fully able to achieve his ideal of separation from "Babylon" in the short term, and he ultimately lost the war of economic isolation and self-sufficiency. But he had been able to minimize what many proclaimed was the inevitable result of such outside influences as the railroad, and he helped Utah avoid the fate of the surrounding territories and states, which found themselves virtual colonies providing raw materials for use by Eastern industries. He also won enough battles to succeed in laying a foundation that continues to provide Latter-day Saints with a vitality and cohesiveness unique among religionists today. The delay in economic accommodation also helped preserve the Mormons as a "peculiar people," which allowed them to grow strong enough to where their singularity and sense of brotherhood could be exported to a worldwide faith. The underlying vision established during this time of being in the world but not of it and of belonging to a larger "community" of Saints and their neighbors continues to characterize the Latter-day Saints.

When Miriam Leslie visited Brigham in late spring 1877, she "spoke of the magnificence of Amelia Palace," a structure then under construction that would serve as a reception center and guest house for official visitors. When he characterized it as "absurdly fine," she proclaimed that the Beehive House "looks to me rather shabby for a man of your position." Responding to her observation, he said: "There it is, there it is; extravagance and ambition come creeping in, and destroy the simplicity of the first ideas. The Beehive was good enough for me, and has been so for many a year, but the world is changing—changing!"[22] While he couldn't stop the world from changing, for thirty years he had been somewhat able to hold it back.

*Indians in front of ZCMI, Main Street, Salt Lake City, 1869*

# ∾ 15 ∾

# CITY PLANNER AND COLONIZER

Under Brigham's leadership, Latter-day Saints settled more than three hundred towns throughout the west between 1847 and 1877—an average of more than ten new communities each year. In establishing these settlements, the Mormons employed a nearly uniform model for laying out their cities that stood in contrast to the often helter-skelter nature of most frontier towns. Mormon settlements were largely laid out using a square grid pattern, featured wide streets, and included building lots with ample land for orchards and gardens.

Brigham has been given much of the credit for what has been dubbed "the Mormon Village," but the plan he implemented followed the basic principles of the plat for the City of Zion outlined by Joseph Smith in 1833. For Brigham, community building was more than just establishing cities, orchards, and farms. If the Saints were to be a light unto the world, they needed to create heaven on earth. The pattern contributed to this goal by creating close-knit communities where the Saints learned how to work, play, and worship together, and provided for the Saints' social, cultural, and religious needs by fashioning a culture based on such values as unity, cooperation, dedication, equality, and neighborliness.

While the City of Zion plat had been implemented in Ohio, Missouri, and Illinois, it proved to be well adapted to the Great Basin, where limited water resources mandated the establishment of small towns. Small communities also allowed neighbors to more easily assist each other and provided greater safety in the event of an Indian uprising than did individual farmsteads. When asked his advice on how the town of Scipio should be settled, Brigham desired them to "take up a block and settle it and then another block and so on" so they "would be close together and could assist one another in case of emergency."[1]

As part of his desire to create heaven on earth, Brigham challenged the Latter-day Saints to embrace a celestial-like manner of thinking and living. "I have Zion in my view constantly," Brigham proclaimed. "We are not going to wait for angels, or for Enoch and his company to come and build up Zion, but we are going to build it. We will raise our wheat, build our houses, fence our farms, plant our vineyards and orchards, and produce everything that will make our bodies comfortable and happy, and in this manner we intend to build up Zion on the earth."[2] Prior to moving to Utah, he implemented his vision at Nauvoo, which he described in 1845 as beginning to look "like a paradise. All the lots and land, which have heretofore been vacant and unoccupied, were enclosed in the spring, and planted with grain and vegetables, which makes it look more like a garden of gardens than a city. . . . Many strangers are pouring in to view the Temple and the city. They express their astonishment and surprise to see the rapid progress of the Temple, and the beauty and grandeur."[3]

Once in Utah, Brigham reminded the Saints: "There is a great work for the Saints to do. Progress, and improve upon, and make beautiful everything around you. Cultivate the earth and cultivate your minds. Build cities, adorn your habitations, make gardens, orchards, and vineyards, and render the earth so pleasant that when you look upon your labours you may do so with pleasure, and that angels may delight to come and visit your beautiful locations."[4] He instructed the Saints to "gravel our streets, pave our walks, water them, keep them clean and nicely swept, and everything neat, nice and sweet."[5] Visitors, used to the filth often associated with other cities, were surprised at the general cleanliness of Mormon towns. In an effort to keep the cities as hygienic as possible, leaders instructed the Saints to keep cows, pigs, and other livestock in places separate from residential areas. In reality, most early Utahns, especially those in smaller communities, found it more convenient to have their domestic animals housed near their homes.

One early visitor to Utah noted that "the city of the Great Salt Lake . . . is laid out upon a magnificent scale, being nearly four miles in length and three in breadth. The municipal regulations as to buildings and streets are of a sagacious character, and if followed out, will make the city a beautiful location."[6] Within days of arriving in the Salt Lake Valley, Brigham undertook the first step toward implementing Joseph's City of Zion plat by choosing a temple site that would serve as the center point for Salt Lake City. Surveyors then began to lay out the city in ten-acre blocks, with each block containing eight lots of one-and-a-quarter acres bounded by streets that ran at right angles to each other. In order that residences could be close to each other and within walking distance of community halls, five-acre lots that could be used as small farms for those who wished to farm were placed outside the city proper, and beyond those were larger farms of ten and twenty acres.

Strict zoning mandated that houses be set back at least twenty feet from the street to allow for sidewalks; trees were to be planted along the street; and commercial districts were to be established. The streets were to be eight rods wide, which would allow a great team of oxen to easily turn a wagon completely around; today those streets appear as if they were tailor-made to accommodate automobile traffic.

Because Brigham desired Utah to be primarily an agricultural-based economy, his plan for providing Salt Lake City with water made him one of the fathers of Western irrigation. A unique system of ditches ran down each street and provided sustenance to the Saints and nourishment for their kitchen gardens and other vegetation growing near their homes. "The streams that pour down from the mountains are tapped at various elevations, the water carried away by canals, big and little, to the gardens," Samuel Bowles reported. "Each one gets his share [usually once a week for a specific portion of the garden]; and when the supply is scant, as is often the case, each one suffers in like degree. . . .

" . . . The gardens in the cities and villages are tropical in their rich greenness and luxuriance. I do not believe the same space of ground anywhere else in the country holds so much and so fine fruit and vegetables as the city of Salt Lake to-day."[7]

Concerning the houses, Brigham was an advocate of personal choice: "Build your houses just the size you want them, whether a hundred feet, fifty feet or five. . . . If there is any one person who has better taste in building than others, and can get up more tasteful houses, make your plans and we will put them up, and have the greatest variety we can imagine."[8] He did, however, recommend that people build two-story homes; the upper story would allow the necessary ventilation for sleeping during the hot summers.

Brigham advocated a characteristically forthright and somewhat idealistic response to the question of how people were to obtain land: "No man should buy or sell land. Every man should have his land measured off to him for city and farming purposes, what he could till. He might till it as he pleases, but he should be industrious and take care of it."[9] Eventually, the government required people to purchase land just like residents in other areas of the country.

Given the hundreds of new arrivals each fall who needed to establish homes and farms, new settlements were continually being built. In 1865, Brigham wrote his son, "It is almost a matter of surprise even to us, who have traveled more or less every Summer throughout the Territory from the first of our settlement here until the present, how the people have increased and are still increasing and spreading abroad. We have been traveling steadily all this summer . . . yet there are a great number of settlements that we have been unable to visit for the want of time."[10] Eventually Latter-day Saint settlements expanded throughout Utah and into Idaho, Wyoming, Arizona, Nevada, and California.

In addition to providing homes for new arrivals, settlements frequently served a double purpose. During the early 1850s, settlements were established along emigration routes to raise grain and hay needed by Mormon pioneers and to cache and store supplies. Some settlements were started to establish a specific industry or to produce needed commodities. Along these lines, Brigham called people on iron missions, cotton missions, lead missions, and coal missions. A final impetus for starting a settlement was to serve as headquarters of Indian missions established to help "civilize" Utah's native residents.

During the early years, concerns about Indian attacks prompted Brigham to regularly admonish settlers to build a fort as quickly as possible and to refrain from taking women and children to the new settlement until their safety could be provided for. He regularly gave instructions concerning how to build a fort. "Your fort walls must be 12 feet high 4 feet thick either good Stone or good dobes and laid in lime mortar," he told a group in 1858.[11] Brigham also encouraged those who were establishing a settlement to work on the fort and their homes during the fall and winter so they could then turn their attention to planting in the spring.

A unique aspect of the establishment of many new settlements was "the call." Certainly new arrivals were often sent to create a new community, but established settlers also were frequently *called* to leave the homes they had worked so hard to build and help settle a new location.

Brigham knew from personal experience the sacrifices people had to make to leave their homes and establish a new settlement, to surrender a summer's work to fulfill an assignment such as picking up emigrants at the Missouri River, or to be away from home for extended periods of time, so he was not cavalier with regard to the Saints and didn't move them around like so many pawns. To the leader of pioneers called to settle Arizona, Brigham wrote: "We sincerely trust [that the brethren] will not become discouraged or slackened in their labors to honorably fulfil the mission of strengthening the kingdom of God by building up its cities on the Little Colorado. It is obvious that you will have some difficulties to encounter, what great enterprise has not, but when you compare your condition with that of those who first set their hands to establish Zion in these mountains, how insignificant are your burdens to what theirs were? You have friends near at hand, who will help you when you need aid. We were a thousand miles from all the world and that world at war with us. Naked, hungry and barefoot we came to these mountains with no base of supplies to fall back upon, whilst you have the necessities of life and your brethren to call upon when you run short."[12]

He also knew the blessing that came from the sacrifices asked of the Saints. Borrowing an image favored by Heber C. Kimball, who had been a potter, he proclaimed, "This people . . . have got to be ground over and worked on the table, until they are made perfectly pliable and in readiness to be put on the wheel, to be turned into vessels of honor."[13] He viewed the calling of people on colonizing efforts as contributing to them being "ground over." He noted when looking for people to help settle the Uintah Valley, "We would like to have good substantial men who are and wish to be saints and who prefer to live with saints."[14] Most of the Saints understood the concept as well. When John Pulsipher was called to the Cotton Mission, he was initially taken aback, for he "had a good home, was well satisfied and had plenty to do. . . . Then the Spirit came upon me so that I felt to thank the Lord that I was worthy to go."[15]

In calling people, Brigham tried to select a balanced group of members that included individuals with the unique skills needed for the particular settlement along with others such as musicians who could provided needed entertainment and make the settlement a community. In establishing a cotton mission at St. George, most of those initially called were converts from southern states who were familiar with the cotton culture. He selected people who had been miners or iron workers in England, Scotland, and Wales for the Iron Mission.

While Brigham sought for the ideal in establishing settlements, it was not always realized. When settlers petitioned to return to their former homes, Brigham's response noted some of the frustration associated with the massive colonizing effort he had undertaken: "You can do as you please. I have given so much counsel to the brethren respecting their locations and the proper methods for them to adopt to secure themselves, their families and stock, and have had it disobeyed, that I do not feel encouraged to [give you] counsel."[16]

An important aspect of Brigham's colonizing effort was the calling of bishops, who oversaw local temporal affairs in the community or settlement. Because of limited contact between Salt Lake and outlying settlements, Brigham also called members of the Quorum of the Twelve to oversee various settlements instead of concentrating leadership in Salt Lake.

*Salt Lake City, ca. 1865*

## 16

# BRIGHAM AS (SUCCESSFUL) INNOVATOR

### *Gathering the Poor*

One of Brigham's most successful innovations centered around gathering the poor from the eastern United States, Europe, and other locations to Zion. With the ultimate goal always in mind, several times he changed how this was to be accomplished. For Brigham, the end result, not the particular program, was of greatest importance. If there was a better way, he was willing to adapt. He employed traditional wagon trains, handcarts, and down-and-back companies. He changed routes that the emigrants traveled—and considered additional changes. He continued to try to improve the system until the railroad no longer made it necessary to refine the process.

For most of the nineteenth century, "the Gathering" played a central role in building the kingdom of God. George Q. Cannon succinctly stated of the concept: "The first duty of the Saints, after becoming associated with the work of God, is very simple, yet very important; it is to place themselves in closer connection with the work, by gathering to the place appointed."[1] Throughout Brigham's presidency, the appointed place was in the Great

Basin and surrounding environs. Brigham declared in 1860 that emigration "upon the first feasible opportunity, directly follows obedience of the first principles of the gospel we have embraced."[2] Because of the importance placed upon the gathering, for much of Brigham's presidency the Church assumed primary responsibility for emigration, with Church emigration agents appointed in both Europe and the eastern United States to assist the effort.

For many Latter-day Saints, however, the idea of gathering to Zion was unrealistic. Struggling to survive, they could little afford to undertake such a journey. Brigham had empathy for the plight of the poor, having been in that position himself. "I have seen the time that I had not food to satisfy the craving of my nature," he recalled. "I know what it is to be in poverty, and to be destitute of the raiment necessary to keep any body warm."[3]

In a revelation Brigham received at Winter Quarters in early 1847, the Lord spoke of the responsibility resting upon the Latter-day Saints to help the poor, the widow, and the fatherless gather to Zion.[4] Once in the Rocky Mountains, Brigham and other leaders experimented with various ways to accomplish the will of the Lord. Of course, there were other needs for funds besides gathering Saints, and not all of their money could go toward that endeavor. The chosen methods of emigration had to meet the needs and resources of both the Church and its members.

The foundation on which the effort to gather the poor was built, and the one constant through the years was the Perpetual Emigration Fund, better known as the P.E.F. When forty-niners passed through Salt Lake on their way to California gold fields, the Latter-day Saints experienced a gold-rush dividend as emigrants passing through sold their possessions for a fraction of their cost and paid a premium for needed food staples. That fall (1849) Brigham proposed that this windfall profit be combined with Church assets and private contributions "to promote, facilitate, and accomplish the Emigration of the Poor" and the P.E.F. was born.[5]

Concerning the P.E.F., the First Presidency wrote in October 1849: "The Lord has been devising, or rather making manifest ways and means to facilitate the gathering of His Saints in these last days. . . . The few thousands [of dollars] we send out by our agent, at this time is like a grain of mustard seed . . . and we expect it will grow and flourish . . . until Israel is gathered from all nations, and the poor can sit under their own vine and inhabit their own house, and worship God in Zion."[6]

The PEF was always designed to be a loan rather than a gift. When the loan was repaid, the money would then be used to help others emigrate, thus providing a perpetual source of funding. In this regard, the PEF did not work exactly as anticipated. Upon reaching Utah, people learning how to farm or earn a living in other ways frequently struggled to make ends meet and would take years to repay their loan. In thousands of other cases, Latter-day Saints could not or would not repay their debts, prompting regular calls for donations to keep the fund operating. Brigham was one of the largest donors, including a donation of personal property in 1855 that totaled nearly $60,000.[7] It was not until 1878, a year after Brigham's death, that real pressure was brought to bear upon those owing money to the fund to pay their debts. The amount owed at that time was more than one million dollars plus interest, a tremendous sum for the day.[8] In spite of these facts, Brigham's critics still erroneously proclaim that the most dangerous place in Utah Territory was between him and a nickel.

While the PEF did not completely function as anticipated, it did succeed in helping around thirty thousand Latter-day Saints gather to Zion—nearly one-third the total number who made the journey—prior to being discontinued in 1887. Unfortunately, there were always more people who wished to emigrate than could be assisted by the fund.

The growing emigration to Zion would have taxed the PEF even under normal circumstances, but in 1855 a devastating drought and grasshopper infestation in the Salt Lake Valley put an additional strain on resources. By the fall of 1855, it was clear that in spite of donations there would not be sufficient money in the PEF to finance the 1856 emigration by the traditional means of wagon and ox team. As a result, Brigham implemented a system that he had considered since watching gold miners pass through the Salt Lake Valley in 1849—emigration by handcarts.

Concerning this possibility, the First Presidency wrote in 1851: "Some of the children of the world, have crossed the mountains and plains, from Missouri to California, with a pack on their back to worship their god— Gold. Some have performed the same journey with a wheel-barrow, some have accomplished the same with a pack on a cow. . . . Can you not do the same? . . . Families might start from Missouri river, with cows, hand-carts, wheel-barrows, with little flour, and no unnecessaries, and come to this place quicker, and with less fatigue. . . . Do you not like this method of travelling? Do you think salvation costs too much? If so, it is not worth having."[9]

Because the Brethren had some concerns about the feasibility of hand-cart travel, it was an innovation of "last resort." In 1855 Brigham instructed Church agents in Europe to send emigrants to "Iowa city or the then termi-nus of the railroad; there let them be provided with hand-carts on which to draw their provision and clothing, then walk and draw them, thereby saving the immense expense every year for teams and outfit for crossing the plains."[10] Not only would a handcart cost less up front, but it would make it easier on those borrowing from the fund to repay their debt since it would be less than if they had traveled by wagon. In 1856, the first two handcart companies, captained by Edmund Ellsworth and Daniel D. McArthur, raced each other to the valley, each arriving at the valley on September 26 and hav-ing experienced few problems. The Edward Bunker company arrived the fol-lowing week, also experiencing few problems. The *Deseret News* wrote of the first three companies: "This journey has been performed with less than the average amount of mortality usually attending ox trains; and all, though somewhat fatigued, stepped out with alacrity to the last, and appeared buoy-ant and cheerful. . . .

"And thus has been successfully accomplished a plan, devised by the wisdom and forethought of our President, for rapidly gathering the poor."[11]

The joy at the arrival of these companies quickly changed. The experi-ences of the fourth and fifth companies, the Willie and Martin companies, were substantially different; they started later than instructed and subsequently became stranded after encountering an early and prolonged winter storm. Although the tragedy of these two companies has largely effected the view of handcart travel, five more companies traveled in their wake between 1857 and 1860, with these pioneers having relatively little difficulty. Their mortality rates were no greater than wagon companies—and the last handcart company had no fatalities at all.

Nevertheless, in 1861 Brigham employed a new way to gather the poor. In the spring of 1860, Brigham's nephew Joseph W. Young led an ox company from Salt Lake to the Missouri River to pick up supplies, merchandise, and machinery. On October 3 the company returned to Salt Lake City, having made the round-trip journey with the same team of oxen in the same season.[12] Everyone "knew" that it was impossible to make the journey down and back with the same team of oxen in the same season—until somebody tried it. At the Church's general conference three days after Joseph W. returned to the Salt Lake Valley, Brigham asked for "enough wagons [to] go to the frontiers to bring all the Saints who wish to come here." He claimed that "it can easily be done, if the people will send back their teams."[13] In presenting the plan, Church leaders noted that "we are rich in cattle, but do not abound in money . . . and desire to so plan and operate as to use our small amount of money and large number of cattle in the best possible manner . . . thereby enabling us to accomplish much with comparatively a very small outlay of money."[14]

Such a system answered the need for a new, efficient, low-cost system to replace the not-so-popular handcart still colored by the Willie and Martin experience. Under this plan, wagons would leave the Great Basin in the spring loaded with food and supplies—some of which was cached along the route to be used on the return trip—and goods to be sold once they reached the Missouri River. They would then return that same year, their wagons filled with emigrants and equipment and other supplies for use in local industries. This innovation avoided the expense of having to spend thousands of dollars on overpriced supplies, wagons, and draft animals to carry out emigration; it also furthered Brigham's oft-stated desire for the Latter-day Saints to become self-sufficient.

Between 1861 and 1868, forty-six down-and-back companies consisting of approximately two thousand wagons made the journey and brought approximately sixteen thousand of the twenty thousand emigrants who traveled to Zion during that time. The decision to implement these companies in 1861 proved fortuitous. While the first down-and-back company was heading east that year, word was traveling west that the Civil War had begun. Because of the war, supplies and draft animals were in short supply and had become extremely expensive to purchase in the States, while the conflict created markets for Utah-produced goods such as cotton.

Initially converts from Europe sailed to New Orleans, then up the Mississippi and Missouri rivers, before undertaking the trip across the plains. In 1854 Brigham suggested that emigrants instead sail to Philadelphia, Boston, and New York to avoid warm-weather illnesses such as malaria.[15] He also considered having European emigrants sail to Panama, travel across the isthmus on foot or wagon, then sail to the western port of San Pedro to avoid "three thousand miles of inland navigation through a most sickly climate and country."[16] A series of settlements was established between Salt Lake and California known as the Mormon Corridor, which included a western terminus at San Bernardino that was designed in part to be an outfitting post for Utah-bound emigrants. While the plan to emigrate through Panama never materialized because few ships regularly ran between Panama and California, the Mormon Corridor aided numerous missionaries and other Latter-day Saints traveling to and from the Pacific.

The arrival of the last Church-organized wagon train from the east in the fall of 1868 marked an end of era. Beginning in 1869 Brigham largely abandoned the use of the Mormon Trail in favor of his last major innovation in gathering the poor—the use of the railroad. A journey that previously took months required only weeks, thanks to steamships and the railroad. On June 2, 1869, a company of Latter-day Saints left Liverpool, England. Twenty-four days later, the *Deseret News* reported that "the first fruits of this year's immigration from Europe reached Ogden [Utah] last evening at five o'clock. ... A little more than three weeks has brought them the whole distance of the weary way that once took the best part of the year to travel."[17]

*Mormon pioneers on the plains, 1866*

## ∽ 17 ∽

# GOVERNOR AND
# SUPERINTENDENT OF
# INDIAN AFFAIRS

Until 1858, Brigham was the political as well as the predominant religious leader of the Great Basin, first when there was no established civil government, then as governor of both the State of Deseret and the Territory of Utah. While both natural and efficient, this mingling of church and state caused controversy that was fueled in part by the fact that Brigham did not always try to distinguish between which hat he was wearing, being more concerned about getting things accomplished than strict formalities. His pragmatic approach to problem solving, coupled with his open dislike of the corrupt and scheming politicians sent to Utah, spawned false charges about his political leadership that resulted in an army being sent to the territory and brought about the end of his governorship.

As governor, Brigham instructed legislators that the laws they passed "should be plain, easy to understand, and few in number," and lectured them about making light of other people's religion and taking the name of Deity in vain, declaring "that it grieved and hurt [his] feelings when present on any occasion where such things were allowed."[1] He also proclaimed, "I am and will be Governor, *and no power can hinder it, until the Lord Almighty says, 'Brigham, you need not be Governor any longer,'* and then I am willing to yield to another Governor."[2] Concerning the public outcry these comments caused in the East, he told the Saints: "The newspapers are teeming with statements that I said, 'President Pierce and all hell could not remove me from office.' I will tell you what I did say, and what I now say; the Lord reigns and rules. . . . He makes Kings, Presidents, and Governors at His pleasure; hence I conclude that I shall be Governor of Utah Territory, *just as long as He wants me to be; and for that time,* neither the President of the United States, nor any other power, can prevent it."[3]

Brigham initially became political leader in the Great Basin out of necessity because there was no established government. In his dual role as spiritual and temporal leader, he oversaw the establishment of laws, the creation of new settlements, the building of roads, and other varied activities designed to benefit the earthly kingdom. Under his direction, the Mormons also created executive, legislative, and judicial branches.

In 1849 the Mormon settlers petitioned Congress to recognize the government they had fashioned for the region by creating the State of Deseret. Instead, Congress, as part of the Compromise of 1850, created the Territory of Utah. The Latter-day Saints would soon learn firsthand that they would indeed be "better without any government . . . than with a Territorial government" that regularly featured "corrupt political men from Washington, as Thomas Kane had warned them."[4]

The State of Deseret continued to operate until early 1851, when word of their territorial status reached Utah. While Brigham was appointed the first governor, other territorial appointments were divided between Mormons and non-Mormons. Given the solidarity of Utah's inhabitants and the political ambitions and attitudes of the outside political appointees, it is not surprising that this well-intentioned effort did not succeed. During the summer of 1851, the non-Mormon officials trickled into the territory. These federal authorities had accepted their positions largely to advance their own careers—Judge Perry Brocchus wanted to be the territorial delegate—and were disappointed by what they found. Rather than being welcomed as a savior when he denounced polygamy, Brocchus and the other outside officials found a territory primarily settled by Latter-day Saints that largely reflected Mormon values and aspirations. By the end of September, all the outside officials had left the territory.

Back east these "runaway officials" raised cries against the Mormons, reporting it was impossible to fulfill their offices because of Brigham's domination over the Saints and his hostility toward the United States. They proclaimed they were viewed as "mere toys of the Governor's power."[5] Fortunately, Utah's delegate to Congress was able to counteract the accusations, and these officials were ultimately discredited.

The departure of these "runaway officials" created a judicial vacuum. To fill this void, Brigham asked the legislature to extend criminal jurisdiction to the local bishop's courts, which were functioning as probate courts. While it has long been claimed that Brigham used prominent Church leaders to ensure that only Mormons could get justice, the evidence indicates otherwise. The judges were far from puppets who rubber-stamped Brigham's predetermined verdicts. In fact, Brigham complained of judges "who do not know their right hands from their left, so far as the principle of justice is concerned. . . . You may go to the Bishops' courts, and what are they? A set of old grannies. . . . We have already dropped many of them."[6] By 1856, most of those who served as judges did not hold any prominent Church office, and later at least one non-Mormon was appointed to preside over a bishop's court.[7] Even if a Mormon judge meted out the perfect judgment Brigham sought, given the prevailing view of the Latter-day Saints, non-Mormons were almost certain to condemn the verdict as partial.

The experience with the first group of appointed officials foreshadowed a problem Brigham had to deal with as governor. While accepting of those who fulfilled their office, conducted themselves as gentleman, and did not display an open animosity to the Mormons, he was less sympathetic to the "infernal, dirty, sneaking, rotten-hearted, pot-house politicians" that Washington sent to Utah.[8] Such was the case with Judge W. W. Drummond, who arrived in Utah with a mistress in tow. His open immorality and his refusal to adhere to universally established judicial procedures prompted the Mormons to look to their own courts rather than an openly corrupt individual for justice. Like his predecessors, Drummond's stay was short-lived. To save face, he too claimed that it was the mingling of church and state that caused him and other officials to be treated as superfluous and not their behavior. Unlike his predecessors, his trumped-up charges of Mormon lawlessness—including religiously controlled and biased courts designed to undermine federal authority and the creation of an unholy alliance between Mormons and Native Americans—were believed in Washington by a new administration.

Unlike most territorial governors, Brigham had the dual responsibility of also serving as Superintendent of Indian Affairs. Prior to assuming this office, he adopted an approach to dealing with the Indians that was not the norm in the American West. Believing that Native Americans were related to the Lamanites mentioned in the Book of Mormon, Brigham proclaimed that the Mormons had an obligation to reach out to them by teaching them the restored gospel and the ways of civilization. His policies of attempting to elevate the Indians, coupled with an emphasis upon patience, were offset by a willingness to chastise and punish when necessary. While hoping for the best, he prepared for the worst. "When we first entered Utah, we were prepared to meet all the Indians in these mountains, and kill every soul of them if we had been obliged so to do. This preparation secured to us peace."[9] He further noted that every settlement had "received strict charges from me, to build, in the first place, a Fort, and live in it until they were sufficiently strong to live in a town; to keep their guns and ammunition well prepared for any emergency; and never cease to keep up a night watch, if any apprehensions of the Indians being hostile were entertained. . . . I have always acknowledged myself a coward, and hope I always may be, to make me cautious enough to preserve myself and my brethren from falling ignobly by a band of Indians."[10]

In addition to the stick, Brigham held out a carrot. In an effort to create and maintain peaceful relations with the Indians, he provided them gifts such as food and clothing, which effort he believed "saved much calamity & bloodshed, and at comparatively trifling expense."[11] He also appointed "farmers to the Indians" to teach them how to farm and also established missions among them. In addition to teaching the gospel, the missionaries were to start schools and to teach habits of cleanliness and virtue. "It has ever been my aim . . . to teach them by example as well as precept, and to endeavor to exercise a good wholesome and salutary influence over them, in order if possible to bring them to appreciate the benefits arising from a civilized existence when contrasted with their own."[12]

In spite of his best efforts, every year he had to deal with altercations between Indians and passing emigrants. "I have preached to the Indians. I have sent them presents, visited them and prayed for them, that they might become peaceable, and let the traveler alone," he reported in August 1857.[13] These conflicts continued in part because his efforts to civilize the Indians were frequently undermined by the actions of passing emigrants, who purposely sought to provoke. His efforts were also not enough to avert the 1853–54 Walker Indian War, a nearly year-long series of clashes that erupted between local Mormon settlers and members of the Ute tribe.

Unable to completely eliminate conflicts, Brigham regularly emphasized forbearance toward Indian depredations and their retaliation for perceived wrongs. "Their sense of matters and things differs so much from ours that we often find it difficult to bear with their indignities and ignorance. . . . What to us is a deep insult and outrage, to them is a small matter" while "a thing of minor importance to us becomes to them a thing of great moment."[14] "Why should men have a disposition to kill a destitute, naked Indian, who may steal a shirt or a horse and thinks it no harm, when they never think of meting out a like retribution to a white man who steals, although he has been taught better?"[15] "This is Indian politics in their savage state, & the white men's should be of a higher grade."[16]

The beginning of the end of Brigham's term as governor came in the spring of 1857, when President James Buchanan ordered an army to Utah along with his choice as Brigham's successor, Alfred Cumming. Although rumors circulated concerning the purpose of this military movement, it was never officially explained. The more Brigham thought about President Buchanan's failure to notify him of his replacement, the more suspicious Brigham became of Buchanan's motives in sending an army. America's Founding Fathers, wary of standing armies, had opposed the creation of a national army, preferring instead to rely upon local militias. For Brigham, the concerns raised by framers of the nation about a chief executive abusing power had been realized. "CITIZENS OF UTAH: We are invaded by a hostile force, who are evidently assailing us to accomplish our overthrow and destruction," he proclaimed.[17] As governor, he assumed the role of commander in chief of the local militia and deployed militiamen, who employed guerrilla tactics to help prevent the army from reaching Salt Lake until 1858.

Around the same time that he ordered out the militia, Brigham reflected on what the Saints had accomplished in working with the Indians. While noting in August 1857 that they had not been able to stop all attacks, Brigham noted that "had it not [been] for our settlements here, the overland emigration would have been stopped years ago." He wrote that if "the United States commence[d] war on us" and the Mormons were forced to abandon their settlements, they would no longer be in a position to help pacify disgruntled Indians.[18]

The following month, when Brigham responded to a letter sent by leaders of the Mountain Meadows Massacre (which letter is no longer extant), he wrote that "the Indians we expect will do as they please, but you should try to preserve good feeling with them." Some historians of the massacre have concluded that the sentence was not a reflection of Brigham's ten years' experience with the Indians, but was instead a coded message ordering mass murder. To make this claim, these individuals have to explain away how the statement reflects both the history of Mormon-Indian relations and how consistent the statement is with Brigham's rhetoric and policies.

When the time came for Brigham to turn over the governorship to Alfred Cumming, he did so with remarkably little fuss. While no longer governor or Superintendent of Indian Affairs after 1858, he continued to exercise influence in both areas. While willing to give up the title of governor, given his views on the interdependency of temporal and religious matters, he had a harder time giving up responsibilities usually reserved for the chief executive, such as directing the repairs of roads. Later he would note: "I believe that Governor Cumming came to the conclusion that he was Governor of the Territory as domain; but that Brigham Young was Governor of the people."[19]

While his efforts with the Native Americans did not succeed as hoped, they stood in stark contrast to much of the nineteenth-century attitude of genocide and ruthless exploitation. Senator Salmon Chase of Ohio stated that "no Governor had ever done so well by the Indians since Wm. Penn as Gov. Young."[20] Upon learning of Brigham's death, one local Indian chief likewise paid him a great compliment: "What shall we do? Who will be our friend?"[21]

# ‰ 18 ‰

# BRIGHAM AS POLYGAMIST

I f Brigham is widely known for any one thing, it is likely for being a polygamist. The fact that he had more than one wife attracted numerous visitors to Salt Lake City, among whom was popular American humorist Artemus Ward, who, after spending a month in Salt Lake in 1864, wittily said of Brigham Young and other Mormon men, "The Mormon's religion is singular and his wives are plural."[1] While some found humor in the situation, most of the ridicule, negative press, and persecution that were directed toward Brigham during his lifetime were the result of polygamy.

Artemus Ward recounted one of the popular stories of the day: "When an immigrant train arrives Brigham Young has all the women march up and down before his block and gobbles up the prettiest ones."[2]

Following his visit to Utah, Albert D. Richardson repeated another popular tale: Among the many people who came to Brigham for help was a woman seeking counsel, and while Brigham pretended to know her, he was finally forced to ask her name.

"'My name!' was the indignant reply; 'why, I am your wife!'"

"'When did I marry you?'

"The woman informed the 'president,' who referred to an account book in his desk, and then said:

"'Well, I believe you are right. I *knew* your face was familiar!'"[3]

Mark Twain reported that next to listening to non-Mormons in Salt Lake City talk about the Danites, the "most interesting thing" was to listen to them "talk about polygamy."[4]

There has always been a great deal of confusion and misunderstanding concerning Brigham the polygamist. He was regularly lampooned, satirized, and condemned as a lecherous scoundrel by critics because of the stories told by those supposedly in the know. After publicly divorcing him, Ann Eliza Webb wrote a tell-all volume that provided an "insider's exposé" on the evils of polygamy. The accuracy of the volume is largely reflected in its title, *Wife 19*, and her claim to have been Brigham's last wife. She was neither.

Because plural marriage ran counter to Victorian sensibilities, it was easy for the public to believe such reports of its depravity. It is also not surprising, given what was being said, that one female visitor to Salt Lake, noting the wall around Brigham's estate, would write: "A high wall surrounds the building [the Lion House] from which his poor wives might as well attempt to fly as to escape. If one of their women attempts to leave them 'tis sheer death. Poor creatures. I know they must be miserable."[5]

As with other aspects of Brigham's life, the reality of his plural marriages differs from the popular perception.

While Brigham was willing to talk generally about the practice of polygamy, he largely kept the specifics about his own plural marriages from prying eyes. An exception to his efforts to protect his family from outsiders occurred in 1870, when he publicly addressed the issue: "A great many men and women have an irrepressible curiosity to know how many wives Brigham Young has. I am now going to gratify that curiosity by saying, ladies and gentlemen, I have sixteen wives. If I have any more hereafter it will be my good luck and the blessing of God. . . . I impart this information to gratify the curiosity of the curious."[6]

His family likewise spoke little of his plural marriages. His daughter Susa Young Gates declared that she "could tell nothing of my father's marital relations, for they were regarded in the family as most sacred. And no one ever knew aught about these matters."[7]

The principle of plural marriage was practiced by ancient prophets such as Abraham, Isaac, and Jacob, and was revealed to Joseph Smith as early as 1831 as part of the promised "restoration of all things."[8] It was not until 1842, however, that Joseph taught it to Brigham and other Church leaders. While plural marriages were discreetly implemented at Nauvoo, it was not until 1852, in Utah, that the Mormon practice of polygamy was publicly announced.

Brigham later recalled his feelings upon being taught the principle:

> Some of these my brethren know what my feelings were at the time Joseph revealed the doctrine; I was not desirous of shrinking from any duty, nor of failing in the least to do as I was commanded, but it was the first time in my life that I had desired the grave, and I could hardly get over it for a long time. And when I saw a funeral, I felt to envy the corpse its situation, and to regret that I was not in the coffin, knowing the toil and labor that my body would have to undergo; and I have had to examine myself, from that day to this, and watch my faith, and carefully meditate, lest I should be found desiring the grave more than I ought to do.[9]

Brigham was not alone in his feelings. When Horace Greeley asked in 1859 how Mormon women felt about polygamy, Brigham responded: "They could not be more averse to it than I was when it was first revealed to us as the Divine will. I think they generally accept it, as I do, as the will of God."[10]

In 1877, during her visit with Brigham, Miriam Leslie asked, "Are all the women of Utah sure to marry? . . . Suppose nobody offers for them?" She reported Brigham's reply this way: "A woman feeling herself drawn in affinity to a man, and feeling inclined to seal herself to him, should make her ideas known to him without scruple. It is her duty, and there can be no indelicacy in obeying the voice of duty."[11] Obeying the "voice of duty" was also at the heart of how he approached polygamy. Not only did his numerous wives and large family add to his burdens, but he also publicly proclaimed that "there are probably but few men in the world who care about the private society of women less than I do."[12] When U.S. Vice President Schuyler Colfax suggested in 1865 that the Mormons abandon polygamy, Fitz Hugh Ludlow reported that Brigham "responded quickly and frankly that he should readily welcome such a revelation; that polygamy was not in the original book of the Mormons; that it was not an essential practice in the church, but only a privilege and a duty, under special command of God."[13]

While the number of Brigham's wives has usually been placed at twenty-seven, he is known to have married fifty-six women, fifty-four of whom were plural wives. The greatest number of Brigham's plural marriages were performed to fulfill the sacred sealing ordinance. These marriages included the traditional ceremony of sealing a man and a woman for time and eternity by priesthood authority, as well as "proxy" marriages in which he was sealed to a woman for "time" while standing in for her deceased husband to whom she was sealed for "eternity," or sealed to a woman for "time" who had previously been married. These proxy marriages reflect an incomplete understanding of the time of the sealing ordinance. They continued until 1894, when Wilford Woodruff received a revelation clarifying the Lord's will on the matter. This occurred four years after Woodruff received Brigham's longed-for revelation ending the Latter-day Saint practice of plural marriage.[14]

The Old Testament injunction that a man had the responsibility to take care of his brother's widow also played a role in Brigham's plural marriages. A number of his wives were widows or divorced. Several were elderly, while others were poor. Another factor was the reality of frontier life, where single women were at an economic disadvantage, especially in outfitting themselves for a journey across the plains. Prior to the move west, Brigham also "married" several teenage girls who needed assistance to reach Utah and who subsequently divorced him after arriving in the valley. The final reason was the Lord's injunction to "raise up seed unto me."[15]

The majority of women sealed to Brigham were not wives in the traditional sense of the word. They never lived as a "sister-wife" in his household, never received financial support from him, and were never publicly known as one of his wives. In response to William Seward's statement that "you are represented as saying that you do not know how many wives you have," Brigham noted that "besides the wives who are married for time, the Mormons believe in sealing other wives only for eternity, and, in regard to such women, he may have made the remark attributed to him."[16]

Only 43 percent of his plural wives became part of his household, and not all of these were conjugal wives.[17] In 1859 Brigham stated of his plural marriages, "Some of those sealed to me are old ladies, whom I regard rather as mothers than wives; but whom I have taken home to cherish and support."[18] When Brigham publicly commented in 1870 about his wives, ten additional living women who did not meet the traditional definition of wife had been sealed to him besides the sixteen he mentioned.

Brigham had children by sixteen of his wives, including the two wives he married prior to becoming a polygamist. He married forty-four women before settling in Utah and twelve after. At least thirty-three of his wives had previously been married. Nineteen wives had a combined total of 112 children prior to being married to Brigham. Many of these children became part of Brigham's already large household. Rather than Brigham selecting a wife from the new arrivals, the women or their families were usually old acquaintances. And rather than Brigham seeking out each wife, several, including Ann Eliza Webb, approached him. Six of these women continued to live with their husbands after being sealed to Brigham. Eighteen of his wives were forty or older when they were sealed to him. Six were between ten and twenty-two years older than he was when they were sealed. Nine wives are known to have divorced him, and two others probably did. Given death and divorce, the greatest number of wives he had at any one time was thirty-two, during 1847–48.

Brigham was sealed to four plural wives in the two years between when he was first taught the principle and Joseph Smith's death. His first plural wife, Lucy Ann Decker Seeley, was the daughter of one of Brigham's long-time friends. She was sealed to Brigham after she and her two children were abandoned by her husband. His second plural wife had gathered to Nauvoo with one child after having left her husband and other children in the East. His third wife had also left her family to join the Mormons and likewise had no relatives at Nauvoo. His fourth plural wife was Lucy's younger sister. All of these women went to Utah, lived as part of his household, and shared in his estate following his death. Three of them bore him children.

In the months immediately following the death of Joseph Smith, Brigham was sealed to fifteen wives. Six of these women were sealed to Joseph for eternity and Brigham for life. Brigham also served as proxy for a young widow who was sealed to her deceased husband. Five of the women sealed to Brigham during this time bore him children, and seven lived in his household in Utah. Three died before the Mormons settled Utah and three others divorced him, including one who filed for divorce before she left for Utah.

Brigham was sealed to nineteen women in the weeks prior to his leaving for the West. Fourteen of these women had been married before and seven were significantly older than he was, including the mothers of the two wives Brigham married prior to entering plural marriage. Six of these women were sealed to dead husbands for eternity (three to Joseph Smith), with Brigham standing as proxy. Two died before reaching Utah, three divorced him (including one who had previously divorced her first husband and agreed to marry him again shortly after being sealed to Brigham), and another two either stayed in the East or died before reaching Utah. Two of these nineteen wives had children by him.

During the journey west, Brigham was sealed to four women. The first, a widow with two young children, requested on her deathbed to be sealed to Brigham. She died four days later. He also married two sisters shortly before leading the first expedition to Utah in 1847. One became part of his household in Utah, while the other divorced him and subsequently remarried four more times. A fourth wife was sealed to him at Winter Quarters in 1848 prior to his return trip to Utah.

Once in Utah, Brigham was sealed to six wives during the 1850s, four in the 1860s, and two in the 1870s. For nine of the twelve, it was their second marriage. The two women sealed to Brigham during 1870s had husbands living at the time and continued to live with them following their sealing (the husband of one was a non-Mormon, and the husband of the other was present during the sealing). Three of the wives he married in Utah bore him one child each. Two divorced him.

In spite of the image presented in the press of a domestic despot, the number of divorces challenges the view of terrified women, enslaved against their will, with unbounded anger against Brigham, Mormonism, and polygamy. Almost all of the divorces occurred in Utah, and the vast majority of his ex-wives lived in the territory, remarried, and continued as faithful Latter-day Saints. Among the divorces were four women sealed to Brigham prior to the journey west who were under the age of twenty at the time and apparently never became part of his household in Utah. Except for Ann Eliza Webb, all the divorces seem to have ended amicably.

The 1873 divorce from Ann Eliza made headlines. She demanded a large financial settlement, and when Brigham refused to pay her $500 a month while the trial was proceeding, the judge ordered him to spend a night in the territorial prison for contempt. The case was eventually dismissed on the grounds that since Ann Eliza was a plural wife, her marriage to Brigham was not legal. Brigham noted the irony: "One day a man is threatened with fine and imprisonment for entering into what they term an illegal marriage, and the next day it is adjudged that he pay alimony to the woman who the day before, it was claimed, was no wife at all. Consistency is said to be a jewel, but it is certainly a treasure not possessed by the aiders and abettors of the anti-Mormon crusade."[19] Unable to obtain the large settlement she desired, Ann Eliza raised money through both her tell-all "memoirs" and anti-Mormon lectures.

Prior to the excitement of Ann Eliza's divorce, United States marshals arrested Brigham in October 1871 on the charge of "lewd and lascivious cohabitation and adultery." In a transparent attempt to end polygamy, civil authorities also indicted him for murder, prompting several non-Mormon merchants who had publicly opposed Brigham's economic policies to speak out against what had transpired. The United States Supreme Court overturned the grand jury indictments.

At the time of his death, Brigham was survived by twenty-three wives, of which seventeen received a share of his estate. The remaining six, while sealed to Brigham, were not wives in the traditional sense. Following his death, several additional women were sealed to him.

*Brigham Young's Lion House and Beehive House, Salt Lake City, ca. 1855*

# BRIGHAM YOUNG FAMILY

| MARRIAGE DATE | NAME OF WIFE | OTHER HUSBANDS |
|---|---|---|

*CHILDREN OF BRIGHAM YOUNG (numbers reflect order of their birth)*

1. 1824 OCT. 8     MIRIAM WORKS, 1806–32
   *1. Elizabeth Young Ellsworth (1825–1903)*
   *2. Vilate Young Decker (1830–1902)*

2. 1834 FEB. 10     MARY ANN ANGELL, 1803–82
   *3. Joseph Angell Young (1834–75)*
   *4. Brigham Young Jr. (Twin) (1836–1903)*
   *5. Mary Ann Young (Twin) (1836–43)*
   *6. Alice Emma Young Clawson (1839–74)*
   *7. Eunice Carolina (Luna) Young Thatcher (1842–1922)*
   *8. John Willard Young (1844–1924)*

3. 1842 JUNE 14     LUCY ANN DECKER, 1822–90     (1) WILLIAM SEELEY
   *9. Brigham Heber Young (1845–1928)*
   *Sally (Adopted, 1847)*
   *19. Fanny Decker (Caroline) Young Thatcher (1849–92)*
   *28. Ernest Irving Young (1851–79)*
   *34. Shemira Young Rossiter (1853–1915)*
   *40. Arta de Christa Young (1855–1916)*

    46. *Feramorz Little Young (1858–81)*
    49. *Clarissa Hamilton Young Spencer (1860–1939)*

4. 1843 Nov. 2    AUGUSTA ADAMS, 1802–86    (1) HENRY COBB

5. 1843 Nov. 2    HARRIET ELIZABETH COOK, 1824–98
    11. *Oscar Brigham Young (1846–1910)*

6. 1844 May 8    CLARISSA CAROLINE DECKER, 1828–89
    23. *Jeannetta Richards Young Easton (1849–1930)*
    29. *Nabbie Howe Young Clawson (1852–94)*
    39. *Jedediah Grant Young (1854–56)*
    45. *Albert Jeddie Young (1858-infant)*
    50. *Charlotte Talula Young Wood (1861–92)*

7. 1844 Sept.    EMILY DOW PARTRIDGE, 1824–99    (1) JOSEPH SMITH
    10. *Edward Partridge Young (1845–52)*
    20. *Emily Augusta Young Clawson (1849–1926)*
    27. *Caroline Partridge Young Cannon (1851–1903)*
    41. *Joseph Don Carlos Young (1855–1938)*
    44. *Miriam Young Hardy (1857–1919)*
    48. *Josephine Young Young (1860–1912)*
    53. *Lura Young (1862–62)*

8. 1844 Sept. 10    CLARISSA ROSS, 1814–58
    15. *Mary Eliza Young Croxall (1847–71)*
    22. *Clarissa Maria Young Dougall (1849–1935)*
    30. *Willard Young (1852–1936)*
    37. *Phebe Louise Young Beatie (1854–1931)*

9. 1844 Sept. 19    LOUISA BEAMAN, 1815–50    (1) JOSEPH SMITH
    12. *Joseph Young (twin) (1846–46)*
    13. *Hyrum Young (twin) (1846–46)*
    14. *Moroni Young (1847–47)*
    17. *Alva Young (twin) (1848–48)*
    18. *Alma Young (twin) (1848–48)*

10. 1844 Oct. 3    ELIZA ROXCY SNOW, 1804–87    (1) JOSEPH SMITH

11. 1844 Oct. 3    ELIZABETH (BETSY) FAIRCHILD,    (2) JAMES D. LYMAN
        1828–1910    (3) JOSEPH McMURRA
                                   (4) JAMES MATTHEWS
                                   (5) W. L. CHASTAIN

12. 1844 Oct. 8    CLARISSA BLAKE, 1796–1863    (1) EDMUND H. MORSE
                                                               (2) LYMAN HOMISTON

13. 1844 Oct. 9    REBECCA GREENLEAF HOLMAN, 1824–49

14. 1844 Oct. 10    DIANA SEVERANCE CHASE, 1827–86    (2) WILLIAM M. SHAW

15. 1844 Oct. 31    SUSANNAH SNIVELY, 1815–92
                                   *Julia (Adopted, 1853–1918)*

16. 1844 Nov. 7    OLIVE GRAY FROST, 1816–45    (1) JOSEPH SMITH

17. 1845 Jan. 15    MARY ANN CLARK, 1816–?    (1) JOHN M. POWERS

18. 1845 Jan. 16    MARGARET PIERCE, 1823–1907    (1) MORRIS WHITESIDES
                                   *36. Brigham Morris Young (1854–1931)*

19. 1845 Jan. 16    MARY HARVEY PIERCE, 1821–47

20. 1845 Apr. 30    EMELINE FREE, 1826–75
                                   *16. Ella Elizabeth Young Empey (1847–90)*
                                   *21. Marinda Hyde Young Conrad (1849–83)*
                                   *26. Hyrum Smith Young (1851–1925)*
                                   *33. Emmeline Amanda Young Crosbie (1853–95)*
                                   *38. Louisa Wells (Nelle) Young Ferguson (1854–1908)*
                                   *43. Lorenzo Dow Young (1856–1905)*
                                   *47. Alonzo Young (1858–1918)*
                                   *51. Ruth Young Healey (1861–1944)*
                                   *54. Daniel Wells Young (1863–63)*
                                   *56. Ardelle Elvira Young Harrison (1864–1900)*

21. 1845 May 22    MARY ELIZABETH ROLLINS, 1818–1913    (1) ADAM LIGHTNER
                                                                (2) JOSEPH SMITH

22. 1846 Jan. 14    MARGARET ALLEY, 1825–52
                                   *25. Evelyn Louisa Young Davis (1850–1917)*
                                   *32. Mahonri Moriancumer Young (1852–84)*

23. 1846 Jan. 15    OLIVE MARTHA ANDREWS, 1818–?    (1) SAMUEL KINGSLEY
                                                                (2) LYMAN O. LITTLEFIELD
                                                                (4) ORRA L. LISH

24. 1846 Jan. 15    EMILY HAWS, 1823–?    (2) WILLIAM WHITMARSH

25. 1846 JAN. 21    MARTHA BOWKER, 1822–90
*Ida Ames (Adopted, 1860–1927)*

26. 1846 JAN. 21    ELLEN ROCKWOOD, 1829–66

27. 1846 JAN. 28    JEMIMA ANGELL, 1803–69    (1) VALENTINE YOUNG
(2) WILLIAM BRYANT STRINGHAM

28. 1846 JAN. 28    ABIGAIL MARKS, 1781–1846    (1) ASA WORKS

29. 1846 JAN. 28    PHEBE MORTON, 1776–1854    (1) JAMES W. ANGELL

30. 1846 JAN. 28    CYNTHIA PORTER, 1783–1861    (1) MR. WESTON

31. 1846 JAN. 31    MARY ELIZA NELSON, 1812–86    (1) JOHN P GREENE
(3) BRUCE I. PHILLIPS

32. 1846 JAN. 31    RHODA RICHARDS, 1784–1879    (1) JOSEPH SMITH

33. 1846 FEB. 2    ZINA HUNTINGTON, 1821–1901    (1) HENRY JACOBS
*24. Zina Presendia Young Card (1850–1931)*    (2) JOSEPH SMITH

34. 1846 FEB. 3    AMY CECILIA COOPER, 1804–?    (1) JOSEPH ALDRICH

35. 1846 FEB. 3    MARY DE LA MONTAGUE, 1805–?    (1) JAMES B. WOODWARD
(3) JAMES B. WOODWARD

36. 1846 FEB. 3    JULIA FOSTER, 1811–91    (1) JONATHAN HAMPTON
(3) THOMAS COLE

37. 1846 FEB. 3    ABIGAIL HARBACH, 1790–1849    (1) JOHN CALVIN HALE

38. 1846 FEB. 3    MARY ANN TURLEY, 1827–1904    (2) JOHN COOK

39. 1846 FEB. 6    NAAMAH CARTER, 1821–1909    (1) JOHN S. TWISS

40. 1846 FEB. 6    NANCY CRESSY, 1780–1871    (1) OLIVER WALKER

41. 1847 FEB. 10    JANE TERRY, 1819–47    (1) GEORGE TARBOX
(2) GEORGE W. YOUNG

42. 1847 MAR. 20    LUCY BIGELOW, 1830–1905
     *31. Eudora Lovina Young Hagan (1852–1921)*
     *42. Susan Amelia (Susa) Young Gates (1856–1933)*
     *55. Rhoda Mabel Young Sanborn (1863–1950)*

43. 1847 MAR. 20    MARY JANE BIGELOW, 1827–68      (2) HORACE ROBERTS
     (3) JOHN BAIR
     (4) DANIEL DURHAM HUNT
     (5) PHILANDER BELL

44. 1848 APR. 18    SARAH MALIN, 1804–58

45. 1852 JAN. 19    AMANDA BARNES, 1808–86      (1) WARREN SMITH
     (2) WARREN SMITH

46. 1852 OCT. 3    ELIZA BURGESS, 1827–1915
     *35. Alfales Young (1853–1920)*

47. 1852 DEC. 16    MARY OLDFIELD, 1793–1875      (1) ELI KELSEY
     (2) JOHN PEARCE
     (3) JOHN GRIBBLE

48. BEFORE 1853    ELIZA BABCOCK, 1828–68      (2) JOHN GROVES

49. 1855 JUNE 10    CATHERINE REESE, 1804–60      (1) ZEPHENIAH CLAWSON

50. 1856 MAR. 14    HARRIET BARNEY, 1830–1911      (1) W. H. H. SAGERS
     *52. Phineas Howe Young (1862–1903)*

51. 1863 JAN. 24    AMELIA FOLSOM, 1838–1910

52. 1865 JAN. 8    MARY VAN COTT, 1844–84      (1) JAMES T. COBB
     *57. Fannie Van Cott Young Clayton (1870–1950)*

53. 1868 APR. 7    ANN ELIZA WEBB, 1844–?      (1) JAMES L. DEE
     (3) MOSES R. DEMING

54. 1869 JULY 3    ELIZABETH JONES, 1813–95      (1) DAVID T. LEWIS
     (2) DAN JONES

55. 1870 MAY 8    LYDIA FARNSWORTH, 1808–97      (1) ELIJAH MAYHEW

56. 1872 DEC. 8    HANNAH TAPFIELD, 1807–86      (1) THOMAS O. KING

## ⨍ 2 0 ⨍

# FAMILY MAN

William H. Seward, the man who purchased "Seward's Folly" (Alaska) for the United States, wrote about Brigham as a family man: "Brigham Young's manner toward his wives is respectful, and toward his children dignified and affectionate. In presenting them severally as they came in groups, with a kind smile for the particular mother, he spoke in this way: 'This is our delicate little Lucy,' 'This is our musical daughter,' 'This is our son George, who has a mathematical genius,' and so on."[1] Seward's comments stand in stark contrast to the public ridicule that Brigham didn't even know all of his children, let alone could provide for their needs.

Brigham seems to have succeeded in meeting his family's physical, emotional, and spiritual needs in a manner that is both exemplary and profound when the demands on his time are considered. While engulfed with public affairs, he did not neglect private life. Once upon learning that one of his children was ill, he dismissed a council meeting, "declaring . . . that the meeting could wait, but his sick child could not."[2]

His children described a loving, caring, and concerned husband and father. Susa Young Gates idealistically recalled a "home of as healthy and happy a family of mothers and children as ever dwelt beneath a roof."[3] She further proclaimed that Brigham "was an ideal father. Kind to a fault, tender, thoughtful, just and firm. . . . None of us feared him."[4] Clarissa Young Spencer portrayed her childhood as "one long round of happiness," and reported that Brigham "had the affection and tenderness of a woman for his family and friends."[5] She stated that while her father "could be stern when occasion demanded . . . he was the wisest, kindest, and most loving of fathers. His constant thoughtfulness for our happiness and well-being endeared him to all of us. The bond between my father and me was as close as if I had been his only child, and I am sure that each of the other children felt the same way."[6] Susa remembered, "Home was as beautiful to me as love and happiness could make it."[7]

For his part, however, Brigham publicly acknowledged that his home was not always the perfect situation his children remembered. Some challenges he faced were unique to his time, while there were others to which parents can well relate today. Regarding his wives, he proclaimed: "Where is the man who has wives, and all of them think he is doing just right to them? I do not know such a man; I know it is not your humble servant."[8] He also conceded that there was probably not one of his wives who at some time didn't wish that the others would go away.[9] He noted that some of his "boys, by the time they are twenty, have not a horse and carriage to drive of their own, [and] they think they are very badly used."[10] On one occasion, when some of his daughters were entertaining young men in the parlor, they decided to change the ambiance by placing books around the coal-oil lamp in the center of the room to create semidarkness. Brigham, upon discovering the situation, removed the books to restore the proper light without saying a word. Then he stated, "The girls will go upstairs to their rooms, and I will say good night to the young men."[11]

Concerning parenting, he told a reporter that it was just as necessary for a mother to receive revelation "in training and rearing her children" as it was for him to receive revelation to lead the Church generally.[12] Given his reliance on the Lord in all aspects of his life, it is not surprising that he brought a remarkable degree of wisdom and understanding to the task of family management, much of which was ahead of its time.

An important part of family life was the evening devotional when the family met together to pray. After prayer, the family would regularly hold council, at which recreational activities were planned, problems were addressed, and counsel and teaching given. When circumstances permitted, Brigham listened to his children sing, recite poems, and play instruments, and watched them perform skits. "There might be wars and rumors of wars, councils and balls, meetings and dinner-parties," one of Brigham's children noted, but family members were expected to be in attendance.[13]

The ideal was not always realized. In 1866 Brigham wrote to his family:

> There is no doubt but that my family, one and all, will acknowledge that my time is as precious to me as theirs is to them. When the time appointed for our family devotion and prayer comes, I am expected to be there; and no public business, no matter how important has been able to influence me to forego the fulfillment of this sacred duty which I owe to you, to myself and to God.
>
> I do not wish to complain of you without a cause; but I have noticed at prayer time that only a portion of my family has been present; some of my wives are absent visiting a sister, a neighbor, a mother or a relative; my children are scattered all over town, attending to this or that; and if at home, one is changing her dress, another her shoes, another getting ready to go to the theater; another has gone to see Mary, and another to see Emily, and I may add, etc., etc., etc.
>
> Now, I have a few words of counsel for my family, which I shall expect them to receive kindly, and obey: namely, when prayer time comes, that they all be at home. If any of them are visiting, that they be at home at half past six o'clock in the evening. I wish my wives and children to be at home at that time in the evening, to be ready to

bow before the Lord to make their acknowledgments to Him for His kindness and mercy and long-suffering towards us.

Your strict attendance to my wishes in this respect will give joy to the heart of your Husband and Father.[14]

George A. Smith was present for one of the devotionals and reported that after a "very fervent prayer" Brigham talked with his family regarding their collective responsibility. He spoke on the need to be examples, since the eyes of both the Church and the world were upon them: "He said it was necessary for him to observe the word of wisdom, not only for his own sake, but his family should set examples. He wished his wives and daughters always to adopt their own fashions and to set an example and as far as possible to manufacture what they wore. He spoke on the absolute necessity of the saints ceasing to follow the fashions of the world."[15]

He tried to make his home a model that others could emulate. The idea of governing as a tyrant and dictator, particularly at home, went against his convictions. He believed that righteous leadership, not compulsion, was the key to marital happiness and raising children, just as it was in directing the Church. "I do not rule my family with an iron hand, as many do," he claimed, "but in kindness and with pleasant words." He concluded that "if soft words would teach them," his family "would know as much as any family on this earth."[16] On another occasion he stated:

I do not believe in making my authority as a husband or a father known by brute force; but by a superior intelligence—by showing them that I am capable of teaching them. . . . If the Lord has placed me to be the head of a family, let me be so in all humility and patience, not as a tyrannical ruler, but as a faithful companion, an indulgent and affectionate father, a thoughtful and unassuming superior; let me be honoured in my station through faithful diligence, and be fully capable, by the aid of God's Spirit, of filling my office in a way to effect the salvation of all who are committed to my charge.[17]

Brigham spoke of the necessity of parents setting "an example before our children that is worthy of their imitation and highest admiration. If we do this, we shall have occasion to rejoice and be exceeding glad, for we shall have influence over them and they will not forsake us."[18] He believed that when children were forced to obey "until duty becomes loathsome to them," then "when they are freed by age from the rigorous training of their parents, they are more fit for companions to devils, than to be the children of such religious parents."[19] He noted that while some children regularly hid from their father "as from a tyrant," his children, "except in the case of their having done something wrong," were not afraid to approach him.[20] He encouraged parents to "always sympathize with [their children] . . . and soothe them. Be mild and pleasant."[21]

For Brigham, discipline was largely a process of educating the child: "It is not by the whip or the rod that we can make obedient children; but it is by faith and by prayer, and by setting a good example before them."[22] He taught that "kindness, love and affection are the best rod to use upon the refractory. Solomon is said to have . . . recommended another kind of rod. I have tried both kinds on children. I can pick out scores of men in this congregation who have driven their children from them by using the wooden rod. Where there is severity there is no affection or filial feeling in the hearts of either party; the children would rather be away from father than be with him."[23] He further stated: "I could break the wills of my little children, and whip them to this, that, and the other, but this I do not do. Let the child have a mild training until it has judgment and sense to guide it. I differ with Solomon's recorded saying as to spoiling the child by sparing the rod."[24]

One of his toddler sons began knocking the dish and spoon to the floor when brought his meal. Brigham recommended to the child's mother that the next time he knocked the dish from her hand, "lean him against the chair, do not say one word to him, go to your work, pay no attention to him whatever." The mother followed the counsel. After the child stood by his chair for a while looking back and forth between his mother and the objects he had knocked to the floor, he picked up the dish and spoon and placed them on the table. "He never tried to knock that dish out of her hand again," Brigham reported. "She might have whipped him and injured him, as a great many others would have done; but if they know what to do, they can correct the child without violence."[25]

During one evening devotional one of his young daughters "was running about and squealing with laughter out of reach of her mother's anxious arms." Brigham stopped praying, took the child to her mother, then returned and knelt by his chair and concluded the family prayer.[26]

Brigham rejected aspects of his typically strict New England Puritan upbringing in favor of a more balanced approach to raising his children. He saw to it that his children were taught music, dancing, and gymnastics, and had ladders to climb, ropes to jump, and swings. His children, however, noted that the Sabbath was always held sacred and that many weekday activities were not permitted on Sunday. He further believed "in indulging children, in a reasonable way. If the little girls want dolls, shall they have them? Yes."[27]

He ran his home like the small community it was. He established accounts for each wife at the family store on his estate as well as at Zion's Cooperative Mercantile Institution (ZCMI). When anyone went out for the evening, they left their lamp on a table near the door. The last person to remove his or her lamp upon returning home was to lock the door for the night.

He observed that if children knew the feelings their parents had when their children did right or wrong, "it would have a salutary influence upon their lives; but no child can possibly know this, until it becomes a parent."[28] Having counseled his son Willard to live at West Point as he would at home—frugally, prayerfully, and chastely, avoiding self-righteousness, being kind and courteous to all, cultivating integrity and honor by making his heart and mouth as one, and remaining true to the faith—Brigham must have delighted to receive the following letter from Willard: "It may be gratifying to you to know that as yet, I have given myself up to none of the temptations which surround me. Perhaps I should not say temptations, for thanks to the good training of my parents, swearing, using tobacco, drinking whiskey, and other kindred vices to which I have alluded, never were a temptation to me. In myself I can perceive no change, but am the same grateful and loving son as when I left home."[29]

Reflecting on his home life, Willard further wrote: "I ever feel grateful towards you, my dear father, for the many great kindnesses and benefits you have heaped upon me, and upon all the children, though it is perhaps impossible for me to appreciate their full worth. How thankful we all ought to be (I really think I am) that we have such a loving and indulgent parent, such a wise instructor, and so worthy an example as you."[30]

*Brigham and Mary Ann Angell Young with their children, 1845–51*

*1) Brigham Young, ca. 1846*

2) *Brigham Young, 1850*

3) *Brigham Young, ca. 1852*

*4) Mary Ann Angell Young, ca. 1853, wife of Brigham Young*

*5) Brigham Young, ca. 1855*

*6) Brigham Young, ca. 1856*

*7) Brigham Young and Margaret Pierce Young, ca. 1852*

*8) Brigham Young and
Amelia Folsom Young, ca. 1863*

*9) Brigham Young, ca. 1863*

10) *Brigham Young, ca. 1864*

11) *Brigham Young, 1864*

12) *Brigham Young's daughters, ca. 1865.* Back row, left to right: *Zina Card, Evelyn Davis, Jeannette Easton, Mary Croxall, and Maria Dougall.* Front row, left to right: *Marinda Conrad, Caroline Cannon, Ella Empey, Emily Clawson, and Fanny Thatcher.*

13) *Brigham Young and brothers, 1866.* Left to right: *Lorenzo Dow Young, Brigham Young, Phineas Howe Young, Joseph Young, and John Young.*

14) *Brigham Young, ca. 1866*

15) *Brigham Young, ca. 1867*

16) *Brigham Young seated with his counselors and the Quorum of Twelve Apostles near his schoolhouse on his Salt Lake City property, October 1868. Left to right: Orson Hyde, Orson Pratt, John Taylor, Wilford Woodruff, George A. Smith, Ezra T. Benson, Charles C. Rich, Brigham Young, Lorenzo Snow, Daniel H. Wells, Erastus Snow, Franklin D. Richards, George Q. Cannon, Brigham Young Jr., and Joseph F. Smith.*

SAVAGE & OTTINGER

*17) Brigham Young, 1869*

*18) Brigham Young and party on the Colorado Plateau, March 1870*

*19) Detail of above.* Seated in the center, left to right: *John Squires, John Willard Young, Brigham Young Jr., Brigham Young (seated on chair), unidentified, Erastus Snow, and George A. Smith.*

20) *Brigham Young. 1871*

*21) Brigham Young, 1871*

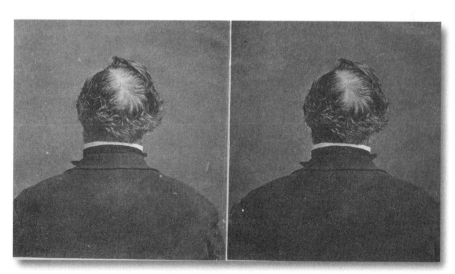

*22) Back of Brigham's head, 1871 (see above)*

23) *Brigham Young's Office, 1871*

24) *Brigham Young, ca. 1875*

*25) Brigham Young, 1875*

*26) Brigham Young, 1876*

*27) Brigham Young, 1876*

*28) Widows of Brigham Young, ca. 1898.* Front row, left to right: *Zina D. Huntington Young and Eliza Burgess Young.* Back row, left to right: *Margaret Pierce Young, Harriet Amelia Folsom Young, Emily Dow Partridge Young, Harriet Barney Young, and Naamah Kendel Jenkins Carter Young.*

29) *Widows and daughters of Brigham Young, 1898.* Front row (first row), left to right: *Rhoda Y. Sanborn, Ruth Y. Healy, Clarissa Y. Spencer, Nabbie Y. Clawson, and Ardell Y. Harrison.* Second row, left to right: *Amelia Folsom Young, Margaret Pierce Young, Zina D. H. Young, Emily Dow Partridge Young, Harriet Barney Young, and Naamah K. J. C. Young.* Third row, left to right: *Clarissa Maria Y. Dougall, Shemira Y. Rossiter, Elizabeth Y. Ellsworth, Fannie Y. Clayton, Eliza Burgess Young, Caroline Y. Cannon, Lucy Bigelow Young, and Josephine Y. Young.* Fourth (top) row, left to right: *Miriam Y. Hardy, Phebe Y. Beatie, Emily Y. Clawson, Zina Y. Card, and Susa Y. Gates.*

# BRIGHAM AS ENTREPRENEUR

Brigham was one of America's great entrepreneurs, but not in the traditional sense of the word. Instead of undertaking projects primarily for personal gain, he was an entrepreneur for the community. His interest was not in building wealth, but in building the kingdom. "The Lord has no objection to his people being wealthy," he taught, "but he has a great objection to people hoarding up their wealth, and not devoting it, expressly, for the advancement of his cause and kingdom on the earth."[1] "We should have only one mess chest, one place of deposit, one store house, one 'pile,' and that is the kingdom of God upon the earth; it is . . . the only safe place of deposit, the only place to invest our capital."[2]

As one person has noted, Brigham was a visible leader "who said, 'Unless you are one in temporal things, how can you be one in spiritual things?' and 'The way the world does business is a sin, the strong build themselves up by putting the weak ones down.'"[3] Decrying the popular attitude of the world, which he called "devilish hoggish," Brigham exclaimed, "It has caused my spirit to weep and mourn to observe their greediness, their cheating and lying, their scheming in every possible way to wring a picayune out of this man, or that woman."[4] "Just as long as every man works for himself," he declared, "we are not the Lord's."[5] He desired that the Saints "should be one family, each seeking to do his neighbour good, and all be engaged to do all the good possible."[6] "We use the terms, 'my farm, my house, my cattle, my horses, my carriage,' &c.," he stated. "But the fact is we do not truly own anything. . . .

"Every man and woman has got to feel that not one farthing of anything in their possession is rightfully theirs, in the strict sense of ownership. When we learn this lesson, where will be my interest and my effort? I do not own anything—it is my Father's. . . . His providence has thrown them into my care; He has appointed me a steward over them, and I am His servant."[7] Brigham believed that "if the Lord has given me means and I spend it needlessly, in rings for my fingers, and jewelry for adornment, I deprive the Priesthood of that which they ought to have to gather the poor, to preach the Gospel, to build temples and to feed the hungry. . . . Every yard of ribbon that I buy that is needless, every flounce, and every gewgaw that is purchased for my family needlessly, robs the Church of God."[8]

Brigham's entrepreneurial efforts were not without controversy. Because he was unable to "define any difference between temporal and spiritual labors," he did not always see the need to make the distinction between enterprises he personally financed and those established through Church funds.[9] His seemingly casual style of operating as if everything was part of the kingdom was both mystifying and maddening to many. One visitor, noting the empire Brigham had helped create, concluded, "Brigham Young is undoubtedly the richest man in the Western Hemisphere."[10] Samuel Bowles was more circumspect: "Brigham Young is at the head of everything. . . . There is immense wealth in his possession; but what proportion of it he calls his own, and what the church's, no one knows,—he apparently recognizes no distinction."[11] His wealth always seemed greater than it was because of the similar and often interchangeable projects he undertook as "Trustee-in-Trust" of the Church.

As an entrepreneur, Brigham was not hesitant to use all available resources, public and private, sacred and profane, human and otherwise, in whatever way inspiration and judgment told him would best benefit the kingdom. While his entrepreneurial skills increased his "personal" wealth and provided security for his family, his efforts benefitted the Church and community even more. Given the relative isolation of the Saints and Utah's growing population, efforts to build the kingdom required the cooperation and the united effort of all—but also provided a benefit to all.

Because Brigham's goal was to always "earn more than I needed," during the early years in Utah he did not see a "need to keep a day-book and ledger in which to keep my accounts."[12] Later, he acknowledged that he had changed this practice. "Some may think that my individual business is so mixed and combined with the public [Church] business that I cannot keep them separate. This is not the case. . . . If you want to know anything about the money, item by item, how it was obtained and how expended, our books are open."[13] Nevertheless, for many people the perception of Brigham is that of an individual casual with Church finances who could not or would not make a distinction between his private enterprises and those of the Church. When this perception is coupled with the fact that much of the Church's property was put into private hands—both Brigham's and other trusted leaders'—to prevent escheatment by federal officials, it is not surprising that the settlement of his estate was both prolonged and involved the courts.

Brigham's task as an entrepreneur was more complicated than the same undertaking would have been in a money-based economy. Because the Saints were largely unable to rely upon the infusion of outside capital or even government assistance, of necessity he implemented an ingenious system by which local manpower and produce such as tallow and turnips were used to finance the importation of machinery and other equipment needed for industry, to finance local construction projects—such as buildings, roads, canals, and irrigation ditches—and to take care of the poor. He helped create a well-organized, relatively self-sufficient "business" that oversaw the establishment of settlements, the implementation of a wide array of businesses and industries, the emigration of skilled workmen from Europe, and the development of agriculture and mineral resources. To maintain a favorable balance of trade, it was necessary for local enterprises to enjoy the advantages of subsidies, central planning, and direction from both Brigham and the Church. It was common practice for Brigham to take the money earned from one endeavor and use it to develop and support other ventures. For instance, the income that he received as governor went toward supporting the Perpetual Education Fund.

Drawing upon his own experience, Brigham spoke of the obligation that men of means possessed to be community entrepreneurs:

> Gather around you the poor and honest of mankind and bestow your charity on them, not by giving them in the way that charity is almost universally understood, but supply them labor that will pay an interest on the outlay of means and, at the same time, afford food, raiment and shelter to the laborer; in this way the man of means becomes a benefactor to his race. Let him instruct those who know not how to cultivate the soil, who know not how to plant gardens and orchards and vineyards, in all these useful and profitable employments. Let him teach them the use of animals and how to profit by their labors and products. After he has taught them how to raise the wool and the flax, let him teach them how to make clothing of various kinds. Now they have their bread, meat, clothing, vege-tables, fruit and dwellings which they have produced by their labor under the direction of the rich, good man whose capital and wisdom have elevated those poor persons from a state of destitution and want to a state of comfort and comparative independence.[14]

The "poor and honest" were also expected to become entrepreneurs in their own right. "Learn . . . how to yoke together a pair of oxen," he taught, and "how to manage and drive them across the plains, how to get timber from the kanyons, how to make brick, and how to hew stone and bring them into shape and position to please the eye and create comfort and happiness for the Saints. These are some of the mysteries of the kingdom."[15] Through these efforts, he envisioned making a nation of "the poor and the ignorant, the low and the degraded who are trodden under foot by the great and the powerful among earth's inhabitants . . . worthy of admiration."[16]

The ultimate resource Brigham made use of was the faith of the Saints, who shared his vision of sacrificing and cooperating for the greater good, whether the task was small or large. When George Goddard, a successful Salt Lake merchant, visited Brigham for business advice, he ended up being called on a mission to "go from door to door with a basket on one arm and an empty sack on the other, enquiring for rags" to be used primarily to create newsprint. Goddard later recalled, "When President Young first made the proposition, the humiliating prospect almost stunned me, but a few moments' reflection reminded me that I came to these valleys . . . for the purpose of doing the will of my Heavenly Father."[17] Goddard's efforts to build the kingdom through his "rag mission" is an example of the varied and countless tasks the Saints willingly undertook.

Brigham also had a knack for looking at a situation and seeing the potential benefit for the kingdom. Knowing that the Saints needed money for their westward journey, one of Brigham's first entrepreneurial projects resulted in the call of the Mormon Battalion. After petitioning the government to build forts along the trail during their journey west, he willingly accepted their counter offer to raise five hundred volunteers to serve during the Mexican War.

The 1847 pioneer company took with them a boat, dubbed the "Revenue Cutter," which was used by the company as a ferry to carry supplies across streams and rivers. The boat was also hired out to ferry Oregon-bound emigrants, thus providing needed supplies and cash. At the Platte River, near present-day Casper, Wyoming, the company built a raft to get themselves across. Brigham then asked ten men to remain behind for a period of time to ferry Oregon emigrants across the river, another profitable venture.

Once in Utah, Brigham turned the gold rush and the later arrival of U.S. Army troops into economic benefits for the Saints, much to the dismay of outsiders. During the gold rush he decried the idea of selling food staples at the same price to those going to the gold fields—where they could earn one hundred and fifty dollars a day—as was charged those who helped build up Utah for a dollar a day. "I say, you men who are going to get gold to make golden images, . . . pay for your flour!"[18] In the aftermath of the Utah War, Brigham's Big Cottonwood Lumber Company provided a major portion of the lumber used by the army during its 1858–61 occupation of Utah and charged handsomely for it. Likewise, he sold excess wheat and other products he produced to the army and bargained well.

As an entrepreneur, Brigham also had a talent of making use of scarce capital, whether in the form of manpower, livestock, or money. For instance, he encouraged Church emigration agents to give priority to those with skills needed in Utah, such as iron and textile workers and "artisans and mechanics of all kinds,"[19] and to have them bring machinery, tools, and blueprints with them.

The scope of the ventures Brigham encouraged is amazing. During the 1850s he built a theater, oversaw the establishment of sugar beet and iron industries, and created the B. Y. Express and Carrying Company (short lived because of the Utah War) that "anticipated the Pony Express, the Ben Holladay Stagecoach line, and the Russell, Majors and Waddell freight trains."[20] Among the ventures during the 1860s were a silk industry, the building of north-south telegraph lines and railroads, and cooperative movements. During the 1870s he expanded into the creation of banks and united orders. Crippled by a lack of knowledge and insufficient start-up capital, some of his endeavors were premature. The sugar and iron industries, for example, came close enough to succeeding that they eventually led others who were better-funded to create successful endeavors.

While some of Brigham's enterprises failed, all contributed to his professed goal of keeping "every man, woman, and child busily employed, that they may have no idle time for hatching mischief in the night, and for making plans to accomplish their own ruin . . . [and] keep everybody busy in building up the kingdom."[21] Since many emigrants often arrived too late in the fall to establish homes before winter, Brigham frequently employed them, sometimes creating marginal or imaginative jobs when substantive work was not available.

To achieve his ideal, Brigham established an ambitious public works program, which regularly provided hundreds of men with work.[22] Among the public works projects were the Salt Lake Temple, the Social Hall, the territorial capitol building, the Salt Lake Theater, irrigation canals, fences, and numerous private houses. Public works enterprises included mills, tanneries, factories, a foundry, a lumber yard, and carpenter, blacksmith, wagon, and other shops.

Individuals who worked on public works projects were regularly paid in "tithing scrip," which was redeemable in merchandise from the local tithing offices, which in an economy initially dependent upon goods rather than money could rightly be viewed as banks. In many regards, Brigham's public works program and his use of "tithing scrip" anticipated by nearly eighty years both the modern Mormon welfare system and Franklin Delano Roosevelt's Works Progress Administration projects.

# 22

# BRIGHAM AT PLAY

Clarissa Young Spencer wrote, "One of Father's most outstanding qualities as a leader was the manner in which he looked after the temporal and social welfare of his people along with guiding them in their spiritual needs."[1] Another daughter, Susa Young Gates, concluded that her father "manifested even more godly inspiration in his carefully regulated social activities and associated pleasure than in his pulpit exercises. He kept the people busy, gave legitimate amusements full sway and encouraged the cultivation of every power, every gift and emotion of the human soul." She based her conclusion on the fact that "people would have had in those grinding years of toil, too few holidays and far too little of the spirit of holiday-making which is the spirit of fellowship and socialised spiritual communion, but for Brigham Young's wise policy."[2]

While the implementation and successful oversight were Brigham's, the inspiration was the Lord's. "The Word and Will of the Lord" that Brigham received in 1847 shortly before the advance pioneer company left Winter Quarters addressed both the spiritual and social needs of Saints. Anticipating the tiring journey the Saints would have across the plains, and their challenges in establishing new homes in an isolated location, the Lord said: "If thou art merry, praise the Lord with singing, with music, with dancing, and with a prayer of praise and thanksgiving. If thou art sorrowful, call on the Lord thy God with supplication."[3]

For Brigham, it was important to give everything its proper time and place. He understood that recreation was an important aspect of life, along with work and worship. He knew that people needed to rest their minds and that their bodies needed to "receive that recreation which is proper and necessary to keep up an equilibrium, to promote healthy action to the whole system."[4] In some ways he subscribed to the maxim of eight hours for rest, eight for work, and eight for recreation. After several years in the valley, he sent a circular letter to local Church leaders recommending that ward socials follow the pattern he established early in the territory by ending with a closing prayer eight hours after the opening prayer.

Although raised in a household where listening "to the sound of a violin was an unforgivable sin," Brigham wholeheartedly accepted the counsel of the Lord and is remembered as a man who "loved all sorts of art and music."[5] Both in crossing the plains and later in Utah, he championed dancing, music, and the theater. In addition to providing a welcome diversion from the harshness of everyday life, these activities helped build a stronger sense of community among the Latter-day Saints.

Because Mormonism provided "food to the mind and exercise to the body," Brigham was able to push aside his harsh, narrow upbringing in favor of a more balanced approach to life, and he became an advocate of activities of which his father would have never approved.[6] "I had not a chance to dance when I was young, and never heard the enchanting tones of the violin, until I was eleven years of age," he recalled, "and then I thought I was on the high way to hell, if I suffered myself to linger and listen to it. I shall not subject my little children to such a course of unnatural training, but they shall go to the dance, study music, read novels, and do anything else that will tend to expand their frames, add fire to their spirits, improve their minds, and make them feel free and untrammeled in body and mind."[7] He couldn't understand "tight-laced religious professors of the present generation [who] have a horror at the sound of a fiddle" and held a negative view of all dancing.[8] John Taylor proclaimed: "We have always considered that there existed on the minds of the religious community, a great deal of unnecessary superstition in relation to dancing, but perhaps this feeling is engendered more through other associations and evils connected with it, than from the thing itself."[9]

Within days of receiving the "Word and Will of the Lord," Brigham proposed a social to show "to the world that this people can be made what God designed them. Nothing will infringe more upon the traditions of some men than to dance." He noted that "for some weeks past I could not wake up at any time of the night but I heard the axes at work. Some were building for the destitute and the widow; and now my feelings are, dance all night, if you desire to so do, for there is no harm in it."[10]

Years later when famed British explorer Sir Richard Burton visited Utah, he noted that the Mormons considered dancing to be "an edifying exercise. The Prophet dances, the Apostles dance, the Bishops dance."[11] Concerning dancing, Brigham proclaimed: "I want it distinctly understood, that fiddling and dancing are no part of our worship. The question may be asked, What are they for, then? I answer, that my body may keep pace with my mind. My mind labors like a man logging, all the time; and this is the reason why I am fond of these pastimes—they give me a privilege to throw every thing off, and shake myself, that my body may exercise, and my mind rest. . . . I do not wrestle, or play the ball; all the exercise I do get is to dance a little."[12] When asked about his fondness for dancing, he replied, "Besides my own [problems] I have the whole people's burdens, and I get rid of them by kicking them off my toes."[13]

In an attempt to ensure that dancing was a wholesome form of recreation that contributed to physical, mental, and social growth, Church leaders took steps to try to eliminate the negative aspects associated with the activity. To control the atmosphere, the Saints were encouraged to hold and attend their own dances rather than going to public dances. Leaders were also instructed to open and close dances with prayer and to be vigilant to keep out worldly influences such as liquor, rowdy behavior, and unsavory individuals. Dancing in a proper setting, Brigham believed, was as wholesome as any other recreational activity: "If you want to dance, run a footrace, pitch quoits or play at ball, do it, and exercise your bodies, and let your minds rest." He also believed that "those who cannot serve God with a pure heart in the dance should not dance. . . . You are just as much prepared for a prayer meeting after dancing as ever you were, if you are Saints."[14]

Dances were held to commemorate Christmas, Easter, Fourth of July, Twenty-fourth of July, elections, and harvest time, among other occasions. They traditionally featured figure or pattern dances, commonly referred to as cotillions or quadrilles. Because some step patterns were complicated and hard to remember, "callers" would announce the next figure. These dances were viewed as appropriate because they required a gentleman touch only the hands or an arm of a lady. The waltz, which was greeted with cries of outrage and shock when first introduced to the United States because "it permitted too much familiarity between partners," was preached against from the pulpit in Utah.[15]

At the request of Brigham, George Wardle began a school in the 1850s to teach the proper art of dancing. Brigham attended and proved to be an adept student.[16] Emma B. Lindsay reported that "he was very light on his feet and good at dancing."[17] Emmeline B. Wells noted that "Pres. Brigham Young was a famous dancer, and certainly one of the most graceful pictures."[18] Charlotte Evans Adams as a youth in Nephi, Utah, attended a party given to honor Brigham and was thrilled when he asked her to dance. She described him as "a graceful dancer, executing the intricate figures of the Lancers, quadrille, and Schottische so beautifully."[19]

Brigham encouraged the building of social halls where dancing, parties, and theatricals could be held. The most famous of these was the Social Hall, located on State Street in Salt Lake, and dedicated New Year's Day, 1853.

When the Social Hall was dedicated, Brigham stated that if he "were placed on a cannibal island and given a task of civilizing its people," he would "straightway build a theatre for the purpose."[20] Concerned that many of the Saints had not had the opportunity "to cultivate their minds, to search into the history of the nations of the earth, [and] to learn the prejudices that are upon the people, their education, feelings, and customs," he emphasized the importance of the stage in isolated Utah.[21] In 1850 he helped organize the Deseret Dramatic Association and in 1862 the Saints dedicated the impressive Salt Lake Theater, which provided both an important means of diversion and a unique partner with the pulpit. Along these lines Brigham stated: "Upon the stage of a theatre can be represented in character, evil and its consequences, good and its happy results and rewards; the weakness and the follies of man, the magnanimity of virtue and the greatness of truth. The stage can be made to aid the pulpit in impressing upon the minds of a community an enlightened sense of a virtuous life, also a proper horror of the enormity of sin and a just dread of its consequences. The path of sin with its thorns and pitfalls, its gins and snares can be revealed, and how to shun it." He further concluded, "The Lord understands the evil and the good; why should we not likewise understand them?"[22]

As with dancing, Brigham's advocacy of the theater stood in stark contrast to hard-line Christians who tended to shun dramatic productions. "Everything that is joyful, beautiful, glorious, comforting, consoling, lovely, pleasing to the eye, good to the taste, pleasant to the smell, and happifying in every respect is for the Saints," he proclaimed.[23] Rather than banning theatrical productions, he tried to control the negative aspects. He forbade profanity on the stage, along with phrases such as "I swear" and "By Heavens."[24] Believing there was enough sorrow in everyday life, he advocated productions that uplifted. "Tragedy [works that have a disastrous or sorrowful conclusion designed specifically to excite pity or terror] is favoured by the outside world," he noted. "I am not in favour of it. I do not wish murder and all its horrors and the villainy leading to it portrayed before our women and children. . . . I want such plays performed as will make the spectators feel well; and I wish those who perform to select a class of plays that will improve the public mind, and exalt the literary taste of the community."[25]

He was known to censor scenes he deemed inappropriate. One instance was the too realistic portrayal of the death of Nancy in Oliver Twist. On another occasion, when a visiting actor presented one scene Brigham deemed too violent, he told the actor that the scene was not to be portrayed again on the Salt Lake stage. The actor responded that either the scene was to be permitted or he would cancel his engagement. Brigham told him to suit himself, but that the scene had to be changed. In the end, the actor acquiesced. Brigham's favorite plays included *The Lady of Lyons,* a romantic comedy by British author Edward Bulwer-Lytton and works by Shakespeare. (During Brigham's lifetime, *Hamlet* was produced nineteen times in the Salt Lake Theater, *Macbeth* eighteen, and *Romeo and Juliet* fourteen.)[26]

For several years Brigham also organized a yearly retreat to Big Cottonwood Canyon to commemorate the anniversary of the Twenty-fourth of July. Here the Saints could escape the heat of the valley, kick up their heels, and momentarily forget their challenges while enjoying Utah's spectacular mountain beauty.

Brigham's Declaration of Independence.

*Brigham Young and the Saints, 24th of July celebration, Big Cottonwood Canyon*

## 23

# BRIGHAM AS (UNSUCCESSFUL) INNOVATOR

## *The Deseret Alphabet*

A lot can be learned about people from their failures. Not everything Brigham tried worked. Not every settlement survived. Not every mission succeeded. While the Lead Mission failed to produce lead, the Iron Mission not only failed to produce iron, but some of those called to produce iron also failed to become true Saints, becoming involved in the infamous Mountain Meadows Massacre. His efforts to build up the kingdom of God through cooperatives and united orders also did not fully achieve their stated purposes. For the most part, the problem was that Brigham's reach exceeded the Saints' collective grasp.

Another reason that not everything Brigham tried worked was that he dared to dream big. Instead of simply gathering to a city, as was the case at Nauvoo, he envisioned the Saints needing an entire state. And not just any-sized state. The State of Deseret that Brigham proposed in 1849, but which the U.S. Congress rejected, creating the Territory of Utah instead, was to have been as large as Texas.

Maybe none of Brigham's endeavors was more ambitious and idealistic than his unsuccessful attempt to rewrite English orthography in the form known as the Deseret Alphabet. His own adventures with English grammar, along with his understanding that he was not alone in this regard, go a long way to help explain why he initiated one of his most unique innovations. The effort also showed his incredible audacity in thinking that he could overhaul such a far-reaching and well-established convention.

It was said of Brigham that "nothing was too small for his mind; nothing was too large."[1] While he displayed an incredible mental capacity on a wide variety of subjects, there is at least one notable exception to this generalization. He did not have an aptitude for languages. Written English did not readily lend itself to his way of thinking, and he never could correctly write the language that had both long-standing inconsistencies and was also rapidly evolving with the adoption of words borrowed from other languages.

If Brigham had written and spoken one of the phonetic languages, there would have been little need for him to tinker with its orthography. But like the famous American grammarian Noah Webster before him, he was frustrated by the fact that the same letter in English could be pronounced more than one way. The letter *a*, for instance, is pronounced differently in *father, fall, man, many,* or *mate.* As was the case with so many deprived of formal education, Brigham tended to spell words as he pronounced them: *City* was spelled *citty; many* as *meny, imagine* as *emagen,* heart as *hart,* and *anxious* as *ancios.* In addition to the commonly practiced "spell it as it sounds" system, Brigham's writing incorporated his own idiosyncracies. He frequently added a "silent" e to the end of words; thus *go* became *goe* and *leg* became *lage* on the written page. He also combined words that sounded alike but were spelled differently, such as *right* and *write.* Self-conscious about his spelling, his letters occasionally included statements similar to the ones he wrote to Mary Ann in 1837, "Please read this and keep it to yourself [and] not expose my poore righting and speling"[2] and to Willard Richards in 1840, "Excuse erours and mestakes you must remember its from me."[3]

His untutored Yankee dialect and grammar, standardized in the published versions of his discourses, were noted by those who heard him speak.

According to reports, he pronounced *impetus* as *im-PEET-us, little* as *leetle,* and *beyond* as *beyend.* He also used terms such as "disremember," "they was," and "ain't you," prompting one visitor to Salt Lake to write that there was "an irrepressible conflict between his nominatives and verbs."[4]

Concerning his lack of formal education, he noted: "Seeing that this was the way I was brought up they cannot expect from me the same etiquette and ceremony as if I had been brought up at the feet of Gamaliel."[5] On another occasion he noted that "when I began to speak in public, I was about as destitute of language as a man could well be. . . . How I have had the headache, when I had ideas to lay before the people, and not words to express them; but I was so gritty that I always tried my best."[6] By persevering he was able to make himself into a dynamic speaker.

While Brigham's ability "to turn a phrase" increased over the years, his ability to then correctly spell what he had spoken showed little improvement. When it was reported in the press that Brigham opposed the free education plan growing in popularity throughout the nation—"I do not believe in allowing my charities to go through the hands of a set of robbers who pocket nine-tenths themselves, and give one-tenth to the poor,"[7] Brigham would note of his position—John Chislett wrote in an open letter published in a Salt Lake newspaper that he expected no less a position from an individual "who cannot write a correct sentence in his mother tongue, and hardly spell half-a-dozen consecutive words correctly."[8]

The fact that Brigham couldn't spell resulted both from his lack of formal education and from how he chose to deal with written English in his later life. He preferred to have his clerks read letters, newspapers, and other items to him, thus depriving himself of the opportunity to improve his spelling through firsthand experience. He also employed scribes whenever he could to write for him. Of the tens of thousands of manuscript pages authored by him over the years, less than 450 are in his own hand.

Shortly after settling at Kirtland, Ohio, Brigham joined Joseph Smith and others in trying to learn a second language—Hebrew. While Joseph proved somewhat adept at the language, Brigham wasn't. Eventually Joseph, noting Brigham's frustration, excused him to work instead on the temple.

A few years later, Brigham learned what it was like to be a stranger in a strange land and have to deal daily with a "foreign" language. True, it was only England and the language was British English, but he experienced firsthand the reality behind the witticism that the United States and England are two countries divided by a common language.

The one thing Brigham did understand about the English language was that he was not alone in his struggles with it. The Latter-day Saints who had gathered to Utah, he recognized, largely shared his lack of formal education. "We have mostly come from the plough and the furrow, from the mechanic shops and the loom, from the spinning-jenny, the kitchen, and wash-room."[9] This fact led him to proclaim that Church members literally fulfilled the scriptural prophecy concerning "the poor and the ignorant" being gathered "from the dens and caves of the earth."[10]

While most of Utah's early residents spoke English, by the early-1850s the gospel net had begun to gather converts from non-English-speaking countries who would need to learn English. As he greeted new arrivals and contemplated what they were going through, his mind surely must have gone back to his own adventures with language, both at home and abroad, and felt sympathy for what they were going through. While he enjoyed the luxury of clerks who would read to him and write for him, the vast majority of the Latter-day Saints would never enjoy a similar experience. Thus it is not surprising that Brigham proposed rewriting English orthography at the same time emphasis was placed upon the gathering of Latter-day Saints from Europe.

In 1853, the year a concerted effort began to gather Saints from continental Europe, Brigham raised with the Utah territorial legislature the idea that would become the Deseret Alphabet: "While the world is progressing with steam-engine power and lightning speed in the accumulation of wealth, extension of sciences, communication, and dissemination of letters and principles, why may not the way be paved for the easier acquisition of the English language, combining, as it does, great extension and varied expression with beauty, simplicity, and power, and being unquestionably the most useful and beautiful in the world. But while we freely admit this, we also have to acknowledge that it is perhaps as much abused in its use, and as complex in its attainment, as any other."[11] If each letter had its own "fixed and unalterable sound,"[12] Brigham concluded, it would be easier for these people to learn to spell, read, and pronounce words.

In January 1854, the committee appointed to deal with the issue unveiled its solution. Instead of the traditional twenty-six letters, the Deseret Alphabet had thirty-eight symbols, based largely upon Pitman shorthand. The traditional five vowels—a, e, i, o, and u—were replaced by seventeen "vowel" symbols; and instead of twenty consonants, the alphabet had twenty-one "consonant" symbols. Each of these thirty-eight characters corresponded to "a determinate and uniform relation between the sign and its sound." Words could now be spelled "with reference to given sounds," the *Deseret News* noted in announcing the new system. "We may derive a hint of the advantage to orthography, from spelling the word *eight*, which in the new alphabet only requires two letters instead of five to spell it, viz: AT."[13] Later in 1854 Brigham wrote his son Joseph A. Young that although "the alphabet or characters" was "not perfect, we intend to go ahead and if necessary amend until the system of orthography and writing is revolutionized."[14]

Many saw the Deseret Alphabet as an attempt to create a uniquely Mormon kingdom. H. H. Bancroft concluded in his *History of Utah* that the Mormons were "a separate people wishing to have a separate language, and perhaps in time an independent literature."[15] Jules Remy wrote in *A Journey to Great Salt Lake City* that "some persons have supposed that the object of this alphabet was to prevent access to the Mormon books and writings" by outsiders.[16]

In the aftermath of the American Revolution, Noah Webster had indeed tried to create an American English different from British English because he believed that residents of the new world needed their own identity in language as well as government. The Deseret Alphabet, however, rather than being an effort to make Mormonism exclusive, grew from Brigham's desire to make the Book of Mormon and other works more readily available to the larger population in Utah and the nation, especially English speakers who had been deprived of formal education, foreign-language-speakers learning English as a second language, and children just beginning to learn to read and write. The Deseret Alphabet was also touted as a way of holding back the world by establishing a library consisting of only "the best books."[17]

Those who gave the Deseret Alphabet a try reported that they were able to master the system in as little as six lessons. Nevertheless, there were a number of drawbacks that could not be overcome. In 1868 first and second readers were published, followed by excerpts from the Book of Mormon, but it was estimated that to publish even a modest library of a thousand titles would cost $5 million—a prohibitively high sum at the time.[18] In addition to the cost, there was also the problem that people from different backgrounds would pronounce the same word differently, possibly resulting in it being spelled differently even under this system. For instance, Brigham's pronunciation of *piano* as *pianna* was different from most of his contemporaries.[19]

In the end, literate individuals had little incentive to learn the Deseret Alphabet, while the unlettered who desired to learn it had relatively little to read. Nevertheless, in July 1877, shortly before his death, Brigham told a gathering of bishops that he desired them to "use their influence, and be interested in the use of the New Alphabet and improved orthography of the English Language. He was fully satisfied, that it would be of incalculable benefit to Foreign Emigrants in learning the English Language after their arrival here from the Old Country."[20] Two weeks later, he reminded the same group that the "Pitman Phonetic Alphabet" was simpler "than the English Alphabet," and told them that "he was very anxious that we should lay aside the . . . old and mysterious way of spelling the English Language, as we have laid aside the mystery of the religious dogmas of the day," the minutes reported.[21] In spite of his pleas, after more than twenty years of limited success, the Deseret Alphabet was laid to rest along with Brigham.

# 24

# A HARD-SPOKEN NEW YORKER WITH A SOFT SIDE

Unlike Teddy Roosevelt, who spoke softly and carried a big stick, Brigham tended to speak loudly but seldom wielded a stick. A widely held view of Brigham, however, is that of an iron-fisted despot who spoke loudly *and* carried a big stick. Those primarily responsible for this caricature have failed to see, or chose to ignore, the "rest of the story." Rather than his harsh language reflecting the reality of the situation, he often purposely overstated his point, and then tempered his harsh rhetoric with kind words and benevolent deeds. When taken in his entirety, the Brigham that emerges is an individual whose bark was worse than his bite. The Saints who had regular contact with Brigham largely understood something lost on the occasional or one-time visitor and ignored by those motivated by an agenda: behind Brigham's tough words was a kind, caring, tolerant, harmless personality.

Concerning his preaching, Brigham confessed: "Often, when I stand up here, I have the feelings of a person that is unable to convey his ideas, because I have not the advantage of language. However . . . I rise to do the best I can and to give the people the best I have for them at the time."[1] While Brigham didn't prepare his talks in advance, he usually took time to review them afterward and edit them for publication. In most cases the editing was relatively minor; but sometimes he made more substantial changes to ensure that the meaning of his comments was clearly conveyed in published form.

Brigham learned his forthright speaking style from Joseph Smith, who taught him that "when you speak to a people or person you must use language to represent your ideas, so that they will be remembered. When you wish the people to feel what you say, you have got to use language that they will remember, or else the ideas are lost to them. Consequently, in many instances we use language that we would rather not use."[2] The typical preaching of the day, Brigham believed, was like "wind" going "into the ear and . . . [soon] forgotten."[3] Because he was on the Lord's errand, he sought to avoid that situation. "I will tell you what this people need, with regard to preaching," he once declared. "You need, figuratively, to have it rain pitchforks, tines downwards. . . . Instead of the smooth, beautiful, sweet, still, silk-velvet-lipped preaching, you should have sermons like peals of thunder, and perhaps we then can get the scales from our eyes. This style is necessary in order to save many of this people."[4]

While his preaching was more silk and velvet than pitchfork and thunder, his language was often strong enough to earn him a reputation as an acid-tongued orator. Once, Utah's delegate to Congress, knowing that he couldn't change Brigham's speaking style, recommended that Brigham's most fiery sermons not be published because of how the press manipulated his words.[5] Although his speaking style cost him in terms of national public relations, that mattered little to him. It was the end result upon the Saints in Utah that concerned him. "As to the opinion of men concerning myself as a man I care no more about it than I do the dust under my feet," he proclaimed. "I don't care what you say about me if you will only serve the Lord our God."[6] His hope was to inspire his listeners to more fully grab hold of the principles of life and salvation. "When we talk to and instruct the people we have to chasten and correct them sometimes, so as to lead their minds to principles more advanced than they are in the habit of practicing."[7]

There was a contrast between Brigham the lawgiver (his pulpit personality) and Brigham the enforcer (his everyday persona). As the lawgiver, there was no compromise. His words were straightforward and designed to make a point. While he forcefully denounced sin and evil, his actions repeatedly reveal charity toward the sinner and evildoer. The difference between his public voice and his private actions, he explained, was because he was not without faults. "There are weaknesses manifested in men that I am bound to forgive," he stated, for "I am right there myself. I am liable to mistakes. . . . But I am where I can see the light."[8] Recognizing that even the best of men fall short of the mark, he proclaimed: "There is no question but every person here who seriously reflects upon his own existence, his being here, and the hereafter which awaits him, must many times feel that he comes short of doing all the good for which our Father in heaven has brought us forth. This I conclude from my own experience."[9] He further noted: "I have told the Latter-day Saints from the beginning that I do not profess much righteousness, but I profess to know the will of God concerning you, and I have boldness enough to tell it to you, fearless of your wrath, and I expect that it is on this account that the Lord has called me to occupy the place I do."[10]

Regarding Brigham's pulpit personality, English adventurer Sir Richard Burton, who spent an extended period of time in Utah, observed that "where occasion requires, [Brigham] can use all the weapons of ridicule to direful effect, and 'speak a bit of his mind' in a style which no one forgets. He often reproves his erring followers in purposely violent language, making the terrors of a scolding the punishment in lieu of hanging."[11] Non-Mormon Frederick Dellenbaugh, who first came to Utah in the 1860s and frequented Utah on a regular basis thereafter, wrote to a critic of Brigham: "Much that Brigham Young shouted from his pulpit was mere balderdash, couched in the language of God in that terrible book, the Old Testament. . . . Brigham Young's tirades were infantile compared with those of the Jew's Divine leader." After noting some of the cursings, scourgings, and desolation with which the Lord threatened disobedient Israel in Leviticus 26, Dellenbaugh concluded: "This kind of tirade was the same fanatical frenzy that Brigham invoked to keep *his* people in line. . . . It was more or less Biblical, and was not always real—only an effort to frighten people one way or the other."[12]

Regarding his hard language, Brigham stated in 1866: "There are some things that Brigham has said he would do; but has never happened to do them; and that is not all, he prays fervently, to his Father and God that he may never be brought into circumstances to be obliged to shed human blood. He never has yet been brought into such a position. . . . The genius of our religion is to have mercy upon all, do good to all, as far as they will let us do good to them."[13]

During Brigham's lifetime, people frequently pulled his words out of context to suit their own purposes, whether to justify their own actions or to create a stereotype, much as people now take his words out of context to perpetuate long-held myths. Then, as now, people have confused how Brigham used the "if clause." He spoke both hyperbolically and conditionally—to understand which he was using, his words need to be examined in context. While it is not clear how his hyperbolic examples— usually given impromptu and frequently featuring frontier violence imagery—compare with his more carefully crafted conditional statements in accomplishing his ultimate goal of turning sinners into saints, it is clear that he did succeed in making his rhetoric memorable through his occasional use of tongue-in-cheek and over-the-top statements.

During the early days in the valley when some people hoarded corn, a frustrated Brigham vented his feelings in extreme terms in a council meeting: "If those that have do not sell to those that have not, we will just take it and distribute among the poor, and those that have and will not divide willingly may be thankful that their heads are not found wallowing in the snow." He then noted that rather than carrying out his threat, he would instead "talk to the people in public. I know the strongest side are willing to do right." When Brigham addressed the Saints, he spoke "of the oppression of the poor; said to those that [have] corn to spare, to let it go on reasonable terms; said to those that had to buy, not to be particular about what they had to pay, for it would be salvation to them but death to the seller that extortioned." Reportedly, "every man that could be touched was stirred by way of rememberence" and the food shortage was averted.[14]

In 1853 Brigham proclaimed: "If you want to know what to do with a thief that you may find stealing, *I say kill him on the spot,* and never suffer him to commit another iniquity.... That is what I wish every man to do, to put a stop to that abominable practice in the midst of this people."[15] His words were designed to cause the wrongdoer pause at a time when Utah was experiencing an increase in crime and did not have a penitentiary in which to incarcerate criminals. While there is no record that thieves following Brigham's proclamation began to experience widespread summary justice, there is evidence that following the completion of the territorial penitentiary the following year thieves began to be incarcerated.

On another occasion Brigham asked, "What shall be done with sheep that stink the flock?" Answering his own question he stated, "We will take them, I was going to say, and cut off their tails two inches behind their ears; however, I will use a milder term, and say, cut off their ears." As with the statement about thieves, this comment has also been frequently put forth as the "real Brigham." What has been overlooked, however, is the sentence immediately following in which Brigham states, "But instead of doing this, we will try to cleanse them; we will wash them with soap."[16]

Shortages in the Perpetual Emigration Fund prompted him in 1855 to warn those with unpaid debts: "I intend to put the screws upon you, and you who have owed for years, if you do not pay up now and help us, we will levy on your property and take every farthing you have on the earth."[17] The fact that he was simply trying to motivate those who could repay their debts is evidenced by a letter he had written one debtor that he had "not the least disposition to oppress the poor or those who are in embarrassed circumstances and not able to pay; such being your situation I would inform you not to be perplexed or distressed about the matter, but always do right and when you get able to pay do it cheerfully and the Lord will bless you."[18] As further evidence of Brigham's intent, he subsequently donated his own property to be used to gather the poor.

During the 1855 grasshopper infestation he asked each household to reduce their rations to help those in need: "If you do not pursue a righteous course, we will separate you from the Church. Is that all? No, if necessary we will take your grain from your bin and distribute it among the poor and needy, and they shall be fed and supplied with work, and you shall receive what your grain is worth."[19] Instead of carrying out his threats, he created work for people in need—an effort that personally cost him thousands of dollars. "I build walls, dig ditches, make bridges, and do a great amount of variety of labour that is of but little consequence only to provide ways and means for sustaining and preserving the destitute. . . . Why? I have . . . articles of food, which I wish my brethren to have; and it is better for them to labour . . . so far as they are able to have opportunity than to have them given to them."[20]

Critics have claimed that the kindness Brigham showed to the Saints did not extend to non-Mormons. On July 24, 1857, after learning that General William Harney, with his reputation for violence, was leading the soldiers bound for Utah during the Utah War, Brigham privately stated that if the army crossed South Pass "the buz[z]ards Should pick [Harney's] bones."[21] He subsequently publicly proclaimed: "Woe, woe to those men who come here to unlawfully meddle with me and this people. I swore in Nauvoo, when my enemies were looking me in the face, that I would send them to hell across lots, if they meddled with me; and I ask no more odds of all hell to-day."[22]

As with other instances, while Brigham talked tough, instead of carrying out his threats he pursued a course that sought to avoid direct contact with the army. He adhered to what he taught the Latter-day Saints at Nauvoo, that it was better to "suffer wrong rather than do wrong," and he followed the word of the Lord to him: "Rather than fight your enemies, go away."[23] That fall, upon hearing reports that the soldiers did not have salt,

Brigham sent them salt.[24] The following spring as the Saints were preparing to abandon their homes rather than fight the army, Brigham heard that the soldiers were short of provisions and offered them meat and flour.[25]

Shortly before implementing the 1856–57 Mormon Reformation, Brigham proclaimed, "How slow many of us are to believe the things of God, O how slow."[26] Wilford Woodruff reported that shortly afterward Brigham, feeling a need to wake the Saints, gave "one of the strongest addresses that was ever delivered to this Church & kingdom" in which he condemned the Saints "for lying, stealing, swareing, commiting Adultery, quarelling with Husbands wives & Children & many other Evils. He spoke in the power of God & the demonstration of the Holy Ghost & his voice & words were like the Thunderings of Mount Sina."[27]

During the Mormon Reformation, Brigham proclaimed that as part of the repentance process, people guilty of serious sin, such as the shedding of innocent blood, might be required to voluntarily forfeit their own lives or submit to whatever other penalty the Lord might require to receive the benefit of the Savior's atonement—a teaching frequently referred to as "Blood Atonement." Taken in context, his comments seem designed to give the unrepentant pause about the need to repent and to forestall people from committing such sins, rather than being a call for immediate action. In December 1856, after listening to Church leaders caught up in the fervor of the Reformation speak of "ridding ourselves of the wicked in our midst" and stating that there were sinners who ought to have their throats cut, a concerned Brigham cautioned his audience: "Can you divide between wild fire and true fire? You will see bushels of wild fire if this reformation continues. The devils will be on hand to pray, to teach, to exhort,—and you will find the fire mixed—heaven and hell mixed. . . . There are plenty who will have wild fire. If you have true fire, you will have wisdom, integrity and knowledge. . . . If not, you will have the bitter. . . . Select out the things of God, and let the things of the Devil alone."[28]

Rather than inciting the widespread shedding of blood, as has widely been claimed—there were instances where individuals seemingly were unable to differentiate between true and wild fires and took justice into their own hands—the actions Brigham took during the reformation to address misdeeds included stopping dances and the theater, briefly discontinuing the sacrament of the Lord's supper because its atoning power wasn't being appreciated by the Saints, preaching repentance, and encouraging the Saints to submit to rebaptism. Noting that "the time has been in Israel under the law of God . . . that if a man was found guilty of adultery, he must have his blood shed [Lev. 20:10]," Brigham assured the Saints that "now I say, in the name of the Lord, that if this people will sin no more, but faithfully live their religion, their sins will be forgiven them without taking life."[29] When Church leaders in Cedar City asked what should be done with an individual who had committed adultery, Brigham echoed what he previously stated by responding that "remission and pardon: even of adultery, are promised to all that truly repent, confess, forsake their sins, and make restitution, when necessary, then, ever after, 'live their religion,' be on the Lord's side, and do right, all such you may bless and encourage in their journey through life."[30] To leaders in Beaver he similarly wrote: "I do not wish to know the names nor the errors of them who are called saints: Let it suffice that they confess and forsake their sins, & live nearer to the Lord than they have hitherto done."[31]

In 1877, following a statement by Brigham that there was a need to prune sinners from the Church, one individual rejoiced about "the proposed cleansing of the church by cutting off all dead branches which it is hoped will soon be inaugurated."[32] As on other occasions, Brigham's bark had little bite. Shortly before his death he told George Q. Cannon that "offending members should be carefully looked after and attended to but not dealt rashly with."[33]

## ∞ 25 ∞

# AMERICA'S BOGEYMAN

After completing an overland journey to Oregon, an emigrant wrote Brigham with a simple question: Where is my cow? In spite of the fact that thousands of emigrants and thousands of head of cattle passed through the territory each year, this man sincerely believed that although he had no direct contact with Brigham while in Utah, the Mormon prophet was personally aware of both him and his lost cow. This story vividly illustrates what was then believed and continues to be believed about Brigham, notwithstanding his claim that he could not know every emigrant or head of cattle. In an effort to prove him a religious imposter and charlatan, his critics have ironically bestowed on him attributes traditionally associated with deity. According to a popular perception, Brigham possessed the Godlike characteristics of being omniscient, omnipresent, and omnipotent. In short, the story goes, there was nothing in Utah that he did not know about or control. Thus the letter from the emigrant.

According to oft-told tales, Brigham used his unparalleled powers to carry out a reign of terror unprecedented in American history. Shortly before his death he was even dubbed "the greatest criminal of the Nineteenth Century."[1] The claim that Brigham had a hand in everything that happened in "hierarchical, tyrannical" Utah not only provided a ready explanation for those who wanted to believe the worst about Brigham and the Mormons but also continues to be an article of faith among adherents of the old-time anti-Mormon religion.

As America's Bogeyman, the mere mention of Brigham Young sent fear into the hearts of many—including passing emigrants who were repeatedly warned about his despotic kingdom—and captivated the lurid interests of a nation. The evil deeds attributed to him were abundantly reported in newspapers, memorialized in tell-all books, and even became the subject of novels. Given the amount and nature of the stories that circulated, one can easily imagine mothers everywhere exhorting their children to be good or "Brigham Young and the Mormons'll get ya."

One tenet of Brigham as Bogeyman declares that for "many years" following the Saints arrival in the valley "nothing, no trivial incident, even, could happen in Utah without being brought to the ears of Brigham Young and his chief counsellors."[2] How Brigham was able to accomplish this feat—given the tens of thousands of settlers in the territory plus the thousands of emigrants passing through, given the fact that for much of this time Utah Territory was more than twice the size of the state of Utah and contained over one hundred far-flung settlements, and finally, given that it often required more than a week to get messages back and forth between outlying settlements and Salt Lake because the telegraph had not been built—has never been explained. Nevertheless, some detractors, choosing to accept the rhetoric rather than examine the reality, continue to proclaim what common sense suggests would have been unimaginable for a mere mortal.

Although it would have been impossible for Brigham to know everything that happened in Utah, he did try to learn as much as possible about what was transpiring. Like most leaders, he asked for, and received, reports from underlings. His extensive correspondence collection reveals, however, that not all reports were created equal. What he knew was dependent upon what was reported and how it was reported.

In addition to relying upon others, he had developed a great power of observation and regularly tried to put this ability into practice. "I have endeavored all my life to follow one portion of the instructions of the Saviour to his disciples, that is, to 'WATCH,'" he proclaimed. "*I am a very watchful man.*"[3] He counseled one of his sons, "Never allow anything to escape your notice. Listen attentively, and observe minutely the manners, customs, and remarks of all." This philosophy, Brigham informed him, had been his "daily and hourly" course.[4] On his yearly travels through the territory, he spent much of his time observing and listening. When he attended the Salt Lake Theater, his daughter noted that between acts he would regularly go where he could be "unobserved but observing."[5]

Another tenet states that Brigham "controls the every act of the Mormon people and makes slaves of his followers."[6] Given the scope of Mormon settlement, it would have been impossible for him to control every act and still have so many far-flung communities grow and thrive. He instructed people on their responsibilities, gave what help he could, but could not micromanage every action.

Rather than lead a people who did everything he asked, he concluded that "to guide the minds of the people and to govern and control them is a greater miracle than to raise the dead." He lamented that even "the Lord Almighty" would have a hard time controlling the Latter-day Saints.[7] "When I look round and see the foolish habits of the people, it is a little mortifying, and I wish it were otherwise. Still we put up with it . . . and talk and preach and set you examples, and teach you how to be Saints in very deed."[8] He noted that he would gladly "tell the people what to pray for," but he also knew that "ten minutes afterwards they [would] pray for something else."[9] On another occasion he noted that he wished what was said of the Saints "was true—that you were all obedient to your President. If you all will be, you will cease sinning, tattling, lying, backbiting, and strife, all will be industrious, prudent, faithful and full of wisdom and good works, and the power of God will be upon us more and more, and we will be able to do more good to the inhabitants of the earth."[10] It was also common for Brigham during visits to outlying settlements to chastise the Saints because they hadn't followed his instructions, such as how they should build their forts. Given what was transpiring, Brigham would not have been human if at times he did not long for the control he was claimed to possess.

Although portrayed by critics as a harsh dictator, Brigham regularly denounced the use of force. When one visitor to Salt Lake observed, "What you say is generally done," Brigham responded, "If it is right it *should* be done, but I would not and could not control: I instruct the people . . . and leave them to choose for themselves."[11] "We have history enough to prove that when [men] have the power their motto is, 'You shall,'" he declared. "But there is no such thing in the economy of heaven."[12] "We could not say, and maintain the faith that we have embraced, you must bow down and profess our religion. . . . If we become Godlike we will be just as full of charity as he is. . . . Our religion will not permit us to command or force any man or woman to obey the Gospel."[13] He proclaimed that if people "do not believe in my advice, teachings, and counsel, they are at perfect liberty to disbelieve them."[14]

A third tenet declares that Brigham taught "Blood Atonement as a religious duty to be performed by the faithful Latter-Day Saints."[15] Rather than blood atonement being the voluntary submission to the will of the Lord by which an individual might have his sins forgiven as Brigham taught, critics twisted his teachings to portray it as the arbitrary and awful means by which Brigham controlled and punished both Mormons and non-Mormons who dared cross or disobey him. Every violent act that happened in the vicinity of Utah was attributed to "blood atonement." The distorted picture that still exists is of Church-instigated murder of dissenters, enemies, and strangers for even minor or non-existent offences.

Mark Twain noted of his visit to Utah: "It is a luscious country for thrilling evening stories about assassinations of intractable Gentiles. I cannot easily conceive of anything more cozy than the night in Salt Lake which we spent in a Gentile den, smoking pipes and listening to tales" of Mormon atrocities, including how "heedless" visitors to Utah "make remarks about Brigham, or polygamy, or some other sacred matter, and the very next morning at daylight such parties are sure to be found lying up some back alley, contentedly waiting for the hearse."[16]

According to the popular story, Brigham not only could order people to carry out blood atonement with the crook of his little finger, but he also regularly and ruthlessly exercised this power. The group held primarily responsible for these bloody deeds was the infamous Danites. Everything that happened in Utah—including even events that didn't occur at all—was blamed on Brigham and the Danites. After arriving in Salt Lake in 1858, Elizabeth Cumming met a Gentile named Knight who introduced himself as being "well known *in the States* as the man the Mormons *killed* . . . under circumstances of peculiar atrocity."[17]

What is most surprising about Brigham's supposedly unlimited power is how he used it. Those who publicly challenged Brigham's authority and policies, such as William Godbe; or those who wrote negative "tell all" books about Brigham and the Mormons, such as Fanny Stenhouse, Ann Eliza Webb, and Bill Hickman, supposedly the "chief Danite" who broke the organization's oath of silence; or even lesser-known figures such as Almerin Grow, who regularly wrote Brigham asking for help with personal problems, did not experience his "crooked finger." Instead, those who were widely claimed to have been "blood atoned" usually had little or no interaction with him or tended to be the same type of individuals murdered in other areas of the country, such as those who got into feuds with acquaintances over money.

The Danites did exist during a brief period in the fall of 1838, when Sampson Avard created this renegade paramilitary organization to avenge anti-Mormon persecutions in Missouri. Ironically, Brigham and his brother Lorenzo played a major role in exposing the activities of this covert band and bringing about its demise. When Joseph Smith learned from Brigham about Avard's actions, the Mormon prophet wrote an open letter from Liberty Jail condemning the Danites: "We have learned . . . that many false and pernicious things which were calculated to lead the saints far astray and to do great injury have been taught by Dr. Avard as coming from the Presidency . . . which the presidency never knew of being taught in the church by any body untill after they were made prisoners. . . . The presidency were ignorant as well as innocent of these things."[18] After Avard was "cut off for his wickedness," he created tales about the Danites that followed the Mormons to Utah.[19] Although there is no solid evidence they ever existed outside Missouri, the stereotype of Danites carrying out blood atonements and other crimes was perpetuated in numerous tell-all books, countless newspaper articles, and even novels.

Few people in the era of "yellow journalism" were as systematically vilified as Brigham. During the nineteenth century, newspapers were largely free to say what they wanted without impunity—and regularly did. After a French court ruled that knowingly publishing bogus information constituted libel, one Salt Lake City newspaper sarcastically editorialized: "And yet, in the face of such opposition, reporters are expected to make the newspapers spicy and interesting. Thank heaven, American newspapers are not handicapped in this matter."[20] Portrayed as domineering, ruthless, power-hungry, greedy, and a bigot, there was little that Brigham wasn't accused of.

"What is now the news circulated throughout the United States?" Brigham asked as the U.S. Army approached Utah during the summer of 1857. "I am guilty of the death of every man, woman, and child that has died between the Missouri river and the California gold mines."[21] While Brigham exaggerated the claim, it was not by much. At the time he made his statement, newspapers portrayed the Mormons as having a career of "marauding, fanaticism, and murder." One newspaper reported that "hundreds of emigrants have been killed, and robbed of everything. . . . It is an undoubted fact that the Mormons were at the head of most of these outrages."[22] Another paper wrote, "We are fully convinced that the Mormon people, and they alone, are responsible for all of the murders and robberies that have been committed upon the immigrants."[23]

While Jules Remy stated that "the Saints acknowledge, with a candour which does them honour, that among their brethren there have been found some unworthy of that appellation," he further noted that during his time in Salt Lake he and Julius Brenchly "were robbed twice." In each instance it was found to "be by the Gentiles. This fact has a very great importance in our eyes," they concluded, "because it authorizes an impartial mind to believe that very often persons have laid to the charge of the Mormons crimes committed by the intruders who have crept among them."[24]

Included among the charges W. W. Drummond leveled against Brigham that contributed to the Utah War was the 1856 murder of Utah Territorial Secretary Almon W. Babbit in what is now Nebraska—purportedly by the Danites. The following year, as President James Buchanan was ordering troops to put down the rumored Mormon rebellion, an investigation into Babbitt's murder seemingly presented an unparalleled opportunity to demonstrate the validity of Drummond's claims. Instead, to the disappointment of many, the investigation revealed that Cheyenne Indians "acknowledge[d] they committed the murder" to avenge the insults and abuse they had experienced by "parties in charge of the mail."[25] In spite of continuing calls by the nation's press for action against Brigham in 1859, the House Committee on Indian Affairs certified the findings of the investigation.[26]

In 1857 one newspaper accused Brigham of being behind the 1854–58 conflict between pro- and antislavery forces that followed the passage of the Kansas-Nebraska Act known as "Bleeding Kansas." Twenty years later the *Salt Lake Tribune* announced that Brigham was guilty of having ordered more than six hundred murders.[27] The evidence to support these claims? They didn't need any. Everybody *knew* it was the case. As with other claims against Brigham, saying was believing. Not only has no direct evidence ever been produced, there is no other evidence beyond a reasonable doubt or even a preponderance of circumstantial evidence.

Concerning his never-ending conviction by innuendo and newspaper, Brigham frustratingly proclaimed in 1866: "Why do you not testify to what you know before the Courts? If President Young is guilty of any such crime, trace it to him. . . . If any man, woman or child that ever lived has said that

Brigham Young ever counseled them to commit crime of any description, they are liars in the face of heaven. If I am guilty of any such thing, let it be proved on me, and not go sneaking around insinuating that Brigham knows all about it."[28]

Brigham once stated that those individuals who initiated these claims of his evil doing were themselves "bosom companions of thieves, liars and murderers."[29] While Brigham likely overstated the case, most people do see things through their own blinders. For example, shortly after publishing the 1934 best-seller *Holy Murder,* a book purportedly recounting Brigham's reign of terror, Hoffman Birney unabashedly wrote his coauthor Charles Kelly, "I quote a valued friend of mine when I say that my one prayer is that before I shuffle off this mortal coil I will be permitted to kill a Jew—preferably two Jews."[30]

Concerning violence in general, Brigham publicly proclaimed: "There are some things which transpire that I cannot think about . . . that are too horrible for me to contemplate. The massacre at Haun's mill, and that of Joseph and Hyrum Smith, and the Mountain Meadow's massacre and the [recent] murder of Dr. Robinson are of this character. I cannot think that there are beings upon the earth who have any claim to the sentiments and feelings which dwell in the breasts of civilized men who could be guilty of such atrocities."[31] Nine years earlier, in January 1857, when "blood atonement" and the "crooked finger" were reportedly at an apex during the Mormon Reformation, Brigham wondered aloud what it would be like in the "hereafter, say 50,000 yrs [in the] spirit world [to] meet a man in my journeys" who asked "'did you not . . . spill my blood 50,000 years ago?'" Brigham concluded that he "never wish[ed] to have this feeling in the eternal world."[32]

In 1860 a distraught friend from Brigham's early adulthood wrote him asking how, given his career as America's Bogeyman, he could stand before God on the judgment day with "your daughter murdered by your Danites," along with "hundreds of others." Brigham responded: "Most of the crimes you mention as being charged to me were never before so much as *heard* of by me. . . . I am as innocent as a nursing babe of committing, counseling, in any way, having anything to do with such deeds—they are most excruciating and horrifying to all my feelings and natural organization." He further asserted that these "disclosures" were "a tissue of gross, death-designed lies, larded here and there with a little truth, when telling the truth does not militate against the effect of those lies concocted with the well known and express design to exterminate us from the earth."[33]

## ❧ 26 ❧

# FUN FACTS

**B**righam was the second youngest President of the Church, being forty-six years old when sustained in December 1847 (Joseph Smith was the youngest). Brigham presided over the Church for thirty-three years, the longest tenure in Church history (this includes both the three and a half years of his apostolic leadership and twenty-nine and a half as Church president). By contrast, Joseph Smith was President of the Church for fourteen years. Brigham is the only man to have sons serve with him in the First Presidency. In 1873, John W. Young and Brigham Young Jr. were among five men called as "assistant counselors."

When a London watchmaker who was a Latter-day Saint offered to create a watch for Brigham while he was serving his mission to England, Brigham requested that it feature his name in place of letters. He wanted B instead of 1, R instead of 2, and so on, until all twelve letters in his name were spelled out.

At the time he counseled the Saints in the Salt Lake Valley to avoid spending their energies seeking after gold and silver, he noted, "I can stand in my door and can see where there is untold millions of the rich treasures of the earth."[1] Sixteen years later an ore sample containing both gold and silver was discovered in Bingham Canyon, setting off the mining industry in Utah. Today the Kennecott Copper Mine, visible from downtown Salt Lake, is one of the world's leading producers of copper and is the leading producer in Utah of both gold and silver. It has been called the richest hole in the world.

President Zachary Taylor, initially somewhat sympathetic to the Latter-day Saints, became a vocal critic and vowed to never let the Saints have their own state or territory. Following Taylor's death in 1850, Brigham announced, "We have just received word that Zachary Taylor is dead and has gone to hell." When asked to apologize for his statement, Brigham stated: "We announced this morning that Zachary Taylor was dead and gone to hell—I am sorry!"[2]

After Brigham determined to give up chewing tobacco, he carried half a plug in his pocket. When he got the urge to chew, he would take it out and ask himself, "Are you, or is Brigham going to be master?"[3] Concerning the use of tobacco he stated: "It is a loathsome practice to use tobacco in any way. A doctor told an old lady in New York, when she insisted upon his telling her whether snuff would injure her brain, 'It will not hurt the brain: there is no fear of snuff's hurting the brain of anyone, for no person that has brains will take snuff.'"[4]

Brigham suffered from persistent dental problems that caused him discomfort and occasional embarrassment. In April 1862, the Historian's Office Journal noted that he had five teeth pulled, "being all the remaining teeth he had left in his head. The President is getting a new set of teeth made."[5]

To the handful of Saints struggling to establish a cotton mission in the heat of southern Utah in 1863, he proclaimed what must have been unimaginable to them at the time. He told them he had seen in vision "a large city built where St. George now stands."[6]

In response to a request from an individual to have her name removed from the records of the Church because she had decided to become a spiritualist, Brigham dictated the following: "Madam . . . I have this day examined the records of baptisms for the remission of sins in the Church of Jesus Christ of Latter-day Saints, and not being able to find the name of 'Elizabeth Green' recorded therein I was saved the necessity of erasing your name therefrom. You may therefore consider that your sins have not been remitted you and you can enjoy the benefits thereof."[7]

While living in Auburn, New York, around 1826, Brigham incurred a three dollar debt with a local druggist. When Brigham tried to pay it, the druggist refused to accept the money, since he could not find a note for the debt. Almost forty years later and nearly a continent away from Auburn, Brigham learned that the note had been found. He asked his son, John W., who was bound for a mission to Europe, to go to Auburn and cancel the debt: "A man by the name of Richard Steel kept a drug store about forty years ago in Auburn, N. Y. He had my note for three dollars ($3.00), which I wished to take up; but he could not find it, and said that I must be mistaken about it. I offered to pay the amount, but he refused to receive it. Years afterwards, I heard, and do not now recollect how I heard, that he had found that note. I wish it settled. He may be dead, but his heir or heirs may be living." Concerning what transpired, a local newspaper reported: "A son of Brigham Young (we didn't learn his number,) was in town this morning, and called at a business house in Genesee St. to settle an account by his numerous progenitor some thirty years ago. Brigham is honest—in some things, but rather slow. The debt discharged by him was, we understand, for borrowed money."[8]

In counseling the Saints not to worry about things they could not control, Brigham colorfully counseled them, "Do not fret thy gizzard." In one 1855 meeting he declared, "I wish to give you one text to preach upon: 'From this time henceforth do not fret thy gizzard.'" In 1860 he wrote Utah's Congressional delegate William H. Hooper to "remember the 13th Commandment: 'Fret not thy gizzard because of sinners.'"[9]

Brigham once stated: "While I attempt to speak to the people I would like their attention, and for them to keep quiet. I do not particularly object to the crying of children, but I do the whispering of the people. . . . I am very happy to hear the children crying when it is really necessary and they cannot be kept from it. One thing is certain, wherever we go there is a proof that the people are keeping the commandments of the Lord, especially the first one—to multiply and replenish the earth."[10]

"I do not profess to be much of a joker," Brigham confessed, "but I do think this to be one of the best jokes ever perpetrated," referring to the event that is known as the "Bogus Brigham." As Brigham tells the story, when

> the mob had learned that "Mormonism" was not dead [following the martyrdom, they] commenced to hunt for other victims. . . .
>
> I was in my room in the Temple . . . [and] learned that a posse was lurking around the Temple, and that the United States Marshal was waiting for me to come down, whereupon I knelt down and asked my Father in heaven, in the name of Jesus, to guide and protect me that I might live to prove advantageous to the Saints. Just as I arose from my knees and sat down in my chair, there came a rap at my door. I said, "Come in," and Brother George D. Grant, who was then engaged driving my carriage and doing chores for me, entered the room.
>
> Said he, "Brother Young, do you know that a posse and the United States Marshal are here?" I told him I had heard so. On entering the room Brother Grant left the door open. Nothing came into my mind what to do, until looking directly across the hall I saw brother William Miller leaning against the wall. As I stepped towards the door I beckoned to him; he came. Said I to him, "Brother William, the Marshal is here for me; will you go and do just

as I tell you? If you will, I will serve them a trick. ". . . Said I, "Here, take my cloak.". . . I threw it around his shoulders, and told him to wear my hat and accompany brother George D. Grant. He did so. . . .

Just as Brother Miller was entering the carriage, the Marshal stepped up to him, and, placing his hand upon his shoulder, said, "You are my prisoner.". . .

When they reached Carthage the Marshal took the supposed Brigham into . . . the hotel, and placed a guard over him, at the same time telling those around that he had got him. . . . Parties came in, one after the other, and asked for Brigham. Brother Miller was pointed out to them. So it continued, until an apostate Mormon, by the name of Thatcher, who had lived in Nauvoo, came in, sat down and [stated] . . ."I can't see any one that looks like Brigham." The landlord told him it was that fat, fleshy man eating. "Oh, h—!" exclaimed Thatcher, "that's not Brigham; that is William Miller, one of my old neighbors.". . .

The Marshal, very much astonished, . . . took brother Miller into a room, and, turning to him, said, "What in h— is the reason you did not tell me your name?"

Brother Miller replied, "You have not asked me my name."

"Well," said the Sheriff, with another oath, "What is your name?"

"My name," he replied, "is William Miller."

Said the Marshal, "I thought your name was Brigham Young. . . . Why did you not tell me this before?"

"I was under no obligations to tell you," replied brother Miller, "as you did not ask me."

Then the Marshal, in a rage, walked out of the room, followed by brother Miller, who [was taken] . . . to a place of safety.[11]

Prior to reading the names of those to be sustained at the April 1860 general conference, Brigham stated: "The first name I shall present to you is that of Brigham Young, President of the Church of Jesus Christ of Latter-day Saints. If any person can say that he should not be sustained in this office, say so. If there is no objection, as it is usual in the marriage ceremony of the Church of England, 'Let them for ever afterwards hold their peace,' and not go snivelling around, saying that you would like to have a better man, and one who is more capable of leading the Church."[12]

Two preachers attending the Rocky Mountain Conference of the Methodist Church held in Salt Lake City in 1875 saw Brigham across the street and dared each other to go and shake his hand. Brigham "cordially" shook their hands and told them "with an amused twinkle in his eyes," "I certainly am glad to shake hands with you. I was a Methodist once myself."[13]

Brigham wrote out instructions for his funeral which, at his request, were read at the services. Concerning his coffin he wrote: "I want my coffin made of plump 1¼ inch redwood boards, not scrimped in length, but two inches longer than I would measure, and from two to three inches wider than is commonly made for a person of my breadth and size, and deep enough to place me on a little comfortable cotton bed with a good suitable pillow for size and quality. . . . The coffin to have the appearance that if I wanted to turn a little to the right or to the left I should have plenty of room to do so."[14]

Brigham and the Danites were featured in the first Sherlock Holmes novel, *A Study in Scarlet,* in which Holmes solves the murder of a man in London killed by a Danite. Arthur Conan Doyle later apologized for his inaccurate characterizations of both Young and the Mormons—many of which persist today.

Brigham had 60 children (57 biological and 3 adopted), 314 grandchildren, and 703 great-grandchildren. While 13,000 direct descendants of Brigham have been positively identified, an estimate places his total posterity between 25,000 and 30,000.

## ❧ 27 ❧

# HIS FINEST HOUR

### *The 1856 Rescue of the Stranded Handcart and Wagon Companies*

S aturday, October 4, 1856, was a beautiful fall day in Salt Lake City. Members and leaders alike were basking in the glow of both the warm weather and the success of the recently completed emigration season, which included the successful arrival of the first three companies to travel by handcart. But the news that Franklin D. Richards and other missionaries returning from England brought with them that day would quickly change the mood of the community and prompt Brigham to immediately spring into action in what was arguably his finest hour.

While leaders in Salt Lake had assumed that the third handcart company was the last of the year's emigrants, Richards informed them that there were two handcart and two wagon companies still on the trail, involving upwards of fifteen hundred emigrants, who had begun their journey after the time specified for departure. "We had no idea there were any more companies upon the Plains, until our brethren arrived," Brigham wrote.[1] Since word had not been received that there were emigrants still on the trail, resupply wagons had not been sent to assist them.

T. B. H. Stenhouse, a contemporary of Brigham and a former Latter-day Saint who had turned critic of the prophet and the Church, described what happened next: "When the news reached Brigham Young . . . he did all that man could do to save the remnant and relieve the sufferers. Never in his whole career did he shine so gloriously in the eyes of the people."[2]

Concerned that the emigrants still on the trail were inadequately clothed for cold weather and would soon be short on food, Brigham immediately called a meeting to discuss the situation. "The object of my wanting the brethren here is to find out what we need to do tomorrow," he told those in attendance.[3] Richards was less concerned about the possibility of a impending disaster, as reflected in his comments the next day. He proclaimed that the emigrants had "this faith and confidence towards God, that He will over-rule the storms . . . and turn them away, that their path may be freed from suffering more than they can bear."[4] While Brigham also believed that God could indeed perform such miracles, he knew that God required His children to do their part.

In the meeting, Brigham showed a remarkable grasp of the situation, the result of a decade of experience with western emigration—including three trips of his own across the trail. He asked about each company and what supplies they might need. While Richards optimistically reported that the Willie company was closer to Salt Lake than it actually was, Brigham envisioned them farther away and in a more precarious predicament. He planned for a worst-case scenario. When someone suggested that the Willie company would need three tons of flour, Brigham responded, "They want 5 tons."[5]

The next day Brigham addressed the Saints and forcefully initiated what turned into a herculean rescue that would involve hundreds of individuals, teams, and wagons, along with tons of food and supplies. The urgency with which he addressed the situation was as much the result of prophetic inspi-ration as trail experience. He seemed to foresee the impending storm at a time when others expected the elements to be tempered. He launched the rescue effort when few believed there could be a disaster of such magnitude and before anyone knew the critical situation faced by the companies. As a result of his quick action, an even greater disaster was averted than what the companies experienced. As events unfolded, a delay of even a few days would have led to even more deaths, while inaction likely would have resulted in the deaths of *all* those stranded on the trail.

Brigham's calls for help prompted Stenhouse to conclude, "In the Tabernacle, he was 'the Lion of the Lord.'"[6] Daniel W. Jones, who traveled with the first group of rescuers to leave Salt Lake, was impressed by Brigham's earnestness, noting that he was "moved by a spirit that would admit no delay."[7]

"I will now give this people the subject and the text for the Elders who may speak to-day and during this conference," Brigham proclaimed.

It is this, on the 5th day of October, 1856, many of our brethren and sisters are on the Plains with hand-carts, and probably many are now seven hundred miles from this place, and they must be brought here, we must send assistance to them. The text will be—to get them here! I want the brethren who may speak to understand that their text is the people on the Plains, and the subject matter for this community is to send for them and bring them in before winter sets in.

That is my religion; that is the dictation of the Holy Ghost that I possess, it is to save the people. . . . This is the salvation I am now seeking for, to save our brethren that would be apt to perish, or suffer extremely, if we do not send them assistance.

I shall call upon the Bishops this day, I shall not wait until to-morrow, nor until the next day, for sixty good mule teams and twelve or fifteen wagons. I do not want to send oxen [they could not travel as fast as mules], I want good horses and mules. They are in this Territory, and we must have them; also twelve tons of flour and forty good teamsters, besides those that drive the teams. This is dividing my texts into heads; first forty good young men who know how to drive teams, to take charge of the teams that are now managed by men, women, and children, who know nothing about driving them; second, sixty or sixty-five good spans of mules, or horses, with harness, whipple-trees, neck-yokes, stretchers, load chains, &c; and, thirdly, twenty-four thousand pounds of flour. . . .

I will tell you all that your faith, religion, and profession of religion, will never save one soul of you in the celestial kingdom of God, unless you carry out just such principles as I am now teaching you. Go and bring in those people now on the Plains, and attend strictly to those things which we call temporal, or temporal duties, otherwise your faith will be in vain; the preaching you have heard will be in vain . . . and you will sink to hell, unless you attend to the things we tell you.[8]

The following day, October 6, during the morning session of general conference, he again called for assistance:

I feel disposed to be as speedy as possible in our cooperation with regard to helping our brethren who are now on the plains. Consequently I shall call upon the people forthwith for the help that is needed. I want them to give in their names this morning, if they are ready to start on their journey tomorrow. And not say, "I will go next week, or in ten days, or in a fortnight hence." For I wish to start tomorrow morning.

I want the sisters to have the privilege of fetching in blankets, skirts, stockings, shoes, etc., for the men, women, and children that are in those handcart companies. . . . I will give you the privilege of bringing hoods, winter bonnets, stockings, skirts, garments, and almost any description of clothing. Our brethren and sisters could not bring much with them on the plains, even if they had had it. . . .

I now want brethren to come forward, for we need 40 good teamsters to help the brethren on the plains; you may rise up now and give your names.[9]

If the people were not ready to heed his call, Brigham noted he was willing to take extreme measures. "If the teams are not voluntarily furnished, there are plenty of good ones in the street and I shall call upon Brother J. C. Little, the marshal, to furnish them."[10]

Brigham did not have to take this extraordinary step. His clarion call was answered. Before the meeting was over, the blacksmiths in the congregation left to begin shoeing horses and mules and to repair the wagons of those planning to leave. Lucy Meserve Smith noted, "The President called for men, teams, clothing and provisions. . . . The sisters stripped off their petticoats, stockings, and everything they could spare, right there in the tabernacle and piled into the wagons to send to the saints in the mountains. . . . I never took more satisfaction and I might say more pleasure in any labor I ever performed in my life, such a unity of feeling prevailed."[11]

The following day, October 7, the first relief party of sixteen wagons and twenty-seven people left Salt Lake. Prior to leaving, these rescuers gathered at Brigham's office to receive instructions and priesthood blessings. Others would soon follow. By the end of the month, 250 or more rescue wagons were on the road.

The early and unrelenting blizzard that eventually stranded the Willie and Martin handcart and Hunt and Hodgetts wagon companies on the high plains did not hit until October 19, two weeks after Brigham's urgent call for assistance. The following day, October 20, the Willie company ran out of food. However, the first rescue wagons with their welcome loads of food and clothing were less than a day away and reached them on October 21. These rescuers seemed "like a thunderbolt out of the clear sky," prompting one individual to conclude that "more welcome messengers never came from the courts of glory."[12]

Leaving some rescuers with the Willie company, the rest pushed on in search of the Martin company. Three express riders located the company on October 28, while the supply wagons reached them three days later. George D. Grant, leader of the rescue company, wrote Brigham that the sight of so many in the company too weak to continue, suffering from frozen and bleeding feet and frozen limbs "is almost too much for the stoutest of us; but we go on doing all we can. . . . I think that not over one-third of br. Martin's company is able to walk. . . . We have prayed without ceasing, and the blessing of God has been with us. Br. Charles Decker has now traveled this road the 49th time, and he says he has never before seen so much snow on the Sweet Water at any season of the year."[13]

While most of those sent from the valley were willing to do all they could, some turned back because of the storm, rationalizing that the emigrants and the advance rescuers had either found a place to winter over or sadly had already perished. Most, however, recalling the urgency with which Brigham spoke, pushed on. When Arza Hinckley met supply wagons heading back, he reminded them of Brigham's resolve and proclaimed, "Brigham Young sent me to find the handcart folks and I will find them or give my life trying."[14] Upon learning that relief wagons were returning to Salt Lake prior to reaching the stranded companies, Brigham sent out messengers ordering them to turn around.

A month after the rescue began, the fate of the emigrants continued to occupy Brigham's mind:

> We can return home and sit down and warm our feet before the fire, and can eat our bread and butter, etc., but my mind is yonder in the snow, where those immigrating Saints are, and my mind has been with them ever since I had the report of their start. . . . I cannot talk about any thing, I cannot go out or come in, but what in every minute or two minutes my mind reverts to them; and the questions—whereabouts are my brethren and sisters who are on the Plains, and what is their condition?—force themselves upon me.[15]

Finally, on November 9, the Willie handcart company reached Salt Lake City. Three weeks later on November 30, wagons carrying the Martin handcart company, along with some members from the Hunt and Hodgetts wagon companies, reached Salt Lake City. On December 15, wagons carrying the last of the Hunt and Hodgetts companies arrived in Salt Lake.

While several hundred emigrants died on the journey—the best estimates place the number of deaths in these companies between 250 and

270—the loss of life diminished after help arrived from the valley, and nearly five times the number who died were saved. The deaths, loss of limbs to frostbite, and the general suffering, terrible as it all was, would have been measurably greater if not for Brigham's firm and immediate call for action before the storms struck, and the Saints' willing response to prophetic leadership.

*Handcart company in a snowstorm*

## 28

# HIS GREATEST DISCOURSE

### *November 30, 1856*

Of the more than eight hundred sermons given by Brigham of which there is at least a partial record—and there were scores of others for which there is not even a summary—the question of which is his greatest is surely a matter of debate. However, for the power of simple and clear language and for a moving expression of pure religion, it is hard to argue with his sermon of Sunday, November 30, 1856, delivered the day the Martin handcart company reached the Salt Lake Valley. The sermon becomes even greater against the background of both the handcart experience in general and also the events that had transpired since the effort to rescue the stranded handcart and wagon companies had begun nearly two months earlier.

After years of having been forced to keep handcart travel "on a back shelf," Brigham so believed in the concept that when he asked his son-in-law to lead a company, Brigham's sadness that he couldn't do it himself is apparent. "We are very ancios to have a company got up in England to cros the planes with hancarts. I due be leve that I could bring a company a cross, with out a team and beet eny ox trane if I could be there my self[.] Would you like to try it?"[1]

As word began to trickle into Salt Lake of the unfolding disaster, criticism aimed directly at Brigham for both the handcart plan in general and the need for the rescue of these companies got under his normally thick skin in a way that criticisms of other enterprises and the comments of outsiders could not hurt him. For many people, the success of the three companies that came through without problems was largely overshadowed by the two stranded companies, and these later companies began to be pointed to as evidence that the handcart plan was not inspired. Brigham was concerned that some people seemed to be losing their faith over what was transpiring.

"There is a spirit of murmuring among the people, and the fault is laid upon brother Brigham," Heber C. Kimball proclaimed on November 2. "If the immigration could have been carried on as dictated by brother Brigham, there would have been no trouble."[2] Brigham's words at this time were likewise defensive. "There is not the least shadow of reason for casting such censure upon me," he declared. "There is no ground or room for . . . suspecting that my mismanagement caused the present sufferings on the Plains." Rather, he proclaimed, it was "pride, arrogance and self esteem" of people who expected God to mitigate the consequences of their decision to send the companies after the appointed starting date that was causing "men and women to die on the Plains."[3]

Brigham was further frustrated by the fact that the decision to send the companies late had necessitated that the Saints' time, energy, and resources be diverted from the vital work that had to be done each fall to assure the well-being and survival of those already in the valley and be directed instead toward assisting the emigrants. He concluded that "it had Cost this Territory more than it would to have bought oxen & brought them through" by the traditional method.[4]

Brigham was so frustrated by both the need for the rescue and the level of criticism that he stated privately that he was "going to inform all Churches people & agents next season who do not take my Council that they shall be suspended from the Church."[5] Publicly, he softened his stance and directed his threat only against Church leaders: "Hereafter I am going to lay an injunction and place a penalty, to be suffered by any Elder or Elders who will start the immigration across the Plains after a given time; and the penalty shall be that they shall be severed from the Church, for I will not have such late starts."[6]

By late November, however, as the magnitude of the suffering of the emigrants was becoming apparent, Brigham put all of that behind him. What must have been among the longest two months of his life was coming to a close, and on November 30 he wanted the Saints to put it behind them as well. To everything there was a season, and now was a time to heal.

As with almost all his talks, Brigham's greatest sermon was given extemporaneously. "I can truly say that I have fulfilled one of the sayings of the Savior tolerably well—to take no thought what ye shall say, for in the very hour or moment when you need it, it shall be given to you," he once stated.[7] Brigham, who described himself as a "minute man" because of his speaking style, truly rose to the occasion:

> I have a few words to say, before this meeting is brought to a close. We expect that the last hand-cart company, br. Martin's, will soon be in the streets by the Council House. What preparations the Bishops have made for their comfortable reception and temporary disposal I know not, but I know what I desire and am going to tell it to the people.
>
> When those persons arrive I do not want to see them put into houses by themselves; I want to have them distributed in this city among the families that have good and comfortable houses; and I wish the sisters now before me, and all who know how and can, to nurse and wait upon the new comers and prudently administer medicine and food to them. To speak upon these things is a part of my religion, for it pertains to taking care of the Saints.
>
> It is a considerable . . . labor to go and preach the gospel to the nations, but we find by experience that that is a very small portion

of the work we have to perform; it is but the first item of the business that is upon us. Our labor constantly becomes more arduous, and we will find that it will increase upon us, instead of decreasing; we understand this perfectly well.

In our traditions we have supposed that we should see the kingdom of God established on the earth and Zion become the joy thereof, by merely gathering to the several Stakes; and that then our labors would be done and we should have nothing to do but sit and 'sing ourselves away to everlasting bliss;' but we will find that preaching the gospel is but a small portion of the labor that is upon us.

We have quite a task upon us this season, for when the last hand-cart company arrives and is comfortably disposed of, we still have about 400 more brethren and sisters [the Hunt and Hodgetts wagon companies] who are yet beyond Fort Bridger, probably near Green river. They are those that came out with teams, or the independent companies. All their gold, all their silver, their cattle and their other property will not enable them to reach here before the snow has overtaken them; and they had plenty of cattle, or money and means; everything that heart could wish, for an outfit for crossing the plains.

To succor those 400 I call out door business; I call it a snow business, a labor, mountain toil and fatigue of a severe description.

Night before last we received a messenger from those two independent trains, by whom we have learned that they are living on their cattle at Green river. The brethren at Fort Supply are striving to get them as far as Fort Bridger.

Our messengers started out night before last to gather fifty more relief teams. We have sent to Utah and Tooele counties.

Until now, this [Salt Lake] and Davis and Weber counties have had to bear the burden. We have sent for those teams to carry flour to Fort Bridger, and load back with people. Some, perhaps, will have to be left there, and if so we will carry supplies to them and keep bringing in the people, until all are comfortably provided for.

Those that are yet back have been living, probably for nearly a week, solely on the cattle that die; they have no flour, and are subsisting upon cattle that drop down through weakness and exposure, which is certainly hard fare. Still, do not be scared, for they will eat and live and come here.

I can say that the great majority of the brethren here, so far as we have called on them to assist this year's immigration, have freely and nobly manifested their faith by their works. True, some that went out have been imprudent, though I think it will all come out right and I can feel to bless them, notwithstanding they have been imprudent and foolish. I will tell them wherein, when I can have them before me in this congregation.

As soon as this meeting is dismissed I want the brethren and sisters to repair to their homes, where their Bishops will call on them to take in some of this company; the Bishops will distribute them as the people can receive them.

I have sent word to Bishop Hunter [Presiding Bishop Edward Hunter] that I will take in all that others will not take. I have house room enough to accommodate the whole of them, if it is necessary; I am willing to take my proportion.

The afternoon meeting will be omitted, for I wish the sisters to go home and prepare to give those who have just arrived a mouthful of something to eat, and to wash them and nurse them up. You know that I would give more for a dish of pudding and milk, or a baked potato and salt, were I in the situation of those persons who have just come in, than I would for all your prayers, though you were to stay here all the afternoon and pray. Prayer is good, but when baked potatoes and pudding and milk are needed, prayer will not supply their place on this occasion; give every duty its proper time and place.

This is what I can say truly, with the rest of your counselors and directors, that no man or woman, that we have knowledge of in the church, has refused to do as requested, with regard to this immigration; they have run by day and night. Our messengers have been traveling from here to the Platte, and back and forth between Bridger, Green river and the Sweetwater; and scores of men have been riding by day and night, without having enjoyed an undisturbed night's rest during the last two months, only occasionally snatching a little sleep when sitting by the camp fire. They have been riding by day and night, hurrying to and fro and laboring with their mights, and have not refused to do what we have required of them; this is to their praise. Works have been most noble when they were needed; we put works to our faith, and in this case we realize that our faith alone would have been perfectly dead and useless, would have been of no avail, in saving our brethren that were in the snow, but by putting works with faith we have been already blest in rescuing many and bringing them to where we can now do them more good.

Some you will find with their feet frozen to their ankles; some are frozen to their knees and some have their hands frosted. They want good nursing, and if you do not know how to treat frozen flesh, let me inform you that the same treatment is needed as in a burn, and by pursuing that method you can heal them.

The Bishops are here, and as soon as the meeting is closed they will meet the company and dispose of them as wisdom shall dictate. And I want you to understand that we desire this people to nurse them up; we want you to receive them as your own children, and to have the same feeling for them. We are their temporal saviors, for we have saved them from death. Br. [John] Chislett, who has just been addressing you, would have been dead long before this, had it not been for the assistance of br. George D. Grant and those who went back with him. The rear companies would never have got over Rocky Ridge, or seen the upper crossing of the Sweetwater, had they not been helped from here.

Now that most of them are here we will continue our labors of love, until they are able to take care of themselves, and we will receive the blessing. You need not be distrustful about that, for the

Lord will bless this people; and I feel to bless them all the time, and this I continually try to carry out in my life.

The two wagon companies still out we are sending for, and will supply flour to such as may have to tarry at Forts Bridger and Supply. We do not calculate to have the winter blast stop us; it cannot stop the Mormon Elders, for they have faith, wisdom and courage; they can perform that which no other men on the earth can perform.

I bless you, in the name of the Lord Jesus Christ, with all the power and authority of the priesthood that it is my right to bless you with; and by faith I seal the blessings of heaven upon you daily, and pray that you may be blessed; you have my good feelings all the time.

I wish all to be faithful in their houses, and to let evil spirits alone; to repent of your heart wanderings and your backslidings and return to the Lord and seek him daily, hourly and momentarily. Cleave to the Lord and all righteous principles, that we may not hear of anything being done, in this, that, or the other part of the city, derogatory to the character of a Christian. May God bless you: Amen.[8]

*The Old Tabernacle and bowery, Salt Lake City, ca. 1863*

# THE DARK CLOUD

## *The Mountain Meadows Massacre*

O n September 7, 1857, John D. Lee led a raid against a California-bound emigrant wagon train camped in southern Utah. Four days later on September 11, he persuaded the emigrants under a flag of truce to abandon their wagon fortress and deceitfully led them into a deadly ambush carried out by local Mormon settlers and Indian allies. Before the day was over, approximately 120 men, women, and children had been killed in the Mountain Meadows Massacre, with only seventeen young children surviving the horrific carnage.

This darkest episode in Mormon history created a cloud that hung over Brigham the rest of his life and largely remains today. He was immediately blamed for the butchery, a claim that has been repeated long and loud in various forms. One version states that "a 'revelation' from Brigham Young . . . was dispatched to President J. [Isaac] C. Haight, Bishop [John] Higbee and J. D. Lee . . . commanding them to raise all the forces they could muster and trust, follow those cursed Gentiles (so read the revelation), [and] attack them. . . . Brigham, and he alone was responsible for the massacre."[1] Others claim that Brigham was more subtle, making his will known through coded messages. Still others claim the genesis for the "massacre was the result of the direct teachings of Brigham Young."[2] Whether it was directly ordered or the result of teachings, the popular view remains that "Lee was simply one of the blind fools and fanatics who executed the will of his superiors. . . . [Brigham] bade him do this bloody work, and he obeyed as the executioner obeys the mandate of a legal tribunal."[3]

Brigham's claims of innocence fell on deaf ears. In 1872 he noted that "again and again" he had offered to help "thoroughly investigate the Mountain Meadow Massacre and bring, if possible, the guilty parties to justice" but that government officials had instead "used every opportunity to charge the crime upon prominent men in Utah, and inflame public opinion against our community." He stated that while his offer "has not yet been accepted, I have neither doubt nor fear that the perpetrators of that tragedy will meet their just reward."[4]

Given the prevailing views that Brigham was responsible for the Mormon practice of polygamy and that both Mormonism and plural marriage would cease with his death, it is not surprising that justice for the victims was largely a secondary concern behind the efforts to tie him to the massacre. Some newspapers made no secret of the fact that their goal in trying to connect him to the Mountain Meadows Massacre was to bring about the ultimate demise of plural marriage. "Of those 'twin relics of barbarism, polygamy and slavery,' the one was more than twelve years ago extinguished in this country, and the time has come for dealing efficiently with the other," the *New York Herald* editorialized in 1877. "If Brigham Young and other Mormon magnates were tried and executed . . . for participation in a horrible and inhuman crime, nobody could raise an outcry that they were persecuted for their religious faith."[5] For nearly twenty years Brigham's enemies worked to implicate him by any means possible.

The Mountain Meadows Massacre took place against the backdrop of the 1857–58 Utah War, in which U.S. troops were ordered to Utah to put down a reported rebellion. Anxieties and passions inflamed by word of approaching soldiers began to boil in Utah and created a unique situation. Twenty years later, in an interview with the *New York Herald* in 1877, Brigham declared that Haight, Lee, and other Mormon leaders in southern Utah "took advantage" of the "disturbed state of the country to accomplish their desires for plunder, which under other circumstances would not have been gratified." In the same interview he stated: "What causes men to steal or commit any sin? Do I prompt them? No; but the devil and his agents do. All evil doing is contrary to our covenants and obligations to God."[6] Along these lines the *Deseret News* also wrote in 1877 that if "fanatical and misguided zeal" on the part of participants indeed led to the massacre, then it was because of "erroneous and distorted views of true principles, and not the legitimate fruits of the principles themselves."[7]

Rather than examining the validity of such statements, those who have written about the massacre have largely rejected these statements as self-serving attempts to misdirect culpability. Instead of putting the question of what Brigham was teaching under the historical microscope, these writers have chosen instead to repeat the long-told claim that his teachings contributed directly to the massacre.

Six motivations for the crime have been given—some by participants, other by the press of the day—and all have since been recited by historians of the massacre: (1) a desire to obtain the possessions of the company; (2) a wish to exact revenge for wrongs suffered by the Saints in Missouri and Illinois; (3) a desire to avenge the blood of Joseph and Hyrum Smith; (4) anger over the recent murder of Parley P. Pratt in Arkansas; (5) fear in response to threats by members of the company that they intended to join with the army and wipe out Mormonism; and (6) a reported attempt by apostate Mormons to escape Utah by joining with the company.

Before the massacre, Brigham did in fact specifically address each of the first four issues. While he didn't directly speak about the two other reasons put forth for the killing of the company, he did generally address the issues of apostates leaving and the approaching army. When his statements on each of these issues are examined, however, they stand in stark contrast to what has long been claimed. They strongly point to the fact that the massacre happened not because people followed his preaching, but because they chose to either ignore or distort it.

Not only did Brigham regularly state that he little cared for worldly goods, but prior to the massacre he regularly counseled the Saints to adopt the same view. Around the time of the massacre he proclaimed, "I am more afraid of covetousness in our Elders than I am of the hordes of hell."[8] Previously he stated, "'Seek FIRST *the kingdom of God,*' . . . and let the gold and silver, the houses, the lands, the horses, the chariots, the crowns, the thrones, and the dominions of this world be dead to you."[9] "Be careful that you love not the world or the things of the world," he declared on another occasion. "We ought to care no more for the silver and the gold, and the property that is so much sought for by the wicked world, than for the soil or the gravel upon which we tread."[10] Ironically, at the same time that some Latter-day Saints in southern Utah were enriching themselves because of the massacre, Brigham was publicly beginning to prepare the minds of the Latter-day Saints in northern Utah to abandon or destroy their homes in the face of the approaching army.

Concerning the past wrongs suffered by the Saints, Brigham repeatedly reiterated what the Lord proclaimed through modern revelation that people must forgive, or "there remaineth in [them] the greater sin. . . . Ye ought to say in your hearts—let God judge between me and thee, and reward thee according to thy deeds."[11] He encouraged the Saints to "cast all bitterness out of your own hearts" as well as "covetousness, and lust."[12] In 1847 Brigham had a dream in which Joseph Smith counseled him to teach Church members to keep the Spirit in their lives, for it would "take malice, hatred, strife and all evil from their hearts; and their whole desire will be to do good, bring forth righteousness and build up the kingdom of God."[13] In March 1852 Brigham proclaimed: "Suppose every heart should say, if my neighbor does wrong to me, I will not complain, the Lord will take care of him. Let every heart be firm, and every one say, I will never contend any more with a man for property, I will not be cruel to my fellow-creature, but I will do all the good I can, and as little evil as possible. . . . I wish men would look upon that eternity which is before them. In the great morning of the resurrection, with what grief would they [say] . . . it is a source of mortification to me to think that I ever should be guilty of doing wrong, or of neglecting to do good to my fellow men, even if they have abused me."[14]

Rather than being bitter about the persecution the Saints experienced in Missouri and Illinois, Brigham proclaimed it was God's will. "Instead of crying over our sufferings, as some seem inclined to do," he stated, "I would rather tell a good story, and leave the crying to others."[15] "They have had the pleasure of driving me five times from my comfortable home; that is nothing," he noted.[16] "When I left Nauvoo, I again left all I had . . . in the hands of the mob, and, said I, 'Eat it up, destroy it, or burn it down, as quick as you please, for "the earth is the Lord's and the fulness thereof." '"[17] "It is very seldom that I refer to past scenes, they occupy but a small portion of my time and attention. Do you wish to know the reason of this? It is because there is an eternity ahead of me, and my eyes are ever open and gazing upon it."[18]

He taught that "in every thing the Saints may rejoice," including persecution, since it was "necessary to purge them, and prepare the wicked for their doom."[19] Concerning the Saints' afflictions he concluded that "if we did not exactly deserve it [at the time], there have been times when we did deserve it. If we did not deserve it at the time, it was good for [us] and gave us an experience."[20] After five years in the valley, he counseled:

"Be humble, be faithful to your God, true to His Church, benevolent to the strangers that may pass through our territory, and kind to all people; serving the Lord with all your might, trusting in him. . . . Very soon we will meet in a larger congregation than this, and have a celebration far superior; we will celebrate our perfect and absolute deliverance from the power of the devil; we only celebrate now our deliverance from the good brick houses we have left, from our farms and lands, and from the graves of our fathers; we celebrate our perfect deliverance from these. . . . By and by we will celebrate a perfect deliverance from all the powers of earth."[21]

While the wounds brought by the martyrdom of Joseph and Hyrum were initially deep, for Brigham they were not long lasting. In 1847 the Lord addressed the martyrdom in "the Word and Will of the Lord": "I took him [Joseph] to myself. Many have marveled because of his death; but it was needful that he should seal his testimony with his blood, that he might be honored and the wicked might be condemned."[22] These words had a profound impact on Brigham, and he tried to instill the same feelings among the Latter-day Saints. "I have never yet talked as rough in these mountains as I did in the United States when they killed Joseph," Brigham noted.[23] In 1849 he told the Saints: "Joseph Smith . . . lived just as long as the Lord let him live. But the Lord said—'Now let my servant seal up his testimony with his blood.'"[24] Four years before the massacre Brigham stated: "Has his [Joseph's] blood been atoned for? No! And why? A martyr's blood to true religion was never atoned for on our earth."[25] Later he reminded the Saints, "If it had been the will of the Lord that Joseph and Hyrum should have lived, they would have lived."[26]

Regarding the May 1857 death of Pratt, Brigham stated in late June 1857 that while it was "hard to acknowledge the hand of God in the death of Parley P. Pratt by as wicked a man as McLain, yet we will have to do it."[27] A little more than a week later Brigham wrote: "The seeing of our faithful Elders, slaughtered in cold blood . . . [is] at times almost to[o] grevious to be borne, but . . . the spirit within me whispers, peace be still."[28]

Years before massacre participants became distressed over threats made by members of the emigrant company that they would join with the army and assist the military to destroy the Mormons, Brigham warned, "Imagined danger always produces the most trouble."[29] In "The Word and Will of the Lord" that Brigham received in 1847, the Lord stated, "Fear not thine enemies, for they are in mine hands and I will do my pleasure with them."[30] The week prior to the massacre, Brigham spoke to the issue: "Cannot this kingdom be overthrown? No. They might as well try to obliterate the sun. . . . God is at the helm. . . . Do not be angry with [the army], for they are in the hands of God. Instead of feeling a spirit to punish them, or anything like wrath, you live your religion."[31] While Lee and Haight may not have had access to Brigham's latest sermon, they were present when Brigham had earlier proclaimed: "I want you to bid farewell to every fear, and say God will take care of his kingdom. . . . It is he who has preserved us—not we. . . . Don't fear about things—God is here—and you mustn't steady the ark."[32] "We need never undertake to guide the ship of Zion," Brigham proclaimed in 1852. "The Lord Almighty can do His own work."[33] During the week of the massacre Brigham included in his response to a letter sent by leaders in Cedar City an assurance that the army would not reach the valley that fall and then repeated his oft-stated advice: "God rules. He has overruled for our deliverance this once again and he will always do so if we live our religion, be united in our faith and good works. All is well with us."[34]

Even before Brigham learned the full details of the massacre, he warned the Saints that "where you find a man who wishes to steady the ark of God, without being called to do so, you will find a dark spot in him. The man [who is] full of light and intelligence discerns that God steadies his own ark, dictates his own affairs, guides his people, controls his kingdom, governs nations, and holds the hearts of all living in his hands."[35]

Rather than advocating that people who were disenchanted with Mormonism and wished to leave Utah should be "blood atoned," Brigham had long openly encouraged them to leave. "I want hard times, so that every person that does not wish to stay, for the sake of his religion, will leave."[36] In January 1857 he wrote: "It is rather warm for the wicked and we expect when spring comes there will be a scattering out of such as cannot abide righteousness and the purifying influences of the spirit of God. Let them go."[37]

Concerning the long-repeated claim that Brigham ordered the massacre, what is clear is that those involved in carrying out the crime acted as if he hadn't. When leaders of the massacre initially discussed the idea with others, several people raised opposition to the plan and requested a messenger be sent to Brigham asking his advice, something that wouldn't have happened if they were fanatics blindly following orders. Once on the killing field, Isaac Haight got into an argument over how to report the massacre to Brigham. If Brigham had ordered it, the argument would have been over *who* got to report it and receive the promised blessing for ardent obedience, not over *how* it was to be reported. Another indication that Brigham didn't order the killing is evidenced by the fact that participants took an oath of silence not to reveal their involvement. If Brigham had ordered it, their participation would have been a badge of honor, not something to hide.

The chief "evidence" against Brigham has long been John D. Lee's posthumous memoir, *Mormonism Unveiled,* published in September 1877 by Lee's lawyer, William W. Bishop. When a summary of this work was published around the time of Lee's March 1877 execution, one newspaper editor concluded that it was "a little Lee and a little lawyer." The editor noted: "The careful perusal of the 'confession,' will convince all persons familiar with 'Mormon' doctrine and history, that the actual statements of Lee have been touched up and interpolated by the writer, until they cover much broader ground and more sweeping charges than the convicted criminal intended, and convey manifest untruths in language that would not be used by any person who had ever been a 'Mormon.'"[38] Historians of the massacre have largely dismissed out of hand this editor's claim as Mormon "sour grapes"—but they have not addressed the volume's numerous internal inconsistencies, which were noted more than 130 years ago. (For example, although Lee correctly referred to Brigham as "prophet, seer and revelator" elsewhere, the phrase that is used in *Mormonism Unveiled* in connection with Brigham's role in the massacre is "prophet, priest, and revelator.") Historians have also failed to address external evidence, such as Bishop's statements prior to the book's publication that he intended to "do some good for the world" with Lee's story by adding "such facts connected with the trial and the history of the case as will make the Book interesting and useful to the public."[39] Given public perception and the clamor of the time, Bishop knew only too well that nothing regarding the massacre would be more "interesting and useful" than the claim of Brigham's involvement. Thus, while *Mormonism Unveiled* has helped to cloud the understanding of the Mountain Meadows Massacre, it does clearly reveal that a forgery doesn't have to be good if no one questions it.

## ⌒ 30 ⌒

# TRUST AND LOYALTY
### *Two Strengths and a Weakness*

Brigham could not have gathered the Saints, settled the Intermountain West, and built the kingdom without trusting people. He regularly gave people varied and challenging responsibilities and then trusted them to carry out their assignments to the best of their abilities. "I love this people so well that I know they love me," he proclaimed. "They have confidence in me, because I have confidence in them. . . . This is what will make a community powerful. But if we lack confidence in each other, and be jealous of each other, our peace will be destroyed. If we cultivate the principle of unshaken confidence in each other, our joy will be full."[1]

Brigham also placed a premium on loyalty by both demonstrating it and demanding it. While many believe that he required loyalty to himself, the loyalty he actually sought was to the kingdom. Joseph had taught: "The advancement of the cause of God and the building up of Zion is as much one man's business as another. . . . Party feelings, separate interests, exclusive designs should be lost sight of in the one common cause."[2] When Franklin D. Richards told Brigham, "You will like Bro Tennant," referring to the man who had paid for much of the 1856 handcart emigration by purchasing property that Brigham had donated to the PEF, Brigham's response was typical of his attitude: "I will like him if he is a saint."[3]

Brigham loved and valued people who were willing to give a sustained effort to build the kingdom in spite of weaknesses and shortcomings. Daniel W. Jones noted: "Brother Young was a true friend to me and understood my disposition. He never allowed anyone to speak against me; he knew my faults, also some of my virtues. One that he always appreciated was my stubbornness; when I started on a trip, I had always stuck to it."[4] On one occasion Jones questioned whether he was the right man to establish a new Latter-day Saint settlement. "I had been used to doing hard service so much that I had gotten in the habit of being arbitrary, and I was afraid I would not have patience to act as a presiding Elder should," he recalled. Brigham responded in essence "that an angel could not please everybody," adding, "You know how to travel, how to take care of teams. You are better acquainted with the roads, the country, the natives and their language, and are better prepared to take charge of the company than any one I know of. Go ahead and do the best you can. When you get things started we can send some 'good' man to take your place."[5]

Time and again Brigham gave ordinary men and women responsibilities that would have challenged giants and told them to "go ahead and do the best you can." People called on difficult colonizing missions were regularly trusted to manage the details the best they could because of limited communication with Salt Lake. Since what Brigham asked of people was not always easy, he knew mistakes would be made. He regularly overlooked missteps and errors, sometimes major ones, if the good of the kingdom seemed to have been the ultimate goal or if the actions had not threatened to jeopardize the kingdom. Such an attitude was consistent with what Joseph Smith wrote while imprisoned in Liberty Jail, reminding the Saints of the importance of "long-suffering . . . love unfeigned" and of "faithfulness . . . stronger than the cords of death."[6] Brigham knew that for the Saints to succeed, they needed to be unified and loyal. "We desire to be a great deal better than we are as individuals and as a people," he proclaimed. "Let all Latter-day Saints learn that the weaknesses of their brethren are not sins. When men or women undesignedly commit a wrong, do not attribute that to them as a sin. Let us learn to be compassionate one with another."[7] Having frequently been the target of others' prejudices, it is not surprising that Brigham counseled the Saints "to understand men and women as they are, and not understand them as you are."[8]

Brigham tended to give people the benefit of the doubt, especially those who had made great sacrifices for the kingdom. As a result, there were instances where he seemed almost cavalier concerning the misdeeds of some Latter-day Saints. Rather than simply turning a blind eye, however, he had adopted an attitude that if an individual's conscience didn't condemn him or her, then neither would he. In taking this approach, he was simply acknowledging the difficulties inherent in trying to render judgment in some cases. "I am very thankful that it is not our province, in our present condition, to judge the world; if it were, we would ruin everything. We have not sufficient wisdom, our minds are not filled with the knowledge and power of God. . . . We must also acquire the discretion that God exercises in being able to look into futurity, and to ascertain and know the results of our acts away in the future, even in eternity, before we will be capable of judging."[9] His view also acknowledged that no man escaped God's judgment and justice, which unlike man's, was always sure. "We talk a good deal about building up the kingdom of God upon the earth. . . . Do you think we are in a kingdom without law? No; the strictest law ever given to mankind is the law of God. If we transgress the law of God, we cannot be sent to the penitentiary, to stay a few years in there; it is before the Lord, and He will judge according to our works, and judge righteous judgment."[10]

While Brigham tolerated mistakes, his attitude changed toward those who were disloyal to or undermined the kingdom. "Personal feelings and friendships and associations ought to sink into comparative insignificance, and have no weight in view of consequences so momentous to the people and kingdom of God," Brigham wrote.[11] The Saints were fighting a war, and

Brigham could be unforgiving of those who aided and abetted the enemy. "Let you be ever so true and faithful to your friends and never forsake them, never turn traitor to the Gospel which you have espoused," he counseled.[12] Susa Young Gates stated that her father's "greatest grief was the defection of men whom he had trusted. His confidence, once lost, was difficult to retrieve." She reported that one prominent individual stated that he regretted the "the loss of Brother Brigham's love and confidence" resulting from his decision to leave Mormonism.[13]

Brigham regularly followed the advice of Joseph Smith: "Never give up an old tried friend, who has waded through all manner of toil, for your sake, and throw him away becau[se] fools may tell you he has some faults."[14] A prime example involved Sydney Rigdon. "Brother Sidney is a man whom I love," Joseph declared. After noting that Rigdon had faults, Joseph proclaimed, "Notwithstanding these things, he is a very great and good man."[15] After Joseph's death, Brigham evidenced the same attitude toward Sidney Rigdon, popular perception to the contrary notwithstanding. Instead of pronouncing Rigdon's "'prophecies' emanations from the devil" and "'handing the false prophet over to the buffetings of Satan for a thousand years'—probably the longest term ever inflicted in Illinois," as has been claimed, Brigham reached out a hand of fellowship.[16] On August 8, 1844, after the Saints had voted to follow the Twelve and the keys, Brigham asked the gathered Saints, "Will this congregation uphold [Rigdon] in the place he occupies by the prayer of faith and let him be one with us and we with him?"[17] The congregation voted in the affirmative, but Rigdon chose to distance himself by continuing to push his claim.

Thomas B. Marsh, whose actions contributed to the Saints being driven from Missouri in 1839, desired to rejoin the Saints and inquired of Brigham in 1857 "if it [was] not too late for him to fill his mission." Brigham declared that while it "was too late" for his mission, he "was willing to forgive him that he may be baptized."[18] Marsh was subsequently rebaptized.

In dealing with those accused of being turncoats, Brigham regularly practiced what Joseph preached to the Twelve: "I will not listen too nor credit, any derogatory report against any of you nor condemn you upon any testimony beneath the heavens, short of that testimony which is infalible, untill I can see you face to face and know of a surity. . . . I do place unlimited confidence in your word for I believe you to be men of truth, and I ask the same of you[!]"[19]

Upon learning that Orson Hyde had accepted employment with W. W. Drummond, a bitter anti-Mormon judge whose lies about Brigham and the Mormons were a contributing factor to the Utah War, Brigham declared that Hyde should be cut off from both the Church and the Twelve: "He is no more fit to stand at the Head of the Quorum of the Twelve than a dog. . . . He is a stink in my nostrils."[20] Brigham did replace Hyde as president of the quorum—but not until more than twenty years had passed. Hyde's actions were not treasonous, only evidenced a need to support his family. When Brigham finally replaced Hyde in 1875, it was the result of a revelation designating that seniority in the Quorum of Twelve was to be by length of consecutive service rather than age.

Although Brigham's trust and loyalty were well founded most of the time and were great strengths, in the aftermath of the Mountain Meadows Massacre, participants in the horrific deed turned them against him. While it was widely reported by 1859 that Lee was at the meadows during the massacre, Brigham seems to have given the benefit of the doubt to Lee's repeated claims that it was an Indian atrocity. Because Brigham knew only too well what it was like to be accused of things he hadn't done—he had to look no further than the inaccurate portrayals of his own involvement with the massacre—he seemingly had greater sympathy for Lee's repeated denials in the face of claims of his involvement than did most individuals.

If Brigham's loyalty and trust did not cause him to believe Lee's claims of innocence long after others quit, he was at least unwilling to take official Church action against Lee and Haight until he had "infalible" evidence—especially since guilt had not been proven in court. Brigham did not have access to all the puzzle pieces now available, in spite of several official investigations into the crime undertaken by Church leaders at his request in its immediate aftermath.

Thanks to the tireless personal efforts of Apostle Erastus Snow and others to ferret out what really took place, the wall of lies was finally broken down. In September 1870 Brigham was provided for the first time with the infallible evidence he needed that Lee and Haight had not only misused the concept of loyalty to get others to help carry out murder, but in the aftermath of the crime they had tried to manipulate loyalty and trust through repeated lies in an attempt to literally get away with murder. When Brigham learned what had really transpired, he sadly noted that Lee "had added to his crime lying and deceit."[21] After thirteen years of trusting those accused of the crime and withholding judgment, in October 1870 Brigham took the only action available to him as a religious leader—he had no civil authority in the matter—and excommunicated the two men most responsible for the slaughter, John D. Lee and Isaac C. Haight.

Even as Lee was facing execution for his role in the crime, he portrayed his actions as a simple mistake. "I have done nothing designedly wrong," he declared.[22] His actions, however, stand in sharp contrast to what Joseph Smith had taught: "When you are obliged to fight be sure you never stain your hands with the blood of women and children, and when your enemies call for quarter be sure to grant it and then will you gain power with your enemies."[23]

As the truth has unfolded, it is clear that Lee and Haight put personal interests above that of the kingdom in planning to attack the company; then they compounded the problem by orchestrating mass murder after things went wrong; and finally they consciously allowed others to take the blame for their actions in an attempted cover-up. "A person who is a thief, a liar, and a murderer in his heart, but professes to be a Saint, is more odious in the sight of God, angels and good men, than a person who comes out and openly declares that he is our enemy," Brigham proclaimed prior to the massacre. "I say, blessings on the head of a wicked Gentile who is my avowed enemy, far sooner than upon an enemy cloaked with a Saint's profession."[24]

Six years after Lee was excommunicated and two years after he was arrested, Brigham, true to his word that he would help in the prosecution of the guilty, gave assistance to government officials when they finally asked for his help to convict Lee. Haight, who like Lee went into hiding when indictments were handed down in 1874, was still a fugitive from the law when Brigham died in 1877.

Lee, Haight, and those who participated in the massacre accomplished what Ann Eliza Webb, other authors of "tell-all" books about Mormonism, and outside critics of the Church could only dream of accomplishing in terms of casting a negative light over Mormonism. Given the focus that the massacre continues to receive, Brigham was right when he proclaimed that the crime was one of the worst things that could have "ever happened."[25]

## ∞ 31 ∞

# BRIGHAM WELCOMES
# THE WORLD

When the Golden Spike was driven at Promontory Summit on May 15, 1869, marking the completion of the transcontinental railroad, Brigham was not present. For many, the reason for his absence was only too obvious. As the railroad pushed its way toward Utah in the late 1860s, it was widely proclaimed that its arrival in the territory would bring about the sudden and dramatic end of Mormonism. While Albert Richardson praised the Mormons for making "the treeless desert indeed blossom as the rose, and [laying] the foundations for a rich and prosperous State," he wrote that "within three years . . . the screaming of the locomotive will be heard in Salt Lake City. Perchance the splendid Mormon temple now rising may yet be the depot of the great Pacific railroad. Brought in contact with our national civilization, the power of Brigham and his associates will cease forever."[1] Along similar lines, one newspaper predicted that "when the United States goes to Utah, Mormonism will disappear like a puddle with Niagara Falls turned into it."[2]

In reality, Brigham was not in attendance because he was on his yearly

visit to southern Utah settlements at the time. He was not the only prominent individual conspicuous by his absence. Utah Governor Charles Durkee
also did not attend.

In spite of gentile hopes and expectations that the railroad would bring
about the dissolution of Mormonism and force Latter-day Saints to assimi-
late into the world, Brigham welcomed the railroad as new technology that
would help build the kingdom. While leading the 1847 vanguard pioneer
company, he helped scout a possible railroad route.[3] He subsequently made
several efforts to secure a railroad to Utah, including petitioning Congress.

While he knew that the railroad could assist "Babylon" to gain a greater
foothold in Zion, he also knew that it provided a great advantage in terms of
gathering converts faster and easier to Zion, sending out missionaries into
various parts of the world, and improved travel and communication within
the kingdom. As the railroad was nearing completion, he proclaimed: "We
want to hear the iron horse puffing through this valley. What for? To bring
our brethren and sisters here."[4] Concerning the prevalent doomsday predic-
tions, he told one non-Mormon that Mormonism "must, indeed, be a . . .
poor religion, if it cannot stand one railroad."[5]

At the time that others were prophesying ruin with the coming of the
railroad, he wrote his son:

> It will be sure to help us, and be advantageous to the Zion of our
> God, though the wicked are contemplating terrible things respect-
> ing us as soon as they can finish the railroad. The waves of civiliza-
> tion to use their own figure will then surge right up against the walls
> of barbarism in which we are entrenched and wash them down. We
> and our religion can then be wiped out and no longer offend the fas-
> tidious tastes and senses of the priests and politicians of this enlight-
> ened(?) age. We shall see. Had we nothing to depend upon but our
> own strength and wisdom, then our condition would be pitiable
> indeed. But can man arrest the diurnal or annual revolution of the
> earth? Can he say to the sun that it shall not shine? . . . His power is
> very limited. . . . In a thousand ways is his weakness apparent, and yet

he presume[s] to measure arms with Jehovah, and declare[s] that
Zion shall not be built up . . . when God has declared that these
things shall be done. . . . Improvements will progress, railroads and
telegraph lines and [transoceanic] cables will be built and stretched;
but instead of these things acting as an aid to our enemies, they will
increase our facilities and accelerate the progress of the work of the
Lord.[6]

Brigham's primary concern with the railroad lay in the fact that it
bypassed Salt Lake City. Shortly after the famous Golden Spike was driven,
he began work on the Utah Central Railroad, one of the few railroads built
without government subsidies, to connect settlements north and south of
Ogden with this great "national highway." The first segment of the Utah
Central, linking the railroad terminus at Ogden with Salt Lake City, was
completed in January 1870. Around fifteen thousand people witnessed the
laying of the last rail and the driving of a ceremonial last spike by Brigham.
Thirty-six guns were fired, one for each mile of track, and a grand ball was
held in the evening to commemorate the accomplishment.

Prior to the coming of the railroad, Brigham had thrown his efforts
behind another project linking Utah with the outside—the transcontinental telegraph, which was completed in October 1861. He contracted to furnish a portion of the "poles, subsistence and transportation" necessary for its
completion.[7] Like the railroad, the east and west portions were joined
together at Salt Lake. He subsequently organized the construction of a telegraph line extending from St. George on the south to the Idaho border on
the north to allow for better communication with the Saints in outlying
areas.

Another popular story states that the Latter-day Saints headed west in
an effort to both isolate themselves and flee the United States. Mormon
scripture, however, proclaims the U.S. Constitution to be a divinely inspired
document that the Mormons were to befriend, not abandon. Besides, even
before leaving Winter Quarters it must have been clear to Brigham that it
was only a matter of time before the Saints' promised land in the Great Basin

would become part of the United States. While the Latter-day Saints were bogged down in the mud of Iowa, he agreed to help the United States accomplish its "manifest destiny" of occupying the continent from coast to coast by raising the "Mormon Battalion" during the 1846–47 Mexican War. As concerns about Mormon loyalty continued to surface, Brigham proclaimed during the American Civil War that the Latter-day Saints had no desire to secede "from the Constitution of the United States" or "the institutions of our country," only "from sin and the practice thereof."[8]

While Brigham was grateful that the place God had reserved for the Latter-day Saints "far away in the west" was an isolated location, he was not an isolationist. Given the Saints charge to carry the gospel into all the world, he realized that not only was it impossible to hide from the world, but it was not desirable. For Brigham, Utah was the starting point for the Saints to accomplish their mission, not the final destination. He viewed the Saints both literally and figuratively as having gone to where they could be a city on a hill:

> Some entertained the idea that we came here to hide ourselves up from the world; but we very soon learned that our light had been placed where the inhabitants of the earth could see that we had the Gospel of Jesus Christ, the Light of the world. We have a mission to preach the Gospel to all nations before the end shall come. It devolves upon the people here to set an example for the nations to pattern after. . . . The Lord wishes us to show to our neighbors, friends and foes, how to live, how to be great.[9]

He was vocal and forthright about the conditions the Saints faced in the Intermountain West and the fact that the primary merit of Utah was that nobody else wanted it. "My soul feels hallelujah, it exults in God, that He has planted this people in a place that is not desired by the wicked. . . . I want hard times, so that every person that does not wish to stay, for the sake of his religion, will leave. This is a good place to make Saints, and it is a good place for Saints to live; it is the place the Lord has appointed, and we shall stay here until He tells us to go somewhere else."[10] He told the Saints that the land was "better adapted to raising Saints than any other article that can be raised here. . . . It is the best country in the world for raising Saints."[11]

To help accomplish the Saints' charge to build the kingdom, Brigham regularly sent out missionaries to preach the gospel and emigration agents to help gather people to Zion. These converts brought with them their culture, which can be seen in the fact that several LDS hymns are sung to popular tunes brought from other countries and the eastern United States and in the fact that the character of many settlements in Utah reflect Old World practices and populations, such as the Swiss of Wasatch County and the Scandinavians of Sanpete County. He also asked missionaries and emigrant agents to be on the lookout for plays that would be appropriate for the Salt Lake stage.

Brigham further encouraged people to get educations outside the territory. In his own family, he had sons attend the military academies of West Point and Annapolis, the University of Michigan, and the Rensselaer Polytechnic Institute in Troy, New York. Brigham called several individuals on missions to study art in Europe, and encouraged a number of women, including members of his own household, to go east to receive medical training.

While recognizing Utah as an ideal location for the Saints, he did not view it as their exclusive property—in spite of claims to the contrary that "Brigham as Territorial Governor made it plain that Mormondom was for the Mormons."[12] In 1867, a Utah gentile banker assured Bishop Daniel Tuttle, an Episcopalian missionary bound for Utah that he would be welcomed by Brigham:

> I am quite intimate with Prest. Young and have very frequently heard him express himself concerning other churches coming in here; and am very sure they will meet a hearty welcome from him, *under certain circumstances.* He is not at all prejudiced against other religions, but is most in favor of his own of course. Have frequently heard him say that the Mormons were not the only people to be

saved. Other denominations would also be redeemed, but they must all, his and every other Christian Church, work and pray, practice and live the religion they profess, etc., etc. They *do profess to live and practice their religion* to greater perfection than other denominations, and have great grounds for making such assertions. In a conversation had with Prest. Young since receipt of your letter he has only reiterated former statements, and assured me no minister, nor any one else, who w'd come here and mind their own business, need have the slightest fear of being disturbed by Mormons.[13]

Following Tuttle's arrival in Utah, Brigham gave him a gift of $500 and a plot of ground on which to build a church. He also provided similar gifts to others, including Catholics and the Jews. In the case of the latter, he also allowed them to hold services in Mormon facilities since their meeting schedules did not conflict.

He was also a vocal advocate of religious toleration, regardless of whether people "worshiped a white dog, the sun, moon, or a graven image."[14] Recognizing that Mormons did not have a monopoly on either good intentions or actual righteousness, he concluded that while people were often steeped in false traditions, mankind possessed "many very excellent and pure ideas, beliefs, faiths and sentiments. . . . All have truth, all have good desires."[15]

When Protestant camp meetings were set up to evangelize Utah, he was little troubled. "I am going to permit every one of my children to go and hear what they have to say."[16] To his son Willard, who was a cadet at West Point, Brigham wrote:

> With regard to your attending Protestant Episcopal service, I have no objections whatever. On the contrary, I would like to have you attend, and see what they can teach you about God and Godliness more than you have already been taught. When the Methodist big tent was here I advised old and young to attend their meetings for that very reason, but I was well satisfied it would not

take our people long to learn what Methodists could teach them more than they had already been taught.[17]

Brigham regularly grumbled about the influences and disorder on Salt Lake's Main Street, which he dubbed "Whiskey Street," Despite decrying the "robbery, theft, drunkenness, lying, deceiving, gambling, whoring, and murder" associated with the street—the elements he wished to secede from—he advocated the use of moral persuasion to combat the problem. Rather than taking drastic actions to destroy or remove offensive business, he refused to walk through this vice-inducive area to the end of his life. He told the Saints concerning non-Mormon merchants: "I would have it distinctly understood that we deport ourselves in a friendly and neighborly manner towards our friends."[18]

*Joining of the Union Pacific and Central Pacific railroads, Promontory, Utah, May 10, 1869*

# 32

# FAMOUS OF HIS TIME

In June 1877, Frank Leslie informed readers of *Leslie's Illustrated Magazine* that he would publish a serial account of his recent journey to California. "Every place of interest on the route was visited. . . . The series will be continued regularly until the entire trip from New York to San Francisco and the Yosemite region, including a visit, on the homeward route, to Brigham Young, at Great Salt Lake City, has been illustrated."[1] Leslie knew, as did numerous other authors, of the great interest in both Brigham and the Mormons.

Concerning his visit to Utah, Mark Twain wrote: "There was fascination in surreptitiously staring at every creature we took to be a Mormon. This was a fairy-land to us, to all intents and purposes—a land of enchantment, and goblins, and awful mystery. We felt a curiosity to ask every child how many mothers it had, and if it could tell them apart; and we experienced a thrill every time a dwelling-house door opened and shut as we passed, disclosing a glimpse of human heads and backs and shoulders—for we so longed to have a good satisfying look at a Mormon family in all its comprehensive ampleness."[2]

For most visitors to Utah, there was no greater "attraction" in "Mormonland" than Brigham himself. One Salt Lake resident observed that those visiting Salt Lake "have not considered to have seen all the sights without seeing B. Y. Some parties expect to see all his wives [and] children, as well."[3] Jules Remy observed that "though aware he is the object of [visitor's] curiosity, this does not in the least embarrass him; on the contrary, he looks upon it as quite natural, and never presumes upon it in any respect."[4] Brigham did draw the line on his family, telling at least one lady who asked to see his wives that they are "not on exhibition."[5]

Nevertheless, thousands of visitors flocked to see Brigham. Between 1871 and 1877 more than three thousand signed a visitors' register. They came from Russia, India, Australia, New Zealand, England, France, Scotland, Brazil, Mexico, and Japan, to name a few countries, and every state in the Union. They included the famous in their own right: Ralph Waldo Emerson; William Seward, Abraham Lincoln's secretary of state; General John Sherman of Civil War fame; President Ulysses S. Grant; Schuyler Cofax, Speaker of the House; Don Pedro, the emperor of Brazil; renowned Norwegian violinist Ole Bull; and famed midget Tom Thumb.

Regarding this seemingly never-ending stream, Brigham wrote in June 1877:

> The constant calls of visitors at my office, all of whom have to be chatted with more or less, are quite a tax on my time and strength yet I am satisfied that such visits are, as a rule, productive of good results. Many a one who comes to Utah filled with all kinds of outrageous ideas with regard to the Mormons in general and Brigham Young in particular, after having visited our City, seen its objects of interest and called at the office, go away with feelings greatly modified, and often afterwards have a kind word for the people of Utah when they hear them assailed, and occasionally will smooth the way of any of our missionaries whom they may chance to meet. This

interviewing, then, though sometimes disagreeable is too valuable a means of correcting false ideas, and removing prejudice to be discontinued, whilst by the blessing of the Lord I am able to meet those who call upon me and extend to them courtisces to which, in some cases, they are probably entirely unworthy.[6]

After first-time visitors to his office had been seated, Brigham took his place behind his desk and would sit quietly for several minutes, whether the visitor began talking or remained silent. During this time he sized up his visitor in an indirect interview and reportedly knew the type of individual he was dealing with and whether their intentions were benign or sinister.

When Remy and his traveling companion, Julius Brenchly, visited Salt Lake City in 1855, they "were not disposed to allow more than a day to elapse without presenting our homage" to Brigham. They noted that Brigham initially "did not condescend to favour us with a word." They concluded that the reason was their "rough costume, which was by no means adapted to create a favourable impression." Upon requesting a private audience, Brigham suggested they go outside. This first of several meetings with Brigham ended when he suddenly "started off, and made towards a team of oxen which were coming up the street without a teamster. He stopped the animals, and stood still before them until the driver returned to his post. 'You allow your oxen to go alone, do you?' asked his Excellency. 'Ah! how do you do, Brother Brigham? these oxen, you see, have been disobedient, like myself sometimes.' This act on the part of the Governor appeared so natural to us, that it seemed rather the result of habitual good-nature than done for the sake of effect."[7]

Sir Richard F. Burton had already achieved fame as an adventurer and explorer prior to traveling to America for the express purpose of observing the Mormons. In addition to serving in the British Army in India, he had made a pilgrimage to Mecca disguised as a Muslim, translated the tales of the Arabian Nights, and spent several years in Africa, including four years exploring the sources of the Nile. During an attack that killed several of his companions, Burton was impaled through the cheeks by a spear that left visible scars.

Shortly after arriving at Salt Lake in 1860, Burton mentioned to Governor Alfred Cumming that he wished "to call upon Mr., or rather, as his official title is, President Brigham Young, and he honored me by inquiring what time would be the most convenient" for Brigham. Burton observed that Brigham was "obliged to use caution in admitting strangers, not only for personal safety, but also to defend his dignity from the rude and unfeeling remarks of visitors, who seem to think themselves entitled, in the case of a Mormon, to transgress every rule of civility." Burton found Brigham's manner during their meeting to be "affable and impressive, simple and courteous. . . . He shows no signs of dogmatism, bigotry, or fanaticism, and never once entered—with me at least—upon the subject of religion. He impresses a stranger with a certain sense of power. . . . His powers of observation are intuitively strong, and his friends declare him to be gifted with an excellent memory and a perfect judgment of character. If he dislikes a stranger at the first interview, he never sees him again."[8] Their conversation covered such varied topics as Indian wars and slavery, and ended with Brigham asking Burton about his "last African exploration, and whether it was the same country traversed by Dr. Livingstone."[9]

In 1859, newspaper reporter Horace Greeley published "Two Hours with Brigham Young," which has been described as "the first full-fledged modern interview with a well-known public figure" published in an American newspaper.[10] Greeley found Brigham "plainly dressed in thin summer clothing," exhibiting "no air of sanctimony or fanaticism" and seeming "to enjoy life and to be in no particular hurry to get to heaven." The reporter noted that Brigham "spoke readily,—not always with grammatical accuracy, but with no appearance of hesitation or reserve, and with no apparent desire to conceal anything; nor did he repel any of my questions as impertinent." Greeley could not detect in Brigham or other Mormon leaders the "cant or snuffle" he anticipated, given the Mormon's reputation in the eastern United States, but found them "looking as little like crafty hypocrites or swindlers as any body of men I ever met."[11]

Twain's celebrated wit comes through in the account of his 1861 visit, made in company with his brother, the recently appointed territorial secretary of the newly created Nevada Territory:

> [We] put on white shirts and went and paid a state visit to the king. . . . He was very simply dressed and was just taking off a straw hat as we entered. He talked about Utah, and the Indians, and Nevada, and general American matters and questions, with our secretary and certain government officers who came with us. But he never paid any attention to me, notwithstanding I made several attempts to "draw him out" on federal politics and his high handed attitude towards Congress. I thought some of the things I said were rather fine. But he merely looked around at me, at distance intervals, something as I have seen a benignant old cat look around to see which kitten was meddling with her tail. By and by I subsided into an indignant silence, and so sat until the end, hot and flushed, and execrating him in my heart for an ignorant savage. But he was calm. His conversation with those gentlemen flowed on as sweetly and peacefully and musically as any summer brook. When the audience was ended and [we] were retiring from his presence, he put his hand on my head, beamed down on me in an admiring way, and said to my brother: "Ah—your child, I presume? Boy, or girl?"[12]

Ralph Waldo Emerson summarized his visit this way: "Apr. 19 [1871], Called on B. Young." One who was with Emerson, however, reported that as they arrived, Brigham's "carriage was waiting for him at the door, but a card was sent in, and we were admitted. 'The President' soon entered the room arrayed for his drive, his long cloak on, and his hat in hand." After shaking hands, "a little talk sprang up—not without its difficulties. Some one spoke to Young of what we had liked about his town, and said that he had had an excellent opportunity to show what combined labor could do, and the directing power of a single man; and he unluckily used the phrase, 'the one-man power.' 'Yes,' said Young, quickly, 'the one-man power! It's easy to talk about that! We have no more of it than they have elsewhere!' Alas, we had not begun well." Brigham never did warm to his famous guest, who had previously written negatively about the Mormons, and throughout the interview "gave no sign of knowing who Mr. Emerson was." As the meeting neared an end, "Brigham's secretary" finally asked, "Is this the justly celebrated Ralph Waldo Emerson?" When Emerson's daughter subsequently told a friend about her father's visit, the lady "laughed to hear he had called on Brigham Young."[13]

Englishman John Mortimer Murphy reported that Brigham "greeted me cordially, though in a dignified manner. . . . He said that he was always glad to meet strangers who were visiting the country, and was willing to show them any kindness he could, but that in most instances he was repaid by slander, contumely, and sarcasm." When Murphy asked if all people treated him that way, Brigham responded that "nearly all did, especially newspaper writers and bookmakers." Acknowledging there were people who treated the Latter-day Saints fairly, Brigham added, "If we had men like that come here often . . . we should soon be known to the world for what we really are—a sober, chaste, God-fearing people."[14]

Frank and Miriam Leslie found "the lion we had come out for to see" "standing in the middle of his Office to receive us, with an expression of weary fortitude upon his face, and a perfunctoriness of manner, suggesting that parties of Eastern visitors, curiosity seekers, and interviewers might possibly have become a trifle tedious in Salt Lake City and the Office of the President." After all were seated, "an awful pause fell upon the assembled company." The silence was finally broken by "a sonorous assertion from the President that it was a pleasant day." After general agreement that the weather was fine, Miriam Leslie boldly asked, "Do you suppose, Mr. President, that I came all the way to Salt Lake City to hear that it was a fine day?" Brigham responded, "I am sure you need not, my dear, . . . for it must be fine weather wherever you are!"

She reported that the conversation then took an "interesting turn," covering a wide variety of topics, but focusing primarily on polygamy. "We felt that what Mr. Young said upon matters of Mormon faith and Mormon practice he said with sincerity and earnestness not always felt in a man's more public and general utterances." At the end of the interview, Brigham took "leave much more impressively than he had greeted us." She found him to be "altogether a man of mark anywhere, and one whose wonderful influence over the minds and purses of men, and the hearts and principles of women, can be much more fully credited after an hour's conversation than before." She hoped that he retained "as pleasant a reminiscence" of the visit as she did.[15]

Word of Brigham's passing prompted her to include the following postscript in a book she wrote of her experiences she and her husband undertook:

> News comes to us of President Young's sudden death, and all that struck us as doubtful, or wrong, or ludicrous in the strange system of life he upheld, and of which he was the centre, disappears in the solemn respect and silence with which one remembers the dead whose lives have, even for an hour, intersected our own. He was an honest and sincere believer in his own theories, and lived up to his own convictions of duty; and how many of those who sneer at him dare say the same? A little selfish regret also mingles with the tribute we would fain pay to the memory of the kindly and courteous patriarch, who made us welcome, and exerted himself to entertain us even when ill and weary himself; for his parting words to us were: "And if you put me in a book, promise at least that you will print me as you have found me, and not as others have described me." We had tried to do so, and now he will never know it; never know how kindly and respectfully we remember him, or how honestly we regret his death. May the world deal as tenderly with his memory as we would do, and above the tomb let us inscribe: "Judgment is Mine, saith the Lord."[16]

# ⤳ 33 ⤳

# BRIGHAM AS SEEN
# BY OTHERS

Government surveyor Captain Howard Stansbury, who spent the winter of 1849–50 in Salt Lake City, noted in a report to his superiors: "Upon the personal character of the leader of [the Latter-day Saints], it may not, perhaps, be proper for me to comment. . . . I may nevertheless be pardoned for saying, that to me, President Young appeared to be a man of clear, sound sense, fully alive to the responsibilities of the station he occupies, sincerely devoted to the good name and interests of the people over which he presides, sensitively jealous of the least attempt to undervalue or misrepresent them, and indefatigable in devising ways and means for their moral, mental, and physical elevation. He appeared to possess the unlimited personal and official confidence of his people."[1]

Like Stansbury, numerous people took the opportunity to write their impressions of Brigham. While some had personal contact with him, for many their only encounter was seeing him at the weekly Sunday service.

One "forty-niner" bound for the California gold fields characterized Brigham as "a very good looking fellow" who "looked every inch a commander."[2] Frenchman Jules Remy concluded: "He is a man of fifty-four years of age, fair, of moderate height, stout almost to obesity. He has regular features, a wide forehead, eyes which convey an idea of finesse, and a smiling expression of a mouth. His general appearance is that of an honest farmer, and nothing in his manner indicates a man of the higher classes."[3]

Twenty-four-year-old Clara Downes, a single woman traveling to California in 1860, described Brigham as "a very good looking man, *very*. There is something noble & commanding in his looks & bearing. He looks about—40 yrs. he is 59 years of age."[4] That same year Sir Richard Burton wrote that while Brigham was

> fifty-nine years of age; he looks about forty-five. . . . Scarcely a grey thread appears in his hair, which is parted on the side, light colored, rather thick, and reaches below the ears with a half curl. . . . The forehead is somewhat narrow, the eyebrows are thin, the eyes between gray and blue, with a calm, composed, and somewhat reserved expression: a slight droop in the left lid made me think he had suffered from paralysis. . . . The nose, which is fine and somewhat sharp-pointed, is bent a little to the left. The lips are close like the New Englander's, and the teeth, especially those of the under jaw, are imperfect. The cheeks are rather fleshy . . . ; the chin somewhat peaked. . . . The hands are well made. . . . The figure is somewhat large, broad-shouldered, and stooping a little when standing. The Prophet's dress was neat and plain as a Quaker's, all gray homespun except the cravat and waistcoat.[5]

Mark Twain, who visited Brigham in 1861, characterized him as "a quiet, kindly, easy-mannered, dignified, self-possessed old gentleman of fifty-five or sixty, and had a gentle craft in his eye that probably belonged there."[6] William H. Knight described him as "a fine-looking, intellectual sort of man, above average in stature . . . vibrant with energy, intelligence, [and] character."[7] Samuel Bowles, who visited Salt Lake in June 1865, portrayed Brigham as "a very hale and hearty looking man, young for sixty four, with a light gray eye, cold and uncertain, a mouth and chin betraying a great determined will—handsome perhaps as to presence and features, but repellent in atmosphere and without magnetism." Bowles concluded that "when his eye did sparkle and his lips soften, it was with most cheering, though not warming, effect; it was pleasant but did not melt you."[8]

In 1867 Albert D. Richardson penned that Brigham was "portly, weighing about two hundred, in his sixty-sixth year, and wonderfully well-preserved. . . . His cheek is fresh and unwrinkled; his step agile and elastic; his curling, auburn hair and whiskers untinged with gray. . . . He has grayish-blue, secretive eyes, eagle nose, and mouth that shuts like a vise, indicating tremendous firmness."[9]

Fitz Hugh Ludlow concluded that he "looked very distinguished" and "his daily homespun detracts nothing from the feeling, when in his presence, that you are beholding a most remarkable man. He is nearly seventy years old, but appears very little over forty. His height is about 'five feet ten.' . . . His figure very well made, and slightly inclining to portliness. His hair is a rich curly chestnut, formerly worn long, in supposed imitation of the apostolic coiffure, but now cut in our practical Eastern fashion. . . . Brigham Young's eyes are a clear blue-gray, frank and straightforward in their look; his nose a finely chiseled aquiline; his mouth exceedingly firm, and fortified in that expression by [his] chin."[10]

A correspondent for the *Chicago Times* wrote of Brigham in 1871:

> His personal appearance is far different from the stereotyped descriptions which have for many years been going the rounds of the newspapers.
>
> Brigham Young is of fine physical structure, rather lymphatic in temperament, small boned, and yet staunchly and compactly built. He stands straightly, about five feet ten inches, shows no sign of age in his walk, and weighs about two hundred pounds. His head is large, well-shaped, well-balanced, and covered with a luxuriant suit of auburn hair, among which, here and there, a silvery few may be seen.

His forehead is ample and high. His eyes are blue, not large, but sharp, searching, and capable of varied and great expression.

His nose is aquiline, quite prominent, but symmetrical, and, with his well formed mouth, which shuts firmly and tightly together, gives indication of great mental energy and indomitable pluck. And altogether, the face of Brigham Young indicates a man of iron inflexibility, much forecast, extraordinary ability and a vast fund of good humor."[11]

In 1872, Elizabeth Kane wrote of Brigham's "keen, blue-gray eyes . . . with their characteristic look of shrewd and cunning insight." She concluded that "his photographs, accurate enough in other respects, altogether fail to give the expression of his eyes."[12]

An acquaintance of Brigham's stated that "his lips came together like the jaws of a bear trap,'" while another individual declared that when Brigham spoke, words "'slipped by the teeth, and [were] finally squeezed through the left half of the almost locked-up' mouth."[13] Burton noted that prior to Brigham rising to preach, that there was "a great silence, which told us that something was about to happen: *that* old man held his cough; *that* old lady awoke with a start; *that* child ceased to squall."[14] Knight, who was in Utah around the same time as Burton, reported that as Brigham "advanced to a railing in front of the pulpit, or altar, he leaned both hands quite heavily upon the rail, as though marshalling his thoughts, preceding delivery. At first he spoke low, but distinctly, then more loudly, but not violently, at the same time indulging in gestures."[15] Burton also observed that Brigham's "discourse began slowly; word crept titubantly after word, and the opening phrases were hardly audible; but as the orator warmed, his voice rose high and sonorous, and a fluency so remarkable succeeded falter and hesitation, that—although the phenomenon is not rare in strong speakers—the latter seemed almost to have been a work of art. The manner was pleasing and animated, and the matter fluent, impromptu, and well turned, spoken rather than preached: if it had a fault it was rather rambling and unconnected. . . . The gestures were easy and rounded, not without a certain grace, though evidently untaught;

one, however, must be excepted, namely, that of raising and shaking the fore-finger; this is often done in the Eastern states."[16]

In 1871, Hamilton Hill reported: "Brigham Young's address was evidently given off-hand, but he spoke with a good degree of fluency; his manner was conversational; his gestures awkward, but they were infrequent; his voice filled the hall, and he was listened to by all with the closest attention."[17] Daniel S. Tuttle, Episcopal bishop of Salt Lake, lauded Brigham's speaking style as one of "conscious ease and strength." According to Tuttle, Young spoke effortlessly "yet so clear was his tone, so well enunciated were his words, and so rapt was the people's attention, that he was easily heard by every one. . . . He speaks, not deliberately, but readily, almost rapidly, and in a businesslike, almost nonchalant way."[18]

Downes concluded that he "speaks very well indeed & has good gestures. . . . he said that the people of the east say that Mormonism is the work of the *devil* 'if that is so' said he 'then glory to the devil, for I am so happy in it.' his remarks were quite funny & some, quite sensible."[19] Bowles, however, found Brigham's sermon to be "a curious medley of scriptural exposition and exhortation, bold and bare statement, coarse denunciation and vulgar allusion, cheap rant and poor cant. . . . It was a very material interpretation of the statements and truths of scripture, very illogically and roughly rendered; and calculated only to influence a cheap and vulgar audience."[20]

Ludlow found Brigham's sermons "cogent and full of common sense, if not elegant or always free from indelicacy."[21]

Remy reported that Brigham "does not preach, he converses; his voice is strong and sonorous." While Brigham employed "puns, jokes, [and] buffooneries" and might "ridicule with point and readiness; he abounds in personalities, and with allusions which the public easily seize, inasmuch as he possesses remarkable talent as a mimic, and does not hesitate to imitate the gestures, voice, and language of those whom he desires to put upon the stage. But this is again another element of success with a popular audience. Besides, under forms that are frequently grotesque, there lies a thoughtful, practical truth, which every man may turn to his profit. The comedian is, in fact, the auxiliary of the pontiff and the moralist."[22] Wilford Murno concluded of Brigham's preaching: "Often he was ungrammatical, occasionally he was witty, sometimes he was slangy and profane, sometimes he was obscene" according to the prevailing Victorian standards of the day, but "his sermons were always to the point. He had a message to put forth, and his language could always be understood by his people. He knew his audience."[23]

Remy agreed with one of Brigham's critics, John Hyde, that "Brigham Young is not an ordinary man. With an extensive knowledge of men, and a fine and delicate tact, he combines unusual strength of mind and remarkable energy of character."[24] Burton reported that "the first impression left on my mind . . . and it was subsequently confirmed, was, that the Prophet is no common man, and that he has none of the weakness and vanity which characterize the common uncommon man."[25] Burton further noted that Brigham's "want of pretension contrasts favorably with certain pseudo-prophets I have seen."[26]

Another English visitor, William Chandless, reported that Brigham demonstrated "no singularity of dress or superiority of manner, and will shake hands freely with brother This and brother That."[27] Ludlow concluded: "There are few courtlier men living. His address is a fine combination of dignity with the desire to confer happiness, of perfect deference to the feelings of others with absolute certainty of himself and his own opinions."[28] Richardson observed that "with an affable and dignified manner he manifests the unmistakable egotism of one having authority. . . . He is universally popular among the Saints and rules them with utmost ease."[29]

A printer who came with the U.S. Army during the Utah War reported that Brigham stated upon meeting him: "I presume you have often put in type 'our own correspondent's' accounts of affairs out here. Now, do you take me for the terrible, treasonable, anathematizing, many-wived[,] law-resisting rascal I have been represented?" The printer concluded: "And, of a truth I should say, no. He has an open, pleasant countenance, that speaks of benevolence, humanity and frankness; there is nothing in his appearance to indicate the bold bad man that the race of Drummonds have represented him to be. . . . He is not very well liked by some of our officers, I admit, but the cause of it is this: He holds the opinion that . . . an honest, upright, sober private soldier is a better man by far than a king without these qualities. . . . I am no friend of Mormonism, or the policy of Brigham Young, but I approve of giving 'the devil his due.'"[30]

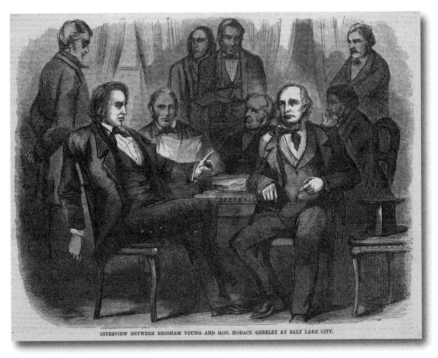

INTERVIEW BETWEEN BRIGHAM YOUNG AND HON. HORACE GREELEY AT SALT LAKE CITY.

*Interview between Horace Greeley and Brigham Young in Salt Lake City, 1859*

# ∾ 34 ∾

# BRIGHAM AS
# RENAISSANCE MAN

Brigham was a Renaissance Man in the tradition of Leon Battista Alberti and Leonardo da Vinci, for he too was an individual with a wide range of accomplishments and intellectual interests. Alberti (1404–72), the original model of a Renaissance Man, was accomplished in poetry, architecture, art, philosophy, cryptography, science, and mathematics. Da Vinci (1452–1519), who is often held up as the greatest example of a Renaissance Man, was a man of seemingly infinite curiosity whose diverse talents led to numerous inventions and designs, many of which were beyond the capacity of the technology of his lifetime.

While Brigham is regarded as an American Moses for directing the westward migration of tens of thousands of his fellow Saints, praised for his work as a colonist and city planner, and recognized as the first governor of Utah, and President of The Church of Jesus Christ of Latter-day Saints for thirty years, his abilities also included craftsman, entrepreneur, innovator, reformer, and architect. When a traveler addressed him by his political and religious titles, Brigham responded, "Sir, you have omitted my most cherished titles: Carpenter, Painter and Glazier."[1] In fact, his scope and expertise were broader than most men of his time.

Brigham revealed himself a Renaissance Man through his continuous search for knowledge; his willingness to use what he learned to benefit his family, church, and community; and his ability to solve problems. Even one of his critics was forced to admit that Brigham "is one of the few Americans deserving of the adjective great. In a situation of precariousness and importance he showed himself a man of resourcefulness and sturdiness."[2]

Awed by all that was before him, Brigham noted, in typical fashion, "It is one of the most happifying subjects that can be named, for a person, or a people, to have the privilege of gaining wisdom enough while in their mortal tabernacle to be able to look through the whys and wherefores of the existence of man, like looking through a piece of glass that is perfectly transparent; and understand the design of the Great Maker of this beautiful creation."[3]

Having been denied a formal education, Brigham undertook a life-long, wide-ranging self-education to satisfy his curiosity about the world around him. While a missionary in London in 1840, he made the traditional tourist stops—the National Gallery, St. Paul's Cathedral, Westminster Abbey, the British Museum—but he also visited the "College of Surgeons, and went through every department."[4] In 1858, he spent one evening observing a comet through a telescope, then shortly afterward devoted most of another to reading about the life of Napoleon, retiring "about 1. A.M."[5] Brigham subsequently asked a missionary son in Hawaii to "bring me all the specemens you can from the water and Iland."[6]

Brigham used his yearly visits through the settlements as occasions to acquire new knowledge. Following his travels in 1861, he reported "a method to make cheese, which he learned from an Englishmen while on his Southern Trip. This brother told him he made his cheese rhinds hard by wrapping cloths round the cheese, and letting them remain in the cheese press sufficient time to form a rhind that would keep the flies from doing any harm."[7]

Early in Brigham's life, because of his mother's consumption, he had both learned and practiced "the domestic arts." This knowledge continued after his first wife Miriam was likewise afflicted with the same debilitating illness. Having acquired some proficiency, he continued to make the home sciences a matter of study. In 1871, a concerned Brigham declared that he would like the privilege "to teach every woman in this Church and kingdom how to keep house, and how to sweep house, cook meat, wash dishes, make bread without any waste, etc. I may go to a house and what do I see? Perhaps the bottom or the top of bread is burnt to a coal. Why did you not do different? 'O, these are accidents.' Yes, because we never think of the business on our hands."[8]

Another area where Brigham expanded upon the lessons learned in his youth was in terms of farming. Visitors to Salt Lake noted that Brigham's fields often produced yields in excess of the average. Samuel Bowles reported that while fifty to sixty bushels of wheat to an acre was common, Brigham once harvested 93 bushels.[9] Fitz Hugh Ludlow concluded that with Brigham's understanding of "soils, stock, tools, rotation, irrigation, manures, and all the agricultural economies so well that he would speedily have the best crops within a hundred miles' radius. With his own hands he would put the best house in the settlement over the heads of himself and his family."[10]

Ludlow also marveled at the fact that "on Sundays [Brigham] can preach sermons cogent and full of common sense" and "on week-days he sits in the Church office, managing a whole nation's temporalities with such secular astuteness that Talleyrand or Richelieu would find him a match should the morning's game be diplomatic, and the Rothschild family could not get ahead of him if the stakes were a financial advantage."[11] Famed British explorer Sir Richard Burton observed that during their meeting Brigham spoke "as an authority upon certain subjects, such as agriculture and stock-breeding." When their discussion turned to Burton's African travels, Albert Carrington arose to locate the spot on the map. When he placed his finger too near the equator, Brigham stated, "A little lower down." An amazed Burton reported that "there are many educated men in England who could not have corrected the mistake as well."[12] Jules Remy noted that Brigham could "philosophize with authority, if not polish, on Voltaire" and then immediately and easily turn his attention to instructing people on the provisions they would need for an extended journey.[13] During one day in 1855, Brigham discussed such widely diverse topics as naval armaments, national politics, and the making of molasses.[14] In February 1857, he gave counsel concerning the design of a windmill for pumping water and improvements to the beet sugar factory.[15]

Like many during the Renaissance, Brigham was also a patron of the arts, even calling missionaries to go to Paris to study art. His personal mediums of expression, however, tended to be architecture and woodworking.

Brigham's skills as a carpenter and builder never lay dormant. "I have built a great many houses, both for myself and for others," he declared. "I have never built two houses alike, and I do not expect to in time or eternity, but I mean to improve every time I begin."[16] His best-known residence, the Beehive House, is a traditional Georgian-style house with Greek revival features. The neighboring Lion House, which he also helped design, is of the Gothic-revival style also popular at the time. It was designed so that each wife had a room and has been called the first apartment building in Utah. His daughter Clarissa noted that Brigham's carpentry skills were "evidenced in such fine features" of the Lion House "as the easy stair treads and graceful banisters—quite perfect for sliding upon."[17]

Brigham also played a major role in the construction of the massive, elliptical, self-supporting roof of the famous Salt Lake Tabernacle, which measured 250 feet long, 150 feet wide, and 80 feet high at its apex. At the time, to construct a building of the size of the Salt Lake Tabernacle without roof supports was unthinkable, given the fact that steel girders were not available for construction. Nevertheless, Brigham wanted a building that was big enough to house the Saints for Sunday meetings but didn't have any interior pillars or posts to obstruct views. (The balcony with its pillar supports was not part of the original structure.) To carry out the design for the roof, Brigham turned to Henry Grow, whose expertise was in building bridges. In consultation with Brigham, Grow employed a modified-lattice truss system widely used on bridges to create a remarkably engineered bridgework of timbers nine feet tall that created huge elliptical arches spanning the width of the structure. The timbers were latticed and pinned together using only wooden pegs and rawhide strips. The tabernacle has been called one of the "world's truly remarkable architecturally designed buildings" and the Society of American Civil Engineering has designated the building as a National Historic Civil Engineering Landmark. Until the Royal Albert Hall opened in London a few years later, it was the largest such structure in the world.

Brigham was actively involved in both the construction and operation of the Salt Lake Theater. During Ludlow's visit to Utah, he attended a play at the theater and was "astonished to find in the desert heart . . . a place of public amusement, which regarding comfort, capacity, and beauty has but two or three superiors in the United States." He noted that the central chandelier was "creditable to any New York firm, apparently a richly carven circle, twined with gilt vines, leaves, and tendrils, blossoming all over with flaming wax-lights, and suspended by a massive chain of gold lustre." He guessed that the Saints had "probably paid a thousand dollars for it in New York." In response, Brigham exclaimed: "'*I made it myself!* That circle is a *cart*-wheel, the wheel of one of our common Utah ox-carts. I had it waxed and gilded it with my own hands. It hangs by a pair of ox-chains, which I also gilded; and the gilt ornaments of the candlesticks were all cut after my patterns out of sheet tin!'"[18]

Brigham's continuing involvement with the theater prompted one individual to conclude that "Brigham Young knew more about the needs of a large stage than any manager now living." Alfred Lambourne reported on one of Brigham's regular inspections of the theater: "Brigham Young was famed for completeness; he possessed a genius for details. Carefully the President examined each watertank, each barrel of salt. He appeared to think that day of the Playhouse's danger from fire. He broke with the end of his gold-headed cane the thick crusts that had formed over the tops in the barrels of salt. I watched him shake his head and compress his lips; there came a frown upon his face. His orders for safety, one could see, had been neglected. He did a labor which should have been remembered and performed by others."[19]

Unlike Da Vinci, Brigham's thinking tended more toward the practical than the theoretical, and he was able to solve a wide range of problems. During the 1848 trek to Utah, Lucy Groves broke her leg, which was set by Brigham. For nine days she traveled in a bed set up in the family wagon until another unfortunate accident occurred and the leg was broken a second time. This time the pain was so severe that she cried out in agony with every step the oxen took, and she told her husband that they had to pull out of the train. With tears rolling down Lucy's cheeks, she explained the situation to Brigham and strongly urged that the train to go on without them. Brigham responded that he would not leave anyone alone. He instead made camp and set about to find a solution. He sawed off the spindles and legs of her poster bed so nothing was left but the frame around the mattress. He then fastened it to the wagon bows so that it would swing easily like a hammock. The family was able to travel with the company to Salt Lake.[20]

When a second set of drawings of the Salt Lake Temple was needed, Brigham worked out an ingenious solution. Rather than going through the laborious task of having an additional set drawn by hand, he took advantage of a relatively new technology and simply had the plans photographed, thus recognizing the value of the camera beyond simply capturing an image.[21]

When the St. George Tabernacle was built, two beautiful free-standing, circular staircases—which were viewed as a crowning achievement—were included. Upon visiting the structure, Brigham discovered that the height of the stairs placed the balcony so high that not everyone who sat in the balcony could see the pulpit. Because the circular staircases could not be changed without destroying them, Brigham devised a resourceful plan by which the staircases could remain as built and yet have people still see the pulpit. Using jacks and braces and the collective strength of two hundred men, a section was taken out of each pillar so that the balcony could be lowered five feet. Those who climb to the top of the magnificent staircases must now step down eight steps to reach the balcony—but all who do so can see the pulpit.[22] The compromise and end result were both the practical functioning of a modern Renaissance Man.

# ∞ 35 ∞

# THE WISDOM OF
# BRIGHAM YOUNG

I f persons neglect to obey the law of God and to walk humbly before Him, darkness will come into their minds and they will be left to believe that which is false and erroneous; their minds will become dim, their eyes will be beclouded and they will be unable to see things as they are."[1]

"From the beginning of the work our enemies have formed an innumerable number of plans for our overthrow, and they have indulged in great hopes respecting the success which would attend their operation . . . but in every instance, their schemes have fallen to the ground. . . . Notwithstanding these repeated failures, the adversary does not appear discouraged. He deludes his servants with the idea that success is sure to attend their efforts, and thus he leads them forward one after another, captives at his will. They are blind to the confusion and overthrow which have befallen those who have preceded them in opposing the work of God."[2]

"Let us live so that we can say we are the Saints of God; and when the finger of scorn is pointed at us and we are held in derision and the nations talk about us, let us show an example before them that is worthy of imitation, that they cannot but blush before all sensible and intelligent persons when they say, 'There is a people that sin; there is a people that are corrupt.' . . . Let them howl and bark against us as much as they please, but let us live so that they will have no reason to say a word."[3]

"Let every person say: 'I will live my religion, though every other person goes to hell! I will walk humbly before my God and deal honestly with my fellow beings.'"[4]

"The man who suffers his passions to lead him becomes a slave to them, and such a man will find the work of emancipation an exceedingly difficult one. Make the doing of God's will and the keeping of His commandments a constant habit with you and it will become perfectly natural and easy for you to walk uprightly before Him."[5]

"Never allow your courage to fail you; man's greatest works have been done by men of patience, perseverance, and a determined *will* which would acknowledge no defeat, rather than by those gifted with a natural ability which made success easy but who lacked the tenaciousness of purpose."[6]

"Some young men seem to entertain the idea that to smoke, to chew, or to use profane language makes them appear more manly. Never was a greater fallacy. [Real] manhood is manifested in serving God and keeping his commandments. The highest type of mankind is shown in such worthies as Enoch, Abraham, Joseph, Nephi, Alma, Joseph Smith, and others. If boys wish to be thought manly, let them copy the best men and their virtues, not inferior and vicious men and their follies and vices."[7]

"It is our attention to our daily duties that makes us men, and if we devote our lives to the service of heaven, our faithfulness therein will eventually fit us with our Heavenly Father in eternity to dwell. . . . No one advances who imagines himself too good or too big for present duties."[8]

"Our daily toil, however humble it may be, is our daily duty, and by doing it will we make it a part of our daily worship."[9]

"Paul says, in his Epistle to the Corinthians, 'But the natural man receiveth not the things of God,' but I say it is the unnatural 'man that receiveth not the things of God.' . . . That which was, is, and will continue to endure is more natural than that which will pass away and be no more. The natural man is of God. We are the natural sons and daughters of our natural parents, and spiritually we are the natural children of the Father of light and natural heirs to his kingdom; and when we do an evil, we do it in opposition to the promptings of the Spirit of Truth that is within us. Man, the noblest work of God, was in his creation designed for an endless duration, for which the love of all good was incorporated in his nature. It was never designed that he should naturally do and love evil."[10]

"I wish you to understand that sin is not an attribute in the nature of man, but it is an inversion of the attributes God has placed in him."[11]

"The inhabitants of the earth imagine that they are enjoying great freedom. It is not so. If they would stop and reflect, they would find that they only place each other in bondage."[12]

"What liberty is there in anything that will be dissolved and return to its native element? What liberty can any intelligence enjoy that is calculated to be destroyed? There is no liberty, no freedom there. The principles of life and salvation are the only principles of freedom; for every principle that is opposed to God . . . will cease to exist."[13]

"There is no man who ever made a sacrifice on this earth for the kingdom of heaven, that I know anything about, except the Savior. He drank the bitter cup to the dregs, and tasted for every man and for every woman, and redeemed the earth and all things upon it. . . . 'But we suffer, we sacrifice, we give something, we have preached so long.' What for? 'Why, for the Lord.' I would not give the ashes of a rye straw for the man who feels that he is making sacrifices for God. We are doing this for our own happiness, welfare and exaltation, and for nobody else's."[14]

"[It] is not the good, religious, sanctified feelings that I have that will present me or any other man blameless and acceptable before the Lord, but it is the good that we do to one another. . . . Esteem it a privilege to help one another that you may have your reward."[15]

"I am very anxious all my sons should be, faithful . . . members in His kingdom. Integrity to the truth and ability to do good are qualities which I hope will characterize you all."[16]

"There is one virtue, attribute, or principle, which, if cherished and practiced by the Saints, would prove salvation to thousands upon thousands. I allude to charity, or love, from which proceed forgiveness, long-suffering, kindness, and patience."[17]

"It is one of the most simple things in the world for people to understand what course they should take; what a pity they do not all understand it! . . . But to enjoy this we must live before the Lord, so that our minds would be like a sheet of white paper . . . then the Lord could and would dictate all our movements. . . . We should all live so that the spirit of revelation could dictate and write on the heart and tell us what we should do, instead of the traditions of our parents and teachers. But to do this we must become like little children. . . . Live so that our consciences are free, clean and clear. This is as simple as anything can be, and yet it is one of the hardest things to get people to understand, or rather to practice."[18]

"It costs no more to raise a good horse, ox, cow, or sheep than it does a poor one, and why cannot we exercise a little common sense and ordinary care and raise the valuable instead of the worthless?"[19]

"'Keep your dish right side up,' so that when the shower of porridge does come, you can catch your dish full."[20]

"If we live our holy religion and let the spirit reign, it will not become dull and stupid, but as the body approaches dissolution the spirit takes a firmer hold on that enduring substance behind the veil, drawing from the depths of that eternal fountain of light, sparkling gems of intelligence, which surround the frail and sinking tabernacle with the halo of immortal wisdom."[21]

"It is to be regretted that . . . men should fail to perceive that there is nothing that the adversary can offer as a temptation to seduce them from the path of righteousness and truth which they cannot obtain by treading in that path undeviatingly. There is no good thing which is not comprehended in the gospel of Jesus. . . . Strange to say, however, not only are the people in the world blind to this great fact, but men and women, who call themselves Latter-day Saints, and who have been taught the principles of salvation, fail to recognize it, and desert the substantial pleasures which they would enjoy eternally, and go in pursuit of their shadows."[22]

"The immoral habits of many of the natives will doubtless impress you very unfavorably, still you must bear in mind that their practices are apt to be as they are traditionated, just as the rest of mankind are in theirs, and we have to deal with people as they are, and by giving them the gospel and show-ing them a good example, strive to make them better."[23]

"It would be as foolish, yes more so, to copy a man's moral blemishes because he has the reputation of being a gentleman, a student, or a good fel-low, as it would be to make an artificial wart upon one's face because some very handsome man had the misfortune to have a natural one on his. . . . All of us are subject to the influences of others, especially of those for whom we have regard, and from our companions both our character and disposition we'll receive a tincture, as water passing through minerals partakes of their taste and efficacy. How careful then ought we to be to associate only with the upright, the good, and the pure."[24]

"It matters not whether you or I feel like praying, when the time comes to pray, *pray*. If we do not feel like it, we should pray till we *do*. . . . You will find that those who wait till the Spirit bids them pray will never pray much on this earth."[25]

"I have seen men who belonged to this kingdom, and who really thought that if they were not associated with it, it could not progress."[26]

"Never ask how big we are, or inquire who we are; but let it be, 'What can I do to build up the kingdom of God upon the earth?'"[28]

"Do we realize that if we enjoy a Zion in time or in eternity, we must make it for ourselves? That all who have a Zion in the eternities of the gods organized, framed, consolidated, and perfected it themselves, and consequently are entitled to enjoy it."[28]

"What in the name of common sense is there to hang on to, if [one] does not hang on to the Church? I do not know of anything. You might as well take a lone straw in the midst of the ocean to save yourselves. . . . There is nothing but the Gospel to hang on to!"[29]

"One generation passes away and another comes on to occupy their places, and so it will continue until we all meet again in our Father's Mansions from whence we came to perform our parts upon this dark orb. . . . Therefore, let us act well our parts in the Theatre of life that we may draw down the applause of him who rules, directs and governs all."[30]

# ∽ 36 ∾

# "THE OBJECT OF THIS EXISTENCE"

## *Brigham on Education*

Brigham was a great advocate for improving the mind. "The object of this existence," he frankly declared, "is to learn."[1] He further noted that "intelligent beings are organized to become Gods, even the sons of God, to dwell in the presence of Gods, and become associated with the highest intelligences that dwell in eternity. We are now in the school."[2] Concerning this school, Brigham stated, "Inasmuch as the Lord Almighty has designed us to know all that is in the earth, both the good and the evil, and to learn not only what is in heaven, but what is in hell, you need not expect ever to get through learning."[3] "Of the time that is allotted to man here on the earth there is none to lose or to run to waste," he taught. "After suitable rest and relaxation there is not a day, hour or minute that we should spend in idleness, but every minute of every day of our lives we should strive to improve our minds and to increase in the faith of the holy Gospel, in charity, patience, and good works, that we may grow in the knowledge of the truth as it is in Jesus Christ."[4]

Brigham's view of education reflected what Joseph Smith taught:

"Whatever principle of intelligence we attain unto in this life, it will rise with us in the resurrection. And if a person gains more knowledge and intelligence in this life through his diligence and obedience than another, he will have so much the advantage in the world to come."[5] Brigham also took as a personal challenge Joseph's teaching that "thy mind, O man! if thou wilt lead a soul unto salvation, must stretch as high as the utmost heavens, and search into and contemplate the darkest abyss, and the broad expanse of eternity."[6] Given Brigham's perspective on learning, education, and knowledge, it is not surprising that he lamented the fact that he was unable to devote more time to these endeavors. It is also appropriate that his name is associated with several universities.

Regarding his own early education, Brigham stated that "Brother Heber [Kimball] and I never went to school until we got into 'Mormonism:' that was the first of our schooling. We never had the opportunity of letters in our youth."[7] One thing that attracted him to Mormonism was that it presented unlimited opportunities to learn. Christian doctrine when "simmered down" could fit in "a snuffbox," Brigham concluded, but "when I found 'Mormonism,' I found that it was higher than I could reach . . ., deeper than I was capable of comprehending, and calculated to expand the mind . . . from truth to truth, from light to light, . . . to become associated with the Gods and angels."[8] While he could learn the basics of other religions in a limited amount of time, that was not the case with Mormonism: "I am proud to say of my religion, I have studied it faithfully for twenty-two years, day and night; at home and abroad, upon the rivers, and upon the lakes, when travelling by sea and by land; [I] have studied it in the pulpit; from morning till night, whatsoever might be my pursuit, I have studied it with as close an application as any college student ever did any subject he wished to commit to memory; and I can say I have only just got into the A B C of it; it leads the vision of my mind into eternity."[9]

For Brigham, one of the beauties of Mormonism was that it embraced "all truth that is revealed and that is unrevealed, whether religious, political, scientific, or philosophical," whether it was found "in heaven and on earth, in the earth, [or] under the earth."[10] He told the Saints, "Not only does the religion of Jesus Christ make the people acquainted with the things of God, and develop within them moral excellence and purity, but it holds out every encouragement and inducement possible, for them to increase in knowledge and intelligence, in every branch of mechanism, or in the arts and sciences, for all wisdom, and all the arts and sciences in the world are from God, and are designated for the good of His people."[11] He believed that "there is no true religion without true science, and consequently there is no true science without true religion."[12] "Our religion will not clash with or contradict the facts of science in any particular. You may take geology, for instance, and it is a true science; not that I would say for a moment that all the conclusions and deductions of its professors are true, but its leading principles are."[13]

He believed that "every accomplishment, every grace, every useful attainment in . . . all science and art belong to the Saints, and they should avail themselves as expeditiously as possible of [this] wealth of knowledge."[14] He encouraged the Saints to seek out truth wherever it could be found, including the sciences, the arts, even other churches. "All truth is the offspring of heaven and is incorporated in the religion which we have embraced," he declared. "[The gospel] is the fountain of light and intelligence; it swallows up the truth contained in all the philosophy of the world, both heathen and Christian; it circumscribes the wisdom of man; it circumscribes all the wisdom and power of the world; it reaches to that within the veil."[15]

Brigham was concerned that if the only books the Saints read were the scriptures, then "you may be nothing but a sectarian after all. It is your duty to study to know everything upon the face of the earth, in addition to reading those books. We should not only study good, and its effects upon our race, but also evil, and its consequences."[16] He also told the Saints: "I would rather that persons read novels than read nothing" but "if it would do any good, I would advise you to read books that are worth reading; read reliable history, and search wisdom out of the best books you can procure. How I would be delighted if [Saints] would do this, instead of continually studying nonsense."[17] To his son Feramorz, who didn't like to read, Brigham later wrote a stronger condemnation of novel reading:

I do not esteem the perusal of novels a wise means of increasing your desire to read. I should be very foolish if because I had a poor appetite I took to making my meals of poisonous herbs or berries because they tasted sweet or were otherwise palatable. It would be better for my appetite to remain poor than that I should destroy my vitality. Novel reading appears to me to be very much the same as swallowing poisonous herbs; it is a remedy that is worse than the complaint. . . . I hope the taste [for reading] will yet be developed in you, but developed by all means with good, healthy, mental food. Read all good books you can obtain, the revelations of God, the writings of His servants, descriptions of His works, as seen in the animal, vegetable and mineral kingdoms; peruse the lives of the good and great of various ages and nationalities; make yourself acquainted with art, science and manufacture, and before long you will find an interest growing in these things that it will be no longer any trouble to read, but you will read eagerly and whilst so doing you will be fitting yourself for future usefulness.[18]

Brigham couldn't understand people who coveted earthly possessions more than knowledge. For him, possessions simply provided people "room and board" while attending "school." Material possessions were "made for the comfort of the creature, and not for his adoration. They are made to sustain and preserve the body while procuring the knowledge and wisdom that pertain to God and his kingdom, in order that we may preserve ourselves, and live for ever in his presence."[19]

Since "every true principle, every true science, every art, and all the knowledge that men possess, or that they ever did or ever will possess is from God," Brigham believed it was impossible to separate worldly and spiritual knowledge and foolish to try.[20] Since education was not merely for time, but for eternity, he proclaimed: "Teach the children, give them the learning of the world and the things of God; elevate their minds, that they may not only understand the earth we walk upon, but the air we breathe, the water we drink, and all the elements pertaining to the earth; and then search other worlds, and become acquainted with the planetary system." Once this foundation was established, Brigham encouraged people to go on to discover "the dwellings of the angels and the heavenly beings, that they may ultimately be prepared for a higher state of being, and finally be associated with them."[21]

For Brigham, education was an important aspect of building the kingdom. "All our educational pursuits are in the service of God, for all these labors are to establish truth on the earth, and that we may increase in knowledge, wisdom, understanding in the power of faith and in the wisdom of God, that we may become fit subjects to dwell in a higher state of existence and intelligence than we now enjoy."[22] "We should not only learn the principles of education known to mankind, but we should reach out further than this, learning to live so that our minds will gather in information from the heavens and the earth until we can incorporate in our faith and understanding all knowledge which is useful and practicable in our present condition and that will lead to life eternal."[23]

In 1850 Brigham helped establish the University of Deseret, later renamed the University of Utah, "so that the old and young, rich and poor, men, women and children throughout the State . . . may have the privilege of acquiring the most perfect education possible."[24] With the increase in secularism among higher education during the nineteenth century, he decried teachers who possessed "a very limited amount of knowledge, and, like a door upon its hinges, move to and fro from one year to another without any visible advancement or improvement. . . . Man is made in the image of God, but what do we know of him or of ourselves?"[25] Not surprisingly, given his views, twenty-five years after the creation of the University of Deseret, he felt a need to establish a second institution:

> We have enough and to spare, at present in these mountains, of schools where young infidels are made because the teachers are so tender-footed that they dare not mention the principles of the gospel to their pupils, but have no hesitancy in introducing into the classroom the theories of Huxley, of Darwin, or of Miall and the false political economy which contends against co-operation and the

United Order. This course I am resolutely and uncompromisingly opposed to, and I hope to see the day when the doctrines of the gospel will be taught in all our schools, when the revelation of the Lord will be our texts, and our books will be written and manufactured by ourselves and in our own midst. As a beginning in this direction I have endowed the Brigham Young Academy at Provo.[26]

Karl G. Maeser, the young German educator Brigham asked to establish the academy, later renamed Brigham Young University, reported that Brigham's instructions to him were succinct: "I want you to remember that you ought not to teach even the alphabet or the multiplication tables without the Spirit of God. That is all. God bless you."[27]

While Brigham generally favored religious-based education, the fact that several of his sons had left Utah to receive additional education caused him great joy: "Amongst the pleasure of my life at the present time is the thought that so many of my sons are acquiring experimental and practical knowledge that will fit them for lives of great usefulness. And with this thought, I associate the hope that by God's mercy that knowledge will be applied in striving to save the souls of men, and building up the kingdom of heaven on the earth."[28]

In addition to learning, Brigham publicly stated that he desired something else of the Saints: "We are trying to teach this people to use their brains."[29] In this regard, he encouraged the Saints to "cling to all the good that you have learned, and discard the bad."[30] Not surprisingly, in his last public sermon, given four days prior to his death, he addressed the subject of learning and knowledge: "We have a multitude of traditions to overcome, and when this people called Latter-day Saints will be free from these traditions, so that they can take hold of the Gospel and build up the kingdom according to the pattern, I am not able to say. . . . When we get to understand all knowledge, all wisdom, that it is necessary for us to understand in the flesh, we will be like clay in the hands of the potter, willing to be moulded and fashioned according to the will of him who has called us to this great and glorious work."[31]

## 37

# "THE EARTH IS THE LORD'S"

## *Brigham As Steward*

While the Saints were at Winter Quarters in 1847, the Lord through revelation to Brigham reminded them of their responsibility to "be diligent in preserving what thou hast, that thou mayest be a wise steward; for it is the free gift of the Lord thy God, and thou art his steward."[1] Recalling the words of the Psalmist that "the earth is the Lord's, and the fulness thereof," for more than thirty years Brigham served as a faithful steward of God's creations, first along the trail and then later in managing the land, water, and other natural resources of the Great Basin.[2] "Not one particle of all that comprises this vast creation of God is our own," Brigham declared.[3] "How long have we got to live before we find out that we have nothing to consecrate to the Lord—that all belongs to the Father in heaven; that these mountains are His; the valleys, the timber, the water, the soil; in fine, the earth and its fulness," he wondered.[4]

Because of the interdependence of the temporal and the spiritual, Brigham saw the contamination of the world and the misuse of resources as a form of wickedness. Since Jesus was the creator of the world, true disciples

241

of Christ could not treat his creations as things of naught. "The enemy and opposer of Jesus . . . Satan, never owned the earth; he never made a particle of it; his labor is not to create, but to destroy; while, on the other hand, the labor of the Son of God is to create, preserve, purify, build up and exalt all things— the earth and its fulness—to his standard of greatness and perfection; to restore all things to their paradisiacal state and make them glorious. The work of the one is to preserve and sanctify, the work of the other is to waste away, deface and destroy."[5]

By word and deed Brigham regularly directed the Saints' attention to their responsibility to both beautify the earth and to use restraint to preserve the earth as close as possible to its paradisiacal glory. "Keep your valley pure, keep your towns as pure as you possibly can, keep your hearts pure," he urged.[6] "Let there be an hallowed influence go from us over all things over which we have any power; over the soil we cultivate, over the houses we build, and over everything we possess."[7] "You are here commencing anew," Brigham counseled the first settlers of one of Utah's valleys. "The soil, the air, the water are all pure and healthy. Do not suffer them to become polluted with wickedness. Strive to preserve the elements from being contaminated by the filthy, wicked conduct . . . of those who pervert the intelligence God has bestowed upon the human family."[8]

Brigham did not believe that God had given mankind the right to selfishly and wastefully exploit the earth. He taught that God required man to distinguish between need and greed and urged the Saints to think of both their neighbors and future generations. He rejected the glorification of profit at the expense of the earth, spoke against the prevailing wasteful, abusive, and destructive ways of living, and condemned the misuse of natural resources, including the selfish use of limited timber and water resources. He also did not believe that mankind had the right to become God's rival by needlessly destroying His creations. Under Brigham's watchful eye, individual enrichment at the expense of God's creations largely took a back seat to the collective well-being.

As a result of the importance Brigham placed upon protecting the land, timber, and water, Utah grew differently than the surrounding states. In contrast to other areas of the American West, where people "exhausted natural resources" and left a "smoking waste" land, Mormon "cooperation and planning caused the desert" to truly blossom as the rose.⁹ Brigham's emphasis upon a better way to live was markedly different from what European outdoorsman William A. Baillie-Grohmann observed during his travels of the western United States in the early 1880s. While he personally liked the people he met on the American frontier, Baillie-Grohmann was troubled by the common mentality that there was nothing wrong with using-up, wasting, wantonly destroying, or appropriating for one's own use the natural resources. "Nothing on the face of the broad Earth is sacred to him," he wrote. "Nature presents herself as his slave" and man treats the world around him in a "shockingly irreverent manner."¹⁰

Indeed, the prevailing attitude of waste and destroy was well entrenched by 1861 when Mark Twain visited the West. In his celebrated account of his travels, he recounted spending four hours trapped in a canoe on Lake Tahoe as he watched a forest fire that he had accidently started. "It was wonderful to see with what fierce speed the tall sheet of flame traveled!" he wrote. He remained "spell-bound" as the flames spread until "as far as the eye could reach the lofty mountain-fronts were webbed as it were with a tangled network of red lava streams. . . . Every feature of the spectacle was repeated in the glowing mirror of the lake! Both pictures were sublime, both were beautiful."¹¹ After returning to shore, Twain recorded his remorse—not for the destruction he had caused, but for having eaten the camp's food. For Twain, it was just another "escape and blood-curdling adventure."¹²

Brigham's regard for nature also stood in contrast to the prevalent wasteful killing of wildlife. At one time vast herds of bison roamed the West, providing food, clothing, shelter, and bedding to both whites and Indians, but by the 1870s their numbers had been drastically reduced, in large part by the popular desire of certain people to say they had "bagged a buffalo." Elizabeth Custer reported being on a train that encountered a "moving mass of buffaloes." She wrote that there was a "wild rush for the windows, and the reckless discharge of rifles and pistols, put every passenger's life in jeopardy" as her fellow travelers tried to kill as many buffaloes as they could.[13]

In a March 1831 revelation given through the Prophet Joseph, the Lord proclaimed that "the beasts of the field and the fowls of the air, and that which cometh of the earth, is ordained for the use of man for food and for raiment," but He warned, "wo be unto man that sheddeth blood or that wasteth flesh and hath no need."[14] Three years later, during the 1834 march of Zion's Camp, Joseph "exhorted the brethren not to kill a serpent, bird, or an animal of any kind during our journey unless it became necessary in order to preserve ourselves from hunger."[15]

During the journey west, Brigham Young reminded the 1847 vanguard pioneer company of the "Prophet Joseph's instructions not to kill any of the animals or birds, or any thing created by Almighty God that had life, for the [mere] sake of destroying it."[16] Two weeks later, the company encountered "immense droves of buffalo," and men, forgetting what they had been taught, began to indiscriminately shoot them. This time Brigham issued an ultimatum: "There should be no more game killed until such time as it should be needed, for it was a sin to waste life and flesh."[17]

Upon reaching the Salt Lake Valley on July 24, 1847, and seeing the dam that had been built for irrigation purposes, Brigham rejoiced that the Saints had begun to plant crops. He regretted, however, the "destruction of the willows and wild roses growing thickly on the two branches of City Creek" in the process.[18]

From the early days in the valley Brigham stressed that the streams and timber "belong to the people: all the people."[19] He desired that they benefit all, not just a few speculators or individuals thinking only of themselves. Invitations to the annual Twenty-fourth of July celebration in Big Cottonwood Canyon noted that "all persons are forbidden to make or kindle fires at any place in the kanyon, except on the camp ground." At the end of the 1860 celebration a reporter noted that Brigham followed through on his statement that he "personally intended to tarry after everyone was gone" to "see that the fires are all well put out" so there was no possibility of an accidental forest fire.[20]

While the first settlers in the valley erected easy-to-build log cabins, Brigham encouraged subsequent pioneers to build adobe homes that featured lumber rather than whole logs, thus making better use of limited timber. Later, when visiting the first settlers in Cache Valley, he repeated his advice to build "saw-mills, and prepare to build with lumber. They are the cheapest and best houses I can think of, under the circumstances. I do not wish the brethren to cut all the timber to put it into log houses. Erect sawmills and make lumber, which will be far better than building log houses. We have no timber to waste."[21]

When Brigham went to the hot springs north of Salt Lake in October 1861 to bathe, as he frequently did, he found a number of horses standing in the water "depositing excremental matter thus rendering the water unfit for bathing purposes." When Brigham enquired who owned the horses, one man "gruffly demanded who he was." Brigham "coolly replied that his name was *Brigham Young!* This announcement changed the man's tone." Brigham ordered that the springs be cleaned "so that it could henceforth be used as a bath."[22]

The long-term efforts of Brigham as steward can be seen in City Creek Canyon, one of Salt Lake City's natural treasures. Today it continues to serve the purpose Brigham envisioned shortly after reaching the valley. Its beauty in large part is the result of his efforts to keep it as pristine as possible. Shortly after reaching the Salt Lake Valley, he lamented that there were individuals who "lay down their religion at the mouth of the kanyon, saying, 'thou lie there, until I go for my load of wood.'" Wanting to show the "community a plan" by which business matters could be "brought to some kind of a system, to the better accommodation of the public," in 1850 Brigham took the extraordinary step of petitioning the legislature "to grant unto him the exclusive control over the timber, rocks, minerals and water, in the City Creek Kanyon."[23]

He made his request not out of a selfish desire to make the canyon his own but out of concern that self-serving individuals were not being good stewards of this resource. Since it was the primary source of life-sustaining water for Salt Lake City, he made the request in an effort to ensure "that the water may be continued pure unto the inhabitants of Great Salt Lake City."

"When we came here [in 1847] the creek was beautifully shaded and cool," he noted after his request was granted. "We unitedly agreed not to cut down a tree or a shrub." But when he returned to Salt Lake in 1848, "there was a mill built and the water fouled. This creek should abound with trees. . . . I will take care of the Creek if this community will keep out of that kanyon."[24] He even threatened to prosecute those who would not keep out, especially those who wanted to take trees.

In 1853, following the creation of a road, he opened City Creek Canyon for limited use: "Leave all the Fir Trees standing, also all such oak and maple saplings as will do for plow handles, beams, hoop poles and other useful purposes, together with the Cedar whether down or standing. Culling or hauling such without express permission [is prohibited]. With these exceptions, take all the wood, clearing the kanyon of the dead wood and the creek of every combustible likely to injure the water, leaving the small timber and shrubbery on its banks to shade it. Observing these regulations, you are entitled to the privilege of the kanyon."[25]

Nearly twenty years after Brigham briefly appropriated City Creek for the purpose of preserving it, Fitz Hugh Ludlow visited Salt Lake City. Like others, he noted the famous open streams that ran down each Salt Lake street, which were still being fed from City Creek Canyon. He was taken aback, however, by the fact that "the inhabitants of Salt Lake City" drew a "supply of water for all purposes whatsoever" from these streams, including culinary use. "All the earlier association of an Eastern man connect the gutter with ideas of sewerage; and a day or two must pass before he can accustom himself to the sight of his waiter dipping up from the street the pitcher of drinking water for which he has rung, or the pailful which is going into the kitchen to boil his dinner. . . . The novelty of the sensation, however, soon disappears when he pushes his investigations from street to street, and nowhere finds impurity of any kind mingling with the rivulet which runs clear and pellucid before his own door. Dead leaves and sand, the same foreign matters as the wind drifts into any forest spring, are necessarily found in such an open conduit; but no garbage, nothing offensive of any kind, disturbs its purity." Ludlow marveled that "the water seems to take care of itself," unaware that the water supply was actually being watched over by a faithful steward.[26]

## ❧ 38 ❧

# HIS ENDURING
# MONUMENTS

*Brigham As Temple Builder*

Temples and temple work were an important aspect of Brigham's life. While many focus upon the numerous settlements established by the Latter-day Saints as his lasting monuments, he likely would prefer people to instead focus upon temples. Among his first contributions in Kirtland was working on the temple, while his last focus before leaving Nauvoo was again on the temple. Among his first concerns after reaching the Salt Lake Valley was choosing a spot for a temple, and among his last activities was the dedication of the St. George Temple and the dedication of temple sites at Manti and Logan. Concerning temples and temple work, Brigham stated, "Your *endowment* is, to receive all those ordinances in the House of the Lord, which are necessary for you, after you have departed this life, to enable you to walk back to the presence of the Father, passing the angels who stand as sentinels, being enabled to give them the key words, the signs and tokens, pertaining to the Holy Priesthood, and gain your eternal exaltation."[1]

Soon after moving his family to Kirtland in 1833, Brigham's talents as a carpenter and glazier were called upon to help in the construction of the temple. He also helped supervise the painting and finishing work on its upper and lower interior courts and worked closely with Artemus Millett, one of his early converts, on the exterior masonry work. Following the March 1836 dedication of the Kirtland Temple, he was privileged to receive the washing and anointing ordinance there.

Work began on the Nauvoo Temple while Brigham was in England. Following his return, Joseph Smith asked him, as president of the Twelve, to "instruct the building committee in their duty" regarding the temple.[2] Additionally, the Twelve published a letter telling members of the blessings they would receive in the temple and warning them that the Church would be "brought under *condemnation* and *rejected* with her *dead*" if they did not build that House of the Lord.[3]

In May 1842 Joseph began teaching Brigham and other members of the Twelve important principles relating to the temple. While introducing "the ancient order of things for the first time in these last days," Joseph taught that "the Church is not fully organized, in its proper order, and cannot be, until the Temple is completed, where places will be provided for the administration of the [higher] ordinances of the Priesthood."[4] Important sessions of learning and the bestowing of blessings relating to temple ordinances and worship occurred between December 1843 and April 1844.

Following the death of Joseph Smith in June 1844, the completion of the Nauvoo Temple became a priority. Under the direction of Twelve, with Brigham at the head, work on the temple occupied much of the Saints' emotional, spiritual, and physical energies. To fulfill the mandate received from Joseph, Brigham rushed the Nauvoo Temple to the point where washings, anointings, endowments, and marriage sealings could be administered. As persecution of the Saints mounted, the commitment to complete their temple grew, and the pace of work on the temple dramatically increased. While it was important to prepare physically for the trek west, Brigham knew that the spiritual strength that could be had only in the House of the Lord was equally important.

At the October 1845 General Conference held in the temple, Brigham presented it to the Lord in prayer "as a monument to the saints' liberality, fidelity, and faith."[5] The following month the attic story was ready for use and was dedicated. Brigham was not only deeply involved in the construction of the temple, but he also participated in the first baptisms conducted in the temple and was one of the first to receive the holy endowment therein (both of which occurred even before it was completed).

During the tumultuous months of December 1845 and January 1846, Brigham directed the administering of the endowment to nearly six thousand Saints. (During this time a "session" took most of day and only a handful of Saints could receive their endowments at one time.) Brigham reported that "such . . . anxiety manifested by the saints to receive the ordinances [of the temple], and such the anxiety on our part to administer to them, that I have given myself up entirely to the work of the Lord in the Temple night and day, not taking more than four hours sleep, upon an average, per day, and going home but once a week."[6]

On Sunday, February 8, 1846, less than a week before he left Nauvoo, Brigham and others knelt in prayer in the southwest corner of the attic of the temple and asked the Lord's "blessing upon our intended move to the west; also asked him to enable us some day to finish the Temple, and dedicate it to him, and we would leave it in his hands to do as he pleased; and to preserve the building as a monument to Joseph Smith. We asked the Lord to accept the labors of his servants in this land. We then left the Temple."[7] In spite of continued opposition from anti-Mormon mobs, nearly two months after Brigham had left Nauvoo, the temple was dedicated in a private service on April 30, 1846, followed by public dedication services on May 1–3.

On July 28, 1847, four days after Brigham declared Salt Lake the right place, Brigham walked to a spot between the forks of City Creek, tapped his walking stick on the ground, and proclaimed, "Here we will build the Temple of our God."[8]

Construction on the Salt Lake Temple began five-and-a-half years later with a ground-breaking ceremony on February 14, 1853, at which Brigham turned the first shovelful of dirt. In his remarks he noted that if someone should ask "have you ever had a revelation from heaven" concerning the temple, he could respond: "It is before me all the time, not only to-day but it was almost five years ago, when we were on this ground, looking for locations, sending our scouting parties through the country, to the right and to the left, to the north and the south; to the east and the west; before we had any returns from any of them, I knew, just as well as I now know, that this was the ground on which to erect a temple."

Noting that the Saints had not been allowed to fully enjoy the previous temples they had built, he stated:

> Perhaps we may in this place, but if, in the providence of God, we should not, it is all the same. It is for us to do those things which the Lord requires at our hands, and leave the result with Him. It is for us to labor with a cheerful good will; and if we build a temple that . . . requires all our time and means, we should leave it with cheerful hearts, if the Lord in His providence tells us so to do. If the Lord permits our enemies to drive us from it, why we should abandon it with as much cheerfulness of heart as we ever enjoy a blessing. It is no matter to us what the Lord does. . . . It is for His people to obey. We should be as cheerful in building this temple, if we knew beforehand that we should never enter into it when it was finished, as we would though we knew we were to live here a thousand years to enjoy it.[9]

Two months later on April 6, 1853, the twenty-third anniversary of the organization of the Church, the cornerstones were laid. During the ceremony, Brigham recounted an experience he had shortly after reaching the valley: "I scarcely ever say much about revelations, or visions, but suffice it to say, five years ago last July [1847] I was here, and saw in the Spirit the Temple not ten feet from where we have laid the Chief Corner Stone. I have not inquired what kind of a Temple we should build. Why? Because it was represented before me. I have never looked upon that ground, but the vision of it was there. I see it as plainly as if it was in reality before me. Wait until it is done. I will say, however, that it will have six towers."[10]

While he rushed to complete the Nauvoo Temple so that the Saints could use it before they went west, it took nearly forty years to complete the Salt Lake Temple, and it would not be dedicated until more than fifteen years after his death. He proclaimed, "I want to see the Temple built in a manner that it will endure through the Millennium."[11] After a sixteen-foot-deep sandstone foundation was finished, cracks began to appear and Brigham ordered the foundation torn out and replaced with granite.

As the Saints pushed forward on the temple, he reminded them in 1863, "There is not a house on the face of the whole earth that has been reared to God's name, which will in anywise compare with his character, and that he can consistently call his house." He then prophesied that someday "there will be hundreds of [temples] built and dedicated to the Lord."[12]

Joseph had instructed Brigham to "organize and systemize all these [temple] ceremonies."[13] Vividly recalling Joseph's instructions and the fact that he had died before all the ordinances were fully implemented in the Nauvoo Temple, Brigham was anxious that history not repeat itself. In November 1871, Brigham selected a site for a second temple to be built at St. George.

When he was in town, Brigham personally supervised the work. Although his health was poor during the winter of 1874–75, he daily went to the temple site to encourage and instruct the workers. Brigham's involvement prompted George A. Smith to write, President Young "is our only architect."[14] In April 1876 he asked for two hundred workers to go to St. George and push the temple to completion. George Q. Cannon noted of Brigham: "You cannot realize . . . how anxious he is to get this temple completed. He feels he is getting old, and is liable to drop off at any time, and he has keys he wants to give in the Temple."[15]

So anxious was Brigham to resume temple work that, as was the case with the Nauvoo Temple, the St. George Temple was dedicated in stages. On

January 1, 1877, the lower story was completed, and twelve hundred Saints gathered for the dedicatory service. Brigham, suffering from rheumatism, had to be carried into the meeting on a chair. Nevertheless, he stood and spoke for thirty minutes, during which he told the Saints:

> We reared up a Temple in Kirtland, but we had no basement in it, nor a font, nor preparations to give endowments for the living or the dead. . . . We built one in Nauvoo . . . , but the Saints did not enjoy it. Now we have a Temple which will all be finished in a few days, and of which there is enough completed to commence work therein. . . . According to the present feelings of many of our brethren, they would arrogate to themselves this world and all that pertains to it, and cease not day nor night to see that it was devoted to the building up of the kingdom of the devil, and if they had the power they would build a railroad to carry it to hell and establish themselves there. Where are the eyes and the hearts of this people? Where is their interest for their own salvation and that of their fore-fathers? . . . Suppose we were awake to this thing, namely, the salvation of the human family, this house would be crowded . . . from Monday morning until Saturday night. . . . The people are still shaking hands with the servants of the devil, instead of sanctifying themselves and calling upon the Lord and doing the work which he has commanded us and put into our hands to do. When I think upon this subject, I want the tongues of seven thunders to wake up the people. Can the fathers be saved without us? No. Can we be saved without them? No.[16]

Wilford Woodruff recorded that President Young added, "I do not know whether the people are satisfied with the services of the dedication of the Temple or not. I am not half satisfied and I never Expect to be satisfied untill the devil is whiped and driven from off the face of the Earth." Elder Woodruff noted that "in the last remark the President made he struck the pulpit with a hickery Cane filled with knots with such power that he buried three of the knots into the solid wood."[17]

Three months later, the completed temple was dedicated as part of the April 1877 general conference. During the weeks following the final dedicatory service, Brigham traveled to Manti and Logan and selected sites for temples in those communities. Reflecting on what had transpired, a grateful Brigham wrote in May 1877, "Within a period of less than six months, one Temple has been completed and dedicated, and the site for two others consecrated to the Lord our God and the work of construction commenced thereon, whilst another (the one in this City) is being pushed forward with greater zeal and energy than has before been manifested since its commencement."[18]

*Truman O. Angell's Salt Lake Temple architectural drawing, east façade, ca. 1854*

## ❦ 39 ❧

# BRIGHAM'S FINAL ACHIEVEMENT

## *The 1877 Priesthood Reorganization*

E ven though Brigham's final achievement has had a far-reaching impact upon Latter-day Saints today, his efforts have largely been overlooked. Beginning in January 1877 and concluding just three days before his death, he devoted the last eight months of his life to setting the Church in order. "After something had been done towards Temple-building," he noted, "the same Spirit whispered to perfect the organization of the Priesthood."[1] This endeavor to bring priesthood practices into closer harmony with the revelations and the teachings of the Prophet Joseph was the final evidence of Brigham as a lifelong student of his mentor-friend.

According to George Q. Cannon, during the last months of Brigham's life, he was "anxious to get the Priesthood organized and the Stakes everywhere set in order."[2] Early in the process, Brigham informed his son that this priesthood reorganization would allow the Latter-day Saints "to more completely carry out the purposes of Jehovah, to give greater compactness to the labors of the priesthood, to unite the Saints, to care for the scattering sheep of Israel, . . . to be in a position to understand the standing of everyone calling himself a Latter-day Saint, and to consolidate the interests, feelings, and lives of the members of the Church. These are some of the reasons why we are now more fully than heretofore organizing the holy Priesthood after the pattern given us of our Father in heaven."[3]

Brigham's efforts paved the way for an important change of emphasis on the part of Church leaders. After spending most of his presidency emphasizing "the gathering to Zion," the structure and pattern he outlined provided the firm foundation that allowed the Church to grow in as orderly a manner as possible and to spread throughout the world. In some ways, Brigham's last accomplishment served notice that the Church had completed its important and necessary adolescence and was ready to move on. Although there have been minor changes, the basic structure he put in place remains today.

Brigham taught that the priesthood was "a perfect system of laws and government," one that "*rules and reigns in Eternity.*"[4] He further proclaimed: "There is no act of a Latter-day Saint—no duty required—no time given, exclusive and independent of the Priesthood. Everything is subject to it, whether preaching, business, or any other act pertaining to the proper conduct of life."[5] Nevertheless, he noted, while the "the keys of the Priesthood are here . . . [it] has been my deep mortification, one that I have frequently spoke of, to think that a people, having in their possession all the principles, keys, and powers of eternal life, should neglect so great a salvation."[6]

While Brigham desired every member to receive all the promised priesthood blessings, it was clear, as Erastus Snow observed in early 1877, that the revelations on the priesthood had "not been generally observed."[7] John Taylor concluded that "the organizations of the Stakes of Zion on account of their rapid growth have become somewhat loose."[8] Between 1844 and 1877, Church membership grew from twenty thousand to more than one hundred thousand. By 1877 there were more than one hundred far-flung wards while in 1844 there were only about a dozen, mostly at Nauvoo. The number of priesthood holders, which likely numbered less than four thousand when the Saints began their journey to the Great Basin, had more than quadrupled.

During this time the revelations on the priesthood given to Joseph Smith were largely left to private interpretation, and not all priesthood leaders and holders understood and carried out their duties in the same manner. Some stake presidents served without counselors. Some stakes lacked a high council, while others did not have elders quorums. The Aaronic Priesthood was largely ignored as individuals were "advanced at once to the higher or Melchizedek Priesthood" with the result that Melchizedek Priesthood holders doubled as priests, teachers, and deacons. "No stake [Aaronic Priesthood] organization would be complete without them [Melchizedek Priesthood holders]," Franklin D. Richards noted.[9] In the early 1870s, John H. Picknell, a seventy, was a counselor in the Salt Lake Stake's deacons quorum presidency. Around the same time Matthias Cowley stated: "I was an Elder before I was a deacon. . . . If we were all to stay away because we are Elders or Seventies, where would the Teachers and Deacons' quorums be?"[10]

Against this background, Orson Pratt observed as the priesthood reorganization began, "Many things have been left apparently at loose ends . . . but the Lord is about to 'right up' the people; and he has inspired him who presides over us, to organize us more fully."[11] The end result was more "concentrated and localized" wards and stakes, each with a consistent organizational structure and local Church leaders being directed by well-defined principles and practices.

Given Brigham's emphasis upon temples and temple work as a place where heaven and earth meet, it is not surprising that the impetus for the organization had its genesis in the dedication of the St. George Temple. With a temple once again available to better connect earth to heaven, Brigham was inspired to refine earthly priesthood operations to better mirror heavenly ones.

Following the first dedicatory service of the St. George Temple in January 1877, Brigham initiated the first part of the reorganization plan.

He worked "all winter to get up a perfect form of Endowments as far as possible" to paper, which effort was completed in late March.[12]

By the time of the final St. George Temple dedicatory session in April 1877, he was ready to launch the second aspect of the plan—the restructuring and reorganization of stakes and wards. Before leaving St. George, he met with the St. George Stake, the first of twenty such "stake conferences" held during the next five months. During this time, the number of stakes increased from 13 to 20, while the number of wards grew from 101 to 241. In addition to increasing the number of units to better meet the needs of Church members, Brigham more clearly defined the relationship between wards and stakes and perfected their respective organizations. Wards were established as the Church's primary units of governance, with bishops designated as the presiding ecclesiastical officer. Prior to this time, bishops were primarily responsible to see that the poor were taken care of and that tithing was collected while another individual was often appointed to look after the spiritual needs of ward members. The roles of stakes were also clarified to make them meaningful units of administration between the wards and the general level. Stake presidencies were given responsibility to oversee all Church matters in their stakes.

The reorganization effort gave Brigham new life. Shortly after it began he gratefully noted in May 1877: "My own health is excellent. . . . The pain which I have so frequently suffered from my stomach after speaking to large congregations, has troubled me but very little of late."[13] By June things had changed. "In my anxiety to see the House of God set in order . . . I have some what overtaxed my strength," he informed Wilford Woodruff.[14] After several weeks of rest, he again returned to presiding over reorganization meetings, attending the last one on August 19, ten days before his death.

The break from his travels allowed Brigham to implement the third aspect of the reorganization. On July 11, 1877, the First Presidency sent out a lengthy circular letter that has been called the first supplemental "handbook" of Church administration to the Doctrine and Covenants. It covered a wide variety of topics and outlined how wards, stakes, and organizations within these units were supposed to properly function.

The letter taught general principles to be followed in administering the priesthood, contained instructions regarding Church government, and outlined the duties of officers and members. For instance, now every Latter-day Saint would be assigned to a geographical unit, with a priesthood leader to watch over him or her. The circular letter also established definite boundaries for priesthood quorums, which paralleled those of wards and stakes—prior to this time members remained part of a quorum even after moving from where it was headquartered—thus allowing for more regular, accessible meetings of quorum members. Stakes and wards would now compile and submit reports to Church headquarters, and membership was to be transferred when people moved to a new ward.

In many locations where there were multiple wards, such as Salt Lake City, all the Saints in the city had gathered together for Sunday preaching service, just as they had done at Nauvoo. Now, the Saints were to meet together as wards for Sunday preaching services (later called sacrament meeting), as well as other meetings. As a result, local ward buildings and meetings became a prominent feature of the Church.[15]

Brigham also encouraged the practice of ordaining all worthy young men to the Aaronic Priesthood, rather than waiting until they were adults to give them the priesthood. "It would be excellent training for the young men if they had the opportunity of acting in the offices of the lesser priesthood," he counseled.[16]

The final aspect of the priesthood reorganization was the clarification of the role of the Quorum of the Twelve Apostles. Until 1877, some members of the Twelve were given responsibility to oversee missions outside of Utah or to establish and direct settlements far removed from Salt Lake City. At the time of the reorganization, half of the members of the quorum were also serving as stake presidents. Because they were scattered to various locations, the Twelve infrequently met together. It was not until October 6, 1868, more than twenty years after the vanguard company reached the Salt Lake

Valley, that the entire Quorum of the Twelve met together in Utah. Under the reorganization, they were freed from local responsibilities and assumed general authority for the entire Church, not primarily focusing their attention on one location or area.

Brigham anticipated that "much good will result" from this final accomplishment and proclaimed there would be "a radical change, a reformation, in the midst of this people."[17] Individuals reported an immediate impact. One ward leader noted that the priesthood reorganization "had the influence of waking Some up that were way off the line of their duty."[18] The Weber Stake reported in October 1877 that "great good . . . had already resulted from organizing the Lesser Priesthood, the young men responding to the call they received in such a manner as enkindled new life and spirit in the hearts of their parents and older members of the Church generally."[19] Not only did people better understand their duties and responsibilities, but many were also given new opportunities to grow and serve in ward and stake positions.

Following Brigham's death, Church leaders praised his final achievement. Erastus Snow stated that it was "a great joy and comfort to know that he had the privilege of living to complete one temple and to see it dedicated, and that he superintended the setting in order of the priesthood and the ordinances for the redemption of the dead . . . something that he greatly desired to see done before he should pass away."[20] George Q. Cannon proclaimed: "He set the priesthood in order as it had never been since the first organization of the Church upon the earth [anciently]. He defined the duties [of all priesthood holders] . . . with plainness and distinction and power—the power of God—in a way that it is left on record in such unmistakable language that no one need err who has the Spirit of God resting down upon him."[21] John Taylor succinctly noted, "The Church is more perfectly organized than ever before."[22]

## 40

# BRIGHAM EDITORIALIZED AND EULOGIZED

The death of Brigham unleashed a virtual flood of comments about both the man and his accomplishments. Not surprisingly, in death, as in life, the opinions were wide ranging and reveal both the love of the Saints and the hatred of much of the nation toward him, an animosity that he knew only too well while alive.

The negative editorials came from far-flung places, and many were written with remarkable bite (though a few had a kernel of grudging admiration):

*Tuscarora (Nev.) Times:* The death of the pretended [vice-regent] of God will be hailed with genuine delight all over the land. Satan will hold a nine days' jubilee, and summon from the lowest depth of hell the fiends incarnate, to welcome the impostor.[1]

*San Jose Mercury:* A fanatical tyrant, kind to his friends, merciless to his foes, Brigham Young was feared not loved. . . . No man ever left a religious faith with so little foundation for it to rest upon as he.[2]

*Stockton (Cal.) Independent:* The pangs of sorrow felt for the loss of a leader by a people of such coarse moral nature as the Mormons, will find immediate, healthful vent in an hour's blubbering, while the more refined portion of mankind will have no tears of regret to shed over the decease of a man who has expanded the energies of his life in an endeavor to lower the standard of morality.[3]

*Virginia (Nev.) Enterprise:* Had he been guided by a lofty principle, and his aim been guided by a lofty principle, and his aim been to lift up the hearts and the souls of those around him, and to fill the wilderness with happy homes, there would have been sorrow everywhere when he came to die. But, unfortunately, he had not a thought which was not selfish; not a desire which was not unhallowed. . . . To carry out his purposes he not only did not shrink from crime, but organized it as a revelation from Heaven. . . . The death of such a man should cause no regret. Nature gave him a brain capable of securing to its possessor an honorable name anywhere among men; but his heart was as dark from the first as is that night into which he yesterday sank, and if his name is rescued from oblivion it should be but as a warning to generations yet to come.[4]

*Salt Lake Tribune:* His habit of mind was singularly illogical, and his public addresses are the greatest farrago of nonsense that ever was put in print. . . . [He] pretended to be in daily intercourse with the Almighty, and yet he was groveling in his ideas, and the system of religion he formulated was well nigh Satanic. . . . He has succeeded . . . in holding absolute sway over a hundred thousand followers, in directing and controlling their every act, and so dominating their confidence and affections as to stand to them as a very Deity. . . .

We believe that the most graceful act of his life has been his death. . . . It has long been apparent that the defrauded followers of the priesthood have grown restive under the heavy exactions imposed upon them . . . and when disintegration once takes on an active shape, the whole decaying structure will rapidly fall to pieces.[5]

*Sacramento Union:* He was a man of mark, a natural leader of men, and possessing capacities which under better cultivation might have made him an honor to the country that now looks askance upon his bold but lawless career.[6]

*Eureka (Nev.) Republican:* Beyond increasing his family the Prophet has no achievement worthy of note to perpetuate his pseudo greatness. . . . In the course of a few decades his name will either be totally forgotten or remembered only as that of a wicked humbug or an arrant knave.[7]

*Gold Hill (Nev.) News:* Had this man been animated by noble motives; had he directed his talents to some legitimate sphere of action, he might have been remembered today as President of the United States instead of President of the infamous Mormon Church. . . .

. . . There he lies, stricken down by the God whose name he has so often blasphemed. . . . The eighteen wives are rejoicing. They have been freed from the worst kind of slavery, and to them the death of Brigham Young is a godsend. And their feelings correspond with those of the world at large. We all admired the genius of the man, who is now gone; but we all despised the man himself; and now that he is dead, we can only remember him as a man of brilliant talents, who abused those talents, and instead of doing good to his fellowman, left to them a heritage of shame and disgrace.[8]

*Denver Tribune:* This man, though his energies were directed in a strange and a wrong direction, though cruel, grasping tyranizing selfishness, and base sensual passion, were the controlling directing principles of his life, was really one of the most remarkable men of his time.[9]

*Springfield (Ill.) Republican:* The most unique, if not really the most remarkable, career that our country has produced came to an end in Salt Lake City yesterday. . . .

It was a rare combination of qualities that made up the man who could have such a record—Yankee shrewdness, tireless energy, executive powers of the highest type, religious cunning, an iron will, a merciless heart—a combination such as it may well be hoped we shall never see again.[10]

*New York Tribune:* The death of Brigham Young closes the story of a strange career, and opens the last chapter in the history of a peculiar people. The priest and politician, despot and pope, is dead, and all his Latter-day

Saints, all his revelations and ordinances, all his wealth and power, could not save him. . . . Even his dupes will find out some day that their prophet was really nothing, but a cunning, clever old rascal, and no prophet at all, and they will wonder how he could have left them without so much as a parting wink, to show that he had enjoyed the joke.[11]

*Philadelphia Times:* It would strain credulity to its utmost bounds to believe that with all his knowledge of human nature, combined with the average quantity of the learning of books, he had any real faith in the religion that he professed and promulgated.[12]

The positive editorials and eulogies, though fewer in number, provide a distinct contrast with those that were more critical and give more of the measure of the man as the Saints knew him:

*Omaha Herald:* We knew Brigham Young through only a slight personal acquaintance. . . . We were much struck with his frankness and candor. . . . Brigham Young then and there, impressed us with the belief that he was a terribly earnest as well as a sincere man. That belief has not been changed by the clamor of his enemies.[13]

*Deseret News:* We feel the weight of this great loss to the world, and cannot at this moment express in the faintest degree, our deep sense of the void occasioned by his departure. He was a GREAT MAN in every sense of the term. And he has left a mark upon the age which the future will never efface, but which will grow brighter and broader as the man, his deeds and his sentiments became better known and appreciated.

To the Latter-day Saints he has been for more than thirty-three years a counsellor, a father, a friend, a guide, and a tower of strength. To all mankind he has been a prophet and a benefactor so far as they would accept his advice and receive of his teachings. . . .

The marks of his genius are stamped on the history and travels of the Church of Jesus Christ of Latter-day Saints. . . .

His goodness, appreciation of the truth, love for that which is pure and right; detestation of vice and iniquity; desires for the welfare of the Latter-day Saints, spiritual and temporal; regard for the benefit of the whole human race, living and dead; his spirituality, refined taste, earnest faith and devotion of God; and his inspirational, prophetic, and soul-winning qualities are know[n] but to the people who have been gathered from all parts of the earth under his administration, and fully understood and appreciated only by those who were intimately acquainted with him.[14]

*George Q. Cannon:* The time will come when the Latter-day Saints will appreciate him as one of the greatest Prophets that ever lived....

From the greatest details connected with the organization of this Church down to the smallest minutiae connected with the work, he has left upon it the impress of his great mind.... Nothing was too small for his mind; nothing was too large. His mind was of that character that it could grasp the greatest subjects, and yet it had the capacity to descend to the minutest details. This was evident in all his counsels and associations with the Saints; he had that power, that wonderful faculty which God gave him and with which he was inspired.[15]

*Twelve Apostles and Counselors in the First Presidency:* During the thirty-three years that he has presided over the Church, since the martyrdom of the Prophet Joseph, his knees have never trembled, his hands have never shook; he has never faltered or quailed. However threatening the surroundings or prospects may have been, he has never been dismayed; but at those times he has exhibited such serene confidence and faith, and uttered such words of encouragement, as to comfort and sustain all the people, and to call forth their love and admiration. The Lord, however, not only blessed him with valor, but He endowed him with great wisdom. His counsels, when obeyed, have been attended with salvation, and as an organizer and administrator he has no superior....

We have the same consolation, however, in this our time of grief and deep affliction, that the Prophet Brigham had upon hearing of the cruel martyrdom of the Prophets Joseph and Hyrum—"the keys of the kingdom are still right here with the Church."[16]

Four years before his death, Brigham authored what in some ways could be considered his own obituary. Responding to a letter from *New York Herald* publisher James Gordon Bennett, who had written following Brigham's announcement that he would no longer serve as Trustee-in-Trust of the Church, Brigham wrote:

> Thank you for the privilege of representing facts as they are. I will furnish them gladly any time you make the request. For over forty years I have served my people, laboring incessantly, and am now nearly seventy two years of age, and need relaxation. My resignation as Trustee in Trust for the Church, as President of Zion's Co-operative Mercantile Institution, and of the Deseret National Bank are made solely for relief from secular cares and responsibilities and do not affect my position as President of the Church. In that capacity, I shall still exercise supervision over business, ecclesiastical and secular, leaving minutiae to younger men. . . .
>
> It has frequently been published that I had a deposit of several millions pounds sterling in the Bank of England were such the case I would most assuredly use the means to gather our poor Church members from the old countries and bring them here where their condition might be improved. All my means are invested here in developing this Territory in Agriculture Manufactures and Commerce.
>
> The result of my labors for the last twenty six years briefly summed up are the peopling of this Territory by the Latter-Day Saints of about 100,000 souls, the founding of over two hundred cities, towns and villages inhabited by our people, which extend into Idaho on the north, Wyoming on the east, Nevada on the West and Arizona on the south, and the establishment of schools, factories, mills and other institutions calculated to benefit and improve our community. All my transactions and labors have been carried on in accordance with my calling as a servant of God. I know no difference between spiritual and temporal labors. God has seen fit to bless me with means and as a faithful steward I use it to benefit my fellow men, to promote their happiness in this world and in preparing

them for the great hereafter. My whole life is devoted to this service and while I regret that my mission is not better understood by the world, the time will come when I will be understood and I leave to futurity the judgment of my labors and their results as they shall become manifest.[17]

*Brigham Young, ca. 1875*

# NOTES

## Introduction

1.  Brigham Young to Jefferson Davis, September 8, 1855, Brigham Young Office Files. Note: Quotations from sources written by Brigham Young's own hand retain the spelling and punctuation errors of the original. Where such errors are found in sources quoting the spoken words of Brigham, the errors are silently corrected.
2.  John F. Kennedy, Yale University commencement address, June 11, 1962.
3.  Rubin, *Forty Ways to Look at Winston Churchill,* 8.
4.  *Journal of Discourses,* 3:320, April 20, 1856.
5.  Jessee, *Letters of Brigham Young,* xxix.
6.  Jessee, *Letters of Brigham Young,* xxix.
7.  *Journal of Discourses,* 10:271, October 6, 1863.
8.  *Journal of Discourses,* 4:24, August 17, 1856.
9.  Gates and Widtsoe, *Life Story of Brigham Young,* 318.
10. John D. Lee, Diary, July 16, 1848, as published in Cleland and Brooks, *Mormon Chronicle,* 1:59. Spelling standardized.
11. *Journal of Discourses,* 11:290, January 13, 1867.
12. *Journal of Discourses,* 6:75, November 22, 1857.
13. *Journal of Discourses,* 5:229, September 13, 1857.
14. *Journal of Discourses,* 1:108, May 8, 1853.
15. Nibley, *Brother Brigham Challenges the Saints,* 471, 520.

16. Gates and Widtsoe, *Life Story of Brigham Young,* 317–18.
17. Hiram S. Rumsfield to Frank, December 26, 1861, in Hulbert in *Letters of an Overland Mail Agent in Utah,* 33–34.
18. Tullidge, *Life of Brigham Young,* 457–58.

## Chapter 1
### A Life of Quiet Desperation: The Early Years

1. Thoreau, *Walden,* 7.
2. Watson, *Manuscript History of Brigham Young, 1801–1844,* xiv.
3. Arrington, Madsen, and Jones, *Mothers of the Prophets,* 29–30.
4. *Journal of Discourses,* 9:104, January 5, 1860.
5. *Journal of Discourses,* 12:287, October 8, 1868.
6. *Journal of Discourses,* 14:103, August 8, 1869.
7. *Journal of Discourses,* 6:290, August 15, 1852.
8. *Journal of Discourses,* 4:112, October 5, 1856.
9. *Journal of Discourses,* 6:290, August 15, 1852.
10. *Journal of Discourses,* 6:290, August 15, 1852.
11. Watson, *Manuscript History of Brigham Young, 1801–1844,* 1.
12. *Journal of Discourses,* 13:176, May 29, 1870.
13. *Journal of Discourses,* 5:97, August 2, 1857.
14. *Journal of Discourses,* 5:97, August 2, 1857.
15. Gates and Widtsoe, *Life Story of Brigham Young,* 2.
16. *Journal of Discourses,* 6:290, August 15, 1852.
17. Brigham Young "to _____," July 23, 1858, as published in Nibley, *Brigham Young: The Man and His Work,* 343.
18. *Journal of Discourses,* 10:360, November 6, 1864.
19. Brigham Young to George Hickox, February 19, 1876, Brigham Young Office Files.
20. Gates and Widtsoe, *Life Story of Brigham Young,* 5.
21. George Washington Allen, "Brigham Young and Mormonism," as cited in Whitley, *Brigham Young's Homes,* 34.
22. Heber C. Kimball, Journal and Record.
23. Holmes, "The Voiceless," 99.

## Chapter 2
### Religious Seeker and Convert

1. Brigham Young, Journal, April 9, 1832, Brigham Young Office Files.
2. *Journal of Discourses,* 9:219, February 16, 1862.
3. Brigham Young, unpublished discourse, April 7, 1850, Brigham Young Office Files.
4. *Journal of Discourses,* 9:365, August 31, 1862.
5. *Journal of Discourses,* 8:129, July 22, 1860.
6. *Journal of Discourses,* 2:94, February 6, 1853.

7. *Journal of Discourses,* 5:127, August 9, 1857.
8. *Journal of Discourses,* 19:65, July 24, 1877.
9. *Journal of Discourses,* 8:38, April 6, 1860; *Journal of Discourses,* 5:73, July 26, 1857.
10. *Journal of Discourses,* 14:197, June 3, 1871.
11. *Journal of Discourses,* 14:198, June 3, 1871.
12. *Journal of Discourses,* 3:320, April 20, 1856.
13. *Journal of Discourses,* 15:165, October 9, 1872.
14. *Journal of Discourses,* 2:249, April 6, 1855.
15. *Journal of Discourses,* 2:123, April 17, 1853.
16. *Journal of Discourses,* 3:91, August 8, 1852.
17. *Journal of Discourses,* 9:141, July 28, 1861.
18. *Journal of Discourses,* 1:90, June 13, 1852.
19. *Journal of Discourses,* 12:281, October 8, 1868.
20. *Journal of Discourses,* 3:321, April 20, 1856.
21. Brigham Young, unpublished discourse, April 7, 1850, Brigham Young Office Files.

## *Chapter 3*
### To Thunder and Roar Out the Gospel: Brigham As Missionary

1. *Journal of Discourses,* 1:313–14, February 20, 1853.
2. Watson, *Manuscript History of Brigham Young, 1801–1844,* 3.
3. *Journal of Discourses,* 16:69, June 28, 1873.
4. *Journal of Discourses,* 11:295, February 3, 1867.
5. Watson, *Manuscript History of Brigham Young, 1801–1844,* 5.
6. Observation of George D. Watt in reporting the October 12, 1865, Zion's Camp reunion, and comments by Levi Hancock, as included in Arrington, *Brigham Young: American Moses,* 40.
7. *Journal of Discourses,* 2:19, July 24, 1854.
8. Brigham Young, Diary, July 23, 1836, Brigham Young Office Files.
9. D&C 118:4.
10. *History of Brigham Young,* 646.
11. *Journal of Discourses,* 13:211, July 17, 1870.
12. Whitney, *Life of Heber C. Kimball,* 265.
13. Watson, *Manuscript History of Brigham Young, 1801–1844,* 61.
14. *Journal of Discourses,* 4:35, August 31, 1856.
15. *Journal of Discourses,* 13:211, July 17, 1870.
16. Allen, Esplin, and Whittaker, *Men with a Mission,* 71.
17. Madsen, *The Lord Needed a Prophet,* 31.
18. *Millennial Star* 25 (November 7, 1863): 712.
19. *Journal of Discourses,* 13:211–12, July 17, 1870.
20. D&C 4:2.
21. *Millennial Star* 26 (January 2, 1864): 7.

## Chapter 5
### FAITHFUL FRIEND AND DEVOTED DISCIPLE: BRIGHAM AND JOSEPH

1. *Journal of Discourses,* 8:129, July 26, 1860.
2. Brigham Young to Mary Ann Young, October 16, 1840, Luna Young Thatcher Collection.
3. Brigham Young to Joseph Young, August 2, 1877, Brigham Young Office Files.
4. Brigham Young, unpublished discourse, October 8, 1866, General Church Minutes.
5. *Journal of Discourses,* 12:269–70, August 16, 1868.
6. *Deseret News,* June 6, 1877.
7. *Journal of Discourses,* 9:332, August 3, 1862.
8. *Millennial Star* 12 (September 15, 1850): 275.
9. Brigham Young, unpublished discourse, June 22, 1861, General Church Minutes.
10. *Journal of Discourses,* 4:77, November 9, 1866.
11. Brigham Young, unpublished discourse, June 27, 1854, General Church Minutes.
12. *Journal of Discourses,* 8:228, October 21, 1860.
13. *Journal of Discourses,* 4:104, September 28, 1856.
14. *Millennial Star* 25 (July 11, 1863): 439.
15. Brigham Young, unpublished discourse, October 8, 1866, General Church Minutes.
16. *Journal of Discourses,* 5:332, October 7, 1857.
17. *History of the Church,* 1:295–96.
18. Charles Lowell Walker, Diary, May 13, 1876, as published in Larson and Larson, *Diary of Charles Lowell Walker,* 2:422.
19. Brigham Young to David P. Smith, June 1, 1853, Brigham Young Office Files.
20. Leslie, *California: A Pleasure Trip,* 97–98.
21. *Journal of Discourses,* 4:297, March 29, 1857.
22. Watson, *Manuscript History of Brigham Young, 1801–1844,* 16.
23. *History of the Church,* 5:412.
24. *Journal of Discourses,* 4:297, March 29, 1857.
25. *Journal of Discourses,* 1:74, September 11, 1853.
26. *Journal of Discourses,* 4:297, March 29, 1857.
27. *Journal of Discourses,* 12:105, November 3, 1867.
28. *Journal of Discourses,* 12:270, August 16, 1868.
29. *History of the Church,* 7:233.
30. Brigham Young, unpublished discourse, October 8, 1866, General Church Minutes.
31. "Reunion of Zion's Camp Veterans," *Deseret News,* October 19, 1865.
32. *Journal of Discourses,* 10:20, October 6, 1862.
33. Reconstructed from two variant minutes of meeting of February 12, 1848, in General Church Minutes, February 12, 1849, and published in Holzapfel and Shupe, *My Servant Brigham,* 69.
34. *Journal of Discourses,* 3:51, July 13, 1855.
35. Gates and Widtsoe, *Life Story of Brigham Young,* 362.
36. *Deseret News,* August 30, 1877.

## Chapter 6
### THE LION OF THE LORD

1. *Times and Seasons* 5 (January 1, 1845): 761.
2. Watson, *Brigham Young Manuscript History, 1846–1847,* 495.
3. *Journal of Discourses,* 8:8, March 4, 1860.
4. *Journal of Discourses,* 8:43, April 8, 1860.
5. *Journal of Discourses,* 1:313, February 20, 1853.
6. *Journal of Discourses,* 13:211, July 17, 1870.
7. *Journal of Discourses,* 12:255, August 9, 1868.
8. *Journal of Discourses,* 4:21, August 17, 1856.
9. Wilford Woodruff, Journal, December, 1856, 524.
10. *Journal of Discourses,* 6:279, August 29, 1852.
11. *Journal of Discourses,* 18:361, May 6, 1877.
12. Watson, *Brigham Young Manuscript History, 1801–1844,* 17.
13. *Journal of Discourses,* 18:243, June 21, 1874.
14. *Journal of Discourses,* 4:297–98, March 29, 1857.
15. Watson, *Brigham Young Manuscript History, 1801–1844,* 16–17.
16. Watson, *Brigham Young Manuscript History, 1801–1844,* 17.
17. Whitney, *Life of Heber C. Kimball,* 113.
18. D&C 118:4–5.
19. Brigham Young and Willard Richards to First Presidency, September 5, 1840, Joseph Smith Collection.
20. D&C 126:1–3.
21. Brigham Young, Journal, January 18, 1842, Brigham Young Office Files.
22. Brigham Young, unpublished discourse, October 8, 1866, General Church Minutes.
23. *History of the Church,* 7:256.
24. Jones, *Forty Years Among the Indians,* 44.
25. Nibley, *Brigham Young: The Man and His Work,* 166.
26. *Journal of Discourses,* 16:143, August 10, 1873.

## Chapter 7
### FAITH: HIS DOMINANT CHARACTERISTIC

1. Brigham Young to the Brethren Supposed to be on the road to this City from their Missions, May 8, 1858, Brigham Young Office Files.
2. Proverbs 3:5–6.
3. *Journal of Discourses,* 14:118, May 14, 1871.
4. *Journal of Discourses,* 5:229, September 13, 1857.
5. Brigham Young to Orson Hyde, July 28, 1850, as published in *Frontier Guardian,* September 14, 1850.
6. *Journal of Discourses,* 13:318, April 17, 1870.
7. *Journal of Discourses,* 11:295, February 3, 1867.

8. *Journal of Discourses,* 11:295–96, February 3, 1867.
9. *Journal of Discourses,* 4:315, April 6, 1857.
10. *Journal of Discourses,* 11:296, February 3, 1867.
11. *Journal of Discourses,* 7:230, April 7, 1860.
12. Brigham Young, Journal, November 26, 1839.
13. Brigham Young, Journal, May 5, 1841.
14. *Journal of Discourses,* 1:279, February 14, 1853.
15. D&C 136:1, 17–18, 30–31, 37, 42.
16. Watson, *Brigham Young Manuscript History, 1846–1847,* 561.
17. *Journal of Discourses,* 8:288, June 7, 1860.
18. Brigham Young, Sermon, February 4, 1849, as reported in James S. Brown, *Life of a Pioneer,* 121–22.
19. Brigham Young to Orson Spencer, as published in *Millennial Star* 10 (April 15, 1848): 115.
20. *Journal of Discourses,* 1:108; April 8, 1853.
21. Samuel W. Richards, Journal, May 6, 1855.
22. *Journal of Discourses,* 8:151, February 12, 1860.
23. Brigham Young, unpublished discourse, August 16, 1857.
24. Manuscript History of the Church, July 8, 1849.
25. *Journal of Discourses,* 2:184, February 18, 1855.
26. *Journal of Discourses,* 5:76, 78, July 26, 1857.
27. Manuscript History of the Church, September 30, 1857.
28. Manuscript History of the Church, August 15, 1858.
29. General Church Minutes, April 24, 1858.
30. *Journal of Discourses,* 7:281, October 7, 1859.
31. *Journal of Discourses,* 13:94–95, January 2, 1870.
32. *Journal of Discourses,* 13:317, April 17, 1870.
33. *Journal of Discourses,* 18:356, April 6, 1877.
34. Brigham Young to Lorenzo Dow Young, June 15, 1877, as published in Jessee, *Letters of Brigham Young,* 291.
35. Charles Lowell Walker, Diary, June 11, 1876, as published in Larson and Larson, *Diary of Charles Lowell Walker,* 1:427.

## *Chapter 9*
### THE PETERBOROUGH EXPERIENCE: BRIGHAM'S DEFINING MOMENT

1. Watson, *Brigham Young Manuscript History 1801–1844,* 169.
2. Reconstructed minutes of a February 12, 1849, meeting, as published in Holzapfel and Shupe, *My Servant Brigham,* 69, 71.
3. Watson, *Brigham Young Manuscript History, 1801–1844,* 171.
4. *History of the Church,* 7:233.
5. Remarks by President Wilford Woodruff, June 2, 1899, as included in *Collected Discourses,* 1:292.

6. *Times and Seasons* 5 (September 15, 1844): 651.
7. Parley P. Pratt, "Proclamation to the Church of Jesus Christ of Latter-day Saints," *Millennial Star* 5 (March 1845): 151.
8. *Times and Seasons* 5 (September 15, 1844), 651.
9. *Journal of Discourses,* 13:164, December 12, 1869.
10. *Journal of Discourses,* 13:164, December 12, 1869.
11. Parley P. Pratt, "Proclamation to the Church of Jesus Christ of Latter-day Saints," *Millennial Star* 5 (March 1845): 151.
12. Wilford Woodruff, Journal, August 7, 1844, 434.
13. *History of the Church,* 7:229, 230.
14. Watson, *Manuscript History of Brigham Young, 1801–1844,* 172.
15. Brigham Young, Journal, August 8, 1844, Brigham Young Office Files.
16. *History of the Church,* 7:232, 233, 235.
17. Wilford Woodruff, Journal, August 8, 1844, 435.
18. Watson, *Brigham Young Manuscript History, 1801–1844,* 172.
19. Brigham Young to Vilate Young, August 11, 1844, Brigham Young Letters to Vilate Young, August 1844; spelling standardized.
20. *History of the Church,* 7:266, September 1, 1844.
21. *Times and Seasons* 5 (October 15, 1844): 675.

## *Chapter 10*
### BRIGHAM AS LEADER

1. Remy, *A Journey to Great Salt Lake City,* 1:495.
2. Ludlow, *The Heart of a Continent,* 372.
3. *Journal of Discourses,* 16:46, May 18, 1873.
4. *Journal of Discourses,* 14:81, April 9, 1871.
5. *Journal of Discourses,* 5:342, October 18, 1857.
6. *History of the Church,* 7:234.
7. Brigham Young, Sermon, September 23, 1860, as published in Nibley, *Brigham Young: The Man and His Work,* 367.
8. *Journal of Discourses,* 5:73–74, 75, July 26, 1857.
9. Brigham Young, Office Journal, January 29, 1857, Brigham Young Office Files.
10. Nibley, *Brigham Young: The Man and His Work,* 58.
11. Brigham Young to Vilate Young, August 11, 1844, Brigham Young Letters to Vilate Young, August 1844.
12. Brigham Young to Jesse C. Little, February 26, 1847, Brigham Young Office Files.
13. Brigham Young, Journal, August 17, 1845, Brigham Young Office Files.
14. *Journal of Discourses,* 5:353, October 25, 1857.
15. *Journal of Discourses,* 15:36, May 26, 1872.
16. Remy, *A Journey to Great Salt Lake City,* 1:497.
17. *Journal of Discourses,* 7:275, October 6, 1859.
18. Twain, *Roughing It,* 107.

19. *Journal of Discourses,* 18:234, September 17, 1876.
20. *Journal of Discourses,* 5:100, August 2, 1857.
21. *Journal of Discourses,* 14:79, April 9, 1871.
22. *Journal of Discourses,* 4:368, June 28, 1857.
23. *Journal of Discourses,* 17:51, May 3, 1874.
24. *Journal of Discourses,* 13:171, May 29, 1870.
25. *Journal of Discourses,* 14:162, June 4, 1871.
26. *Journal of Discourses,* 13:176–77, May 29, 1870.
27. *Journal of Discourses,* 12:257, August 9, 1868.

## *Chapter 11*
### Brother Brigham

1. *Millennial Star* 22 (November 3, 1860): 701.
2. Marshall, "Salt Lake City and the Valley Settlements," 107.
3. Hyde, *Mormonism: Its Leaders and Designs,* 170.
4. *Journal of Discourses,* 1:33, March 4, 1852.
5. D&C 121:43–44.
6. *Journal of Discourses,* 9:125, February 17, 1861.
7. *Journal of Discourses,* 1:49, April 9, 1852.
8. Holzapfel and Shupe, *Brother Brigham,* 33.
9. *Millennial Star* 5 (December 1844): 100.
10. *Journal of Discourses,* 13:318, April 17, 1870.
11. *Millennial Star* 12 (April 8, 1850): 276.
12. *Journal of Discourses,* 11:130, August 1865.
13. Gates and Widtsoe, *Life Story of Brigham Young,* 212.
14. *Journal of Discourses,* 16:113, June 27, 1873.
15. Thomas Bullock, Journal, June 16, 1847.
16. John D. Lee, Diary, June 15, 1848, as published in Brooks and Cleland, *A Mormon Chronicle,* 1:39.
17. Arrington, *Brigham Young: American Moses,* 309.
18. *Journal of Discourses,* 1:104, May 8, 1853.
19. Kane, *Twelve Mormon Homes,* 5.
20. *Millennial Star* 22 (November 3, 1860): 702.
21. Journal History, September 28, 1846.
22. Brigham Young to the high council at Council Point, September 27, 1846, as included in Journal History, September 28, 1846.
23. Mary Goble Pay, Autobiographical Sketch, 5.
24. Gates and Widtsoe, *The Life Story of Brigham Young,* 212.
25. *Millennial Star* 30 (October 10, 1868): 643.
26. *Millennial Star* 30 (October 10, 1868): 643.
27. *Millennial Star* 15 (February 19, 1853): 113–14.
28. Brigham Young to Horace Eldredge, February 16, 1871, Brigham Young Office Files.

29. Kane, *Twelve Mormon Homes,* 101.

30. Historian's Office, Journal, August 13, 1854.

31. Larson, *Erastus Snow,* 601.

32. Arrington, *Brigham Young: American Moses,* 308.

33. Jones, *Forty Years Among the Indians,* 43–44.

34. Kane, *Twelve Mormon Homes,* 5.

35. General Church Minutes, May 12, 1850.

## *Chapter 12*
### BRIGHAM ON BRIGHAM

1. Hirshson, *The Lion of the Lord,* ix–x.

2. Elizabeth Cumming to Anne Eliza Cumming Smith, July 9, 1858, as published in Mulder and Mortensen, *Among the Mormons,* 312.

3. Twain, *Roughing It,* 136.

4. Remy, *A Journey to Great Salt Lake City,* 1:v.

5. Remy, *A Journey to Great Salt Lake City,* 1:201.

6. *Journal of Discourses,* 1:105, May 8, 1853.

7. *Journal of Discourses,* 3:237, February 24, 1856.

8. *Journal of Discourses,* 13:252, September 25, 1870.

9. *Journal of Discourses,* 5:97, August 2, 1857.

10. *Journal of Discourses,* 19:68, July 19, 1877.

11. *Journal of Discourses,* 10:191, May 31, 1863.

12. *Journal of Discourses,* 13:317, April 17, 1870.

13. *Journal of Discourses,* 9:248, March 23, 1862.

14. *Journal of Discourses,* 14:225, August 27, 1871.

15. *Journal of Discourses,* 1:364, August 1, 1852.

16. *Journal of Discourses,* 6:39, November 15, 1857.

17. *Journal of Discourses,* 9:29, April 7, 1861.

18. *Journal of Discourses,* 5:97, August 2, 1857.

19. James H. Martineau, Journal, January 30, 1856.

20. General Church Minutes, December 5, 1847.

21. *Journal of Discourses,* 1:166, July 31, 1853.

22. *Journal of Discourses,* 12:151, January 12, 1868.

23. *Journal of Discourses,* 7:281, October 7, 1859.

24. *Journal of Discourses,* 3:276, March 23, 1856.

25. *Journal of Discourses,* 8:185, September 23, 1860.

26. *Journal of Discourses,* 8:8–9, March 4, 1860.

27. Brigham Young, Diary, August 19, 1857, as published in Cooley, *Diary of Brigham Young 1857,* 62.

28. *Journal of Discourses,* 11:111, June and July 1865.

29. *Journal of Discourses,* 4:370, June 28, 1857.

30. *Journal of Discourses,* 6:351, October 25, 1857.

31. *Journal of Discourses,* 11:281, December 23, 1866.
32. *Journal of Discourses,* 10:108, March 8, 1863.
33. *Journal of Discourses,* 11:348, April 6, 1867.
34. *Journal of Discourses,* 8:125, July 15, 1860.
35. *Journal of Discourses,* 11:297, February 3, 1867.
36. Nibley, *Brigham Young: The Man and the Work,* 322.
37. *Journal of Discourses,* 18:261, October 8, 1876.
38. *Journal of Discourses,* 1:376, December 16, 1851.
39. *Journal of Discourses,* 1:340, December 5, 1853.
40. *Journal of Discourses,* 7:138, December 18, 1859.
41. Notation of Brigham Young penned to a letter from Miles Anderson, June 27, 1851, Brigham Young Collection.
42. Brigham Young, Office Journal, June 19, 1861, Brigham Young Office Files.
43. General Church Minutes, April 24, 1859.
44. Brigham Young to Hiram McKee, May 3, 1860, Brigham Young Office Files.
45. *Journal of Discourses,* 19:4, April 29, 1877.
46. *Journal of Discourses,* 10:191, May 31, 1863.
47. Brigham Young to Henry G. Sherwood, May 29, 1856, Brigham Young Office Files.
48. *Journal of Discourses,* 3:49, October 6, 1855.
49. General Church Minutes, April 24, 1859.
50. *Journal of Discourses,* 7:228, April 7, 1860.
51. *Journal of Discourses,* 13:177, May 29, 1870.
52. *Journal of Discourses,* 13:139, July 11, 1869.
53. *Journal of Discourses,* 4:20–21, August 17, 1856.
54. *Journal of Discourses,* 8:42, April 8, 1860.
55. *Journal of Discourses,* 19:6–7, April 29, 1877.
56. *Journal of Discourses,* 6:147, December 27, 1857.
57. *Journal of Discourses,* 13:308, November 13, 1870.
58. *Journal of Discourses,* 16:46, May 18, 1873.
59. *Journal of Discourses,* 13:316, April 17, 1870.
60. *Journal of Discourses,* 5:205, October 12, 1856.
61. *Journal of Discourses,* 2:94, February 6, 1853.
62. *Journal of Discourses,* 6:353, July 24, 1859.
63. *Journal of Discourses,* 11:44, January 8, 1865.
64. *Journal of Discourses,* 7:338, October 8, 1859.
65. *Journal of Discourses,* 18:357, April 6, 1877.
66. *Journal of Discourses,* 4:132, December 4, 1856.

# Chapter 13
## BRIGHAM AS AMERICAN MOSES

1. *Journal of Discourses,* 4:41, August 31, 1856.
2. *History of the Church,* 5:85.

3. Brigham Young to Joseph Stratton, Feb. 18, 1847, Brigham Young Office Files.

4. Salt Lake Stake, High Council Record, 1869–1872, 83-84.

5. *Sangamo Journal* (Springfield, Illinois), July 23, 1846.

6. Brigham Young to Joseph Young, March 9, 1846, Brigham Young Office Files.

7. Benjamin Critchlow, Reminicenses, 3.

8. Brigham Young, Vision, February 17, 1847, Brigham Young Office Files.

9. General Church Minutes, March 8, 1847.

10. Willard Richards, Journal, March 3, 1847.

11. Norton Jacob, Journal and Reminiscence, April 16, 1847, as published in Barney, *The Mormon Vanguard Brigade of 1847*, 104.

12. Sylvester H. Earl, Autobiographical Sketch, 5.

13. Madsen, *The Lord Needed a Prophet*, 36.

14. *Deseret News*, June 20, 1869.

15. William Clayton, Journal, April 18, 1847, as published in Smith, *An Intimate Chronicle*, 300.

16. Patty Bartlett Sessions, Diary, April 6, 1846, as published in Smart, *Mormon Midwife*, 41.

17. Bagley, *The Pioneer Camp of the Saints*, 18.

18. *Journal of Discourses*, 12:286–87, October 8, 1868.

19. Wilford Woodruff, Journal, July 24, 1847.

20. *The Utah Pioneers*, 23.

21. Manuscript History of the Church, July 23, 1847.

## Chapter 14
### BRIGHAM HOLDS BACK THE WORLD

1. Norton Jacob, Journal and Reminiscence, July 28, 1847, as published in Barney, *The Mormon Vanguard Brigade of 1847*, 229.

2. *Journal of Discourses*, 9:269, April 6, 1862.

3. *Journal of Discourses*, 1:314, February 20, 1853.

4. Manuscript History of the Church, July 8, 1849.

5. Brigham Young to Morris Young, September 7, 1874, as published in Jessee, *Letters of Brigham Young*, 250.

6. Third General Epistle of the First Presidency, April 12, 1850, as published in *Millennial Star* 12 (August 15, 1850): 244.

7. *Journal of Discourses*, 5:341, October 18, 1857.

8. *Journal of Discourses*, 13:176, May 29, 1870.

9. Brigham Young to Brigham Young Jr., August 30, 1862, as published in Jessee, *Letters of Brigham Young*, 28.

10. Brigham Young, unpublished discourse, May 18, 1855, General Church Minutes.

11. England, *Brother Brigham*, 215.

12. Historian's Office, Journal, May 22, 1868.

13. Derr, Cannon, and Beecher, *Women of Covenant*, 105.

14. *Journal of Discourses*, 13:4, April 7, 1869.
15. *Journal of Discourses*, 15:161, October 9, 1872.
16. *Journal of Discourses*, 15:132, August 18, 1872.
17. *Journal of Discourses*, 14:19, May 6, 1870.
18. *Journal of Discourses*, 13:2, April 7, 1869.
19. Arrington, *Great Basin Kingdom*, 339.
20. *Journal of Discourses*, 18:356, April 6, 1877.
21. Young, *Memoirs of John R. Young*, 226.
22. Leslie, *California: A Pleasure Trip*, 99–100.

## Chapter 15
### CITY PLANNER AND COLONIZER

1. Brigham Young to Thomas Callister, October 31, 1867, Brigham Young Office Files.
2. *Journal of Discourses*, 9:284, February 23, 1862.
3. *History of the Church*, 7:431.
4. *Journal of Discourses*, 8:83, June 12, 1860.
5. *Journal of Discourses*, 15:221, October 9, 1872.
6. *Gleason's Pictorial Drawing-Room Companion* (January 3, 1854), 345.
7. Bowles, *Across the Continent*, 89, 90–91.
8. *Journal of Discourses*, 15:221, October 9, 1872.
9. Roberts, *Comprehensive History of the Church*, 3:269.
10. Brigham Young to Brigham Young Jr., October 18, 1865, as published in Jessee, *Letters of Brigham Young*, 55.
11. Brigham Young to Bro. John Rees and the Other Brethren whose names are on the List, September 6, 1858, Brigham Young Office Files.
12. Brigham Young to Lot Smith, July 29, 1876, Brigham Young Office Files.
13. *Journal of Discourses*, 4:23, August 17, 1856.
14. Brigham Young to Bishops and Brethren in Utah County, August 25, 1861, Brigham Young Office Files.
15. Curtis, "History of the St. George Temple," 9-10.
16. Brigham Young to Edwin Bryant, Edmund Marchant, Thomas Gibbons, and eighteen others, August 18, 1866, Brigham Young Office Files.

## Chapter 16
### BRIGHAM AS (SUCCESSFUL) INNOVATOR: GATHERING THE POOR

1. Manuscript History of the Church, April 28, 1861.
2. Brigham Young to A. Lyman et al., and Saints in the British Isles, August 2, 1860, BY Letterbooks, Brigham Young Office Files.
3. *Journal of Discourses*, 9:294, May 25, 1862.
4. D&C 136:8.

5. An Ordinance Incorporating the Perpetual Emigrating Fund Company, as published in Morgan, *The State of Deseret*, 152.

6. Letter of First Presidency to Orson Hyde, October 16, 1849, as published in the *Millennial Star* 12 (April 15, 1850): 124, 125.

7. Brigham Young to Franklin D. Richards, August 31, 1855, Brigham Young Office Files.

8. *Names of Persons and Sureties Indebted to the Perpetual Emigrating Fund Company*, [1].

9. Sixth General Epistle of the First Presidency, September 22, 1851, as published in *Millennial Star* 14 (January 15, 1852): 23.

10. Thirteenth General Epistle of the First Presidency, October 29, 1855, as published in *Millennial Star* 18 (January 26, 1856): 54.

11. *Deseret News*, October 15, 1856.

12. *Deseret News*, October 10, 1860.

13. Slaughter and Landon, *Trail of Hope*, 135.

14. Manuscript History of the Church, Feb. 28, 1861.

15. Brigham Young to Franklin D. Richards, April 2, 1854, Brigham Young Collection.

16. Fifth General Epistle of the First Presidency, April 7, 1851, as published in *Millennial Star*, 13 (July 15, 1851): 214.

17. *Deseret News*, June 26, 1869.

## *Chapter 17*
### GOVERNOR AND SUPERINTENDENT OF INDIAN AFFAIRS

1. *Governor's Message to the Legislative Assembly*, December 11, 1855; Manuscript History of the Church, January 2, 1853.

2. *Journal of Discourses*, 1:187–88, June 19, 1853.

3. *Journal of Discourses*, 2:183, February 18, 1855.

4. Journal History, November 26, 1849.

5. Report of Messrs. Brandebury, Brocchus, and Harris to the President of the United States, Appendix to the Congressional Globe, 32nd U. S. Congress, 1st Session, House, 87.

6. *Journal of Discourses*, 3:225-26, March 2, 1856.

7. Johnson, "Was Being a Probate Judge in Pioneer Utah a Church Calling?"

8. Brigham Young to John Bernheisel, February 28, 1854, Brigham Young Office Files.

9. *Journal of Discourses*, 1:105, May 8, 1853.

10. *Journal of Discourses*, 1:105, 106, April 8, 1853.

11. Brigham Young to George Maypenny, December 31, 1853, Brigham Young Office Files.

12. Brigham Young to Garland Hurt, February 11, 1857, Brigham Young Office Files.

13. Brigham Young, unpublished discourse, August 16, 1857, General Church Minutes.

14. Brigham Young to George W. Bradley, June 13, 1854, Brigham Young Office Files.

15. Manuscript History of the Church, January 1, 1850.

16. Brigham Young to Alexander Williams, September 23, 1854, Brigham Young Office Files.

17. Broadside Proclamation, September 15, 1857, as published in Hafen and Hafen, *The Utah Expedition*, 63.
18. Brigham Young, unpublished discourse, August 16, 1857, General Church Minutes.
19. *Journal of Discourses*, 11:324, February 10, 1867.
20. Manuscript History of the Church, June 17, 1855.
21. Telegraph of D. B. Huntington, August 30, 1877, as cited in Holzapfel and Shupe, *My Servant Brigham*, 33.

# Chapter 18
## BRIGHAM AS POLYGAMIST

1. Artemus Ward, Programme for lecture on the Mormons, November 13, 1866, as published in Reed, Johnson, McCarthy, and Bergh, *Modern Eloquence*, 4:126.
2. Twain, *Roughing It*, 119.
3. Arrington, *Brigham Young: American Moses*, 326.
4. Richardson, *Beyond the Mississippi*, 355.
5. "Journal Across the Plains; kept by Miss Clara E. Downes," as published in Woods, "Surely This City is Bound to Shine," 342.
6. *Journal of Discourses*, 13:173, May 29, 1870.
7. Recollection of Susa Young Gates as published in Johnson, "Determining and Defining Wife," 58.
8. Acts 3:21; D&C 132:45.
9. *Journal of Discourses*, 3:266, July 14, 1855.
10. "Two Hours with Brigham Young," *Millennial Star* 21 (September 17, 1859): 610.
11. Leslie, *California: A Pleasure Trip*, 102.
12. *Journal of Discourses*, 5:99, August 2, 1857.
13. Bowles, *Across the Continent*, 111.
14. Irving, "The Law of Adoption," 311–12.
15. Jacob 2:30.
16. Seward, *William H. Seward's Travels*, 22.
17. Johnson, "Determining and Defining Wife," 59.
18. "Two Hours with Brigham Young," *Millennial Star* 21 (September 17, 1859): 610.
19. Brigham Young to Arta D. and Lorenzo Dow Young, October 21, 1876, as published in Jessee, *Letters of Brigham Young*, 285.

# Chapter 20
## FAMILY MAN

1. Seward, *William H. Seward's Travels Around the World*, 22.
2. Gates and Widtsoe, *Life Story of Brigham Young*, 340.
3. Gates and Widtsoe, *Life Story of Brigham Young*, 326.
4. Gates and Widtsoe, *Life Story of Brigham Young*, 356.
5. Spencer and Harmer, *Brigham Young at Home*, 16–17.

6. Spencer and Harmer, *Brigham Young at Home*, 35–36.

7. Gates and Widtsoe, *Life Story of Brigham Young*, 321.

8. *Journal of Discourses*, 17:160, August 9, 1874.

9. *Journal of Discourses*, 9:195, February 9, 1862.

10. *Journal of Discourses*, 16:11, April 7, 1873.

11. Spencer and Harmer, *Brigham Young at Home*, 35.

12. "Remarkable Interview with the Salt Lake Prophet," *New York Herald*, May 6, 1877.

13. Gates and Widtsoe, *Life Story of Brigham Young*, 356.

14. As published in Jessee, *Letters of Brigham Young*, xxv–xxvi.

15. As published in Jessee, *Letters of Brigham Young*, xxvi–xxvii.

16. *Journal of Discourses*, 9:39, April 7, 1861.

17. *Journal of Discourses*, 9:307, June 15, 1862.

18. *Journal of Discourses*, 14:193, June 3, 1871.

19. *Journal of Discourses*, 2:94, February 6, 1853.

20. *Journal of Discourses*, 9:196: February 9, 1862.

21. *Journal of Discourses*, 19:69, July 19, 1877.

22. *Journal of Discourses*, 11:117, Summary of Instructions given June and July 1865.

23. *Journal of Discourses*, 9:195-96, February 9, 1862.

24. *Journal of Discourses*, 9:196, February 9, 1862.

25. *Journal of Discourses*, 19:70, July 19, 1877.

26. Gates and Widtsoe, *Life Story of Brigham Young*, 355.

27. *Journal of Discourses*, 9:173, January 26, 1862.

28. *Journal of Discourses*, 2:21, July 24, 1854.

29. Willard Young to Brigham Young, April 14, 1873, as published in Jessee, *Letters of Brigham Young*, 179.

30. Willard Young to Brigham Young, April 14, 1873, as published in Jessee, *Letters of Brigham Young*, 180.

# *Chapter 21*
## BRIGHAM AS ENTREPRENEUR

1. *Journal of Discourses*, 11:294, February 3, 1867.

2. *Journal of Discourses*, 10:210, June 14, 1863.

3. Young, *Memoirs of John R. Young*, 226–27.

4. General Church Minutes, August 22, 1847; *Journal of Discourses*, 3:118, October 8, 1855.

5. *Journal of Discourses*, 15:166, October 9, 1872.

6. *Journal of Discourses*, 1:314, February 20, 1853.

7. *Journal of Discourses*, 4:28, 29, August 17, 1856.

8. *Journal of Discourses*, 14:18, May 6, 1870.

9. *Journal of Discourses*, 2:95, February 6, 1853.

10. Ludlow, *Heart of the Continent*, 318.

11. Bowles, *Our New West*, 215.

12. *Journal of Discourses*, 18:260, October 8, 1876.

13. *Journal of Discourses*, 8:201–2, October 8, 1860.
14. *Journal of Discourses*, 10:193, May 31, 1863.
15. *Journal of Discourses*, 10:25, October 6, 1862.
16. *Journal of Discourses*, 12:259, August 9, 1868.
17. *Deseret Weekly*, April 4, 1896.
18. *Deseret News*, July 20, 1850.
19. *Millennial Star* 12 (May 1, 1850): 141.
20. Arrington, *Great Basin Kingdom*, 162.
21. *Journal of Discourses*, 2:144, December 3, 1854.
22. *Journal of Discourses*, 10:206, June 7, 1863.

## Chapter 22
### BRIGHAM AT PLAY

1. Spencer and Harmer, *Brigham Young at Home*, 169.
2. Gates and Widtsoe, *Life Story of Brigham Young*, 266.
3. D&C 136:28–29.
4. *Journal of Discourses*, 1:29, March 4, 1852.
5. Elizabeth Haven Barlow, Autobiography, in *Our Pioneer Heritage*, 19:319.
6. *Journal of Discourses*, 8:80, June 12, 1860.
7. *Journal of Discourses*, 2:94, February 6, 1853.
8. *Journal of Discourses*, 9:244, March 6, 1862.
9. *Times and Seasons* 5 (March 1, 1844): 459.
10. Watson, *Manuscript History of Brigham Young, 1867–1847*, 520–21.
11. Burton, *City of the Saints*, 253.
12. *Journal of Discourses*, 1:30, 31, March 4, 1852.
13. Madsen, *The Lord Needed a Prophet*, 38.
14. *Journal of Discourses*, 6:148–49, December 27, 1857.
15. Dean Chesley Robison, quoted in "Utah Pioneer Recreation Centers," in *Our Pioneer Heritage*, 8:473.
16. "George Wandle–Musician" in *Our Pioneer Heritage*, 2:492.
17. Emma B. Lindsay, "Christmas When I Was a Girl," in *Our Pioneer Heritage*, 20:186.
18. "Told by Emmeline B. Wells," in *Our Pioneer Heritage*, 14:535.
19. Charlotte Evans Adams as quoted in "Brigham Young–His Wives and Family," in *Our Pioneer Heritage*, 1:447.
20. Spencer and Harmer, *Brigham Young at Home*, 147.
21. *Journal of Discourses*, 6:70, November 22, 1857.
22. *Journal of Discourses*, 9:243, March 6, 1862.
23. *Journal of Discourses*, 9:244, March 6, 1862.
24. Arrington, *Brigham Young: American Moses*, 290.
25. *Journal of Discourses*, 9:245, March 6, 1862.
26. Arrington, *Brigham Young: American Moses*, 293.

## Chapter 23
### Brigham As (Unsuccessful) Innovator: The Deseret Alphabet

1. Remarks of George Q. Cannon at Brigham Young's funeral, as published in *Deseret News*, September 3, 1877.
2. Brigham Young to Mary Ann Young, March 24, 1837, as published in Arrington, *Brigham Young: American Moses*, 58.
3. Brigham Young to Willard Richards, June 17, 1840, as published in Allen, Esplin, and Whittaker, *Men with a Mission*, 387.
4. Burton, *City of the Saints*, 239; Ludlow, *The Heart of the Continent*, 368; Richardson, *Beyond the Mississippi*, 353.
5. *Journal of Discourses*, 14:103, August 8, 1869.
6. *Journal of Discourses*, 5:97, August 2, 1857.
7. *Journal of Discourses*, 18:357, April 6, 1877.
8. *Salt Lake Tribune*, April 9, 1873.
9. *Journal of Discourses*, 6:70, November 22, 1857.
10. *Journal of Discourses*, 14:121, May 21, 1871.
11. Neff, *History of Utah*, 851.
12. *Deseret News*, January 19, 1854.
13. *Deseret News*, January 19, 1854.
14. Brigham Young to Joseph A. Young, August 31, 1854, as published in Jessee, *Letters of Brigham Young*, 8.
15. Bancroft, *History of Utah*, 712.
16. Remy, *A Journey to Great Salt Lake City*, 2:184.
17. D&C 88:118; *Deseret News*, August 19, 1868.
18. Monson, "Deseret Alphabet," 56-57.
19. Brigham Young to Vilate Young, August 11, 1844, Brigham Young Letters to Vilate Young, August 1844.
20. Bishops' Meeting minutes, 1871–1879, July 12, 1877, 616.
21. Bishops' Meeting minutes, 1871–1879, July 26, 1877, 619–20.

## Chapter 24
### A Hard-Spoken New Yorker with a Soft Side

1. *Journal of Discourses*, 5:97, August 2, 1857.
2. *Journal of Discourses*, 12:298–99, April 8, 1868.
3. *Journal of Discourses*, 15:62, June 9, 1872.
4. *Journal of Discourses*, 3:222, March 2, 1856.
5. John M. Bernheisel to Brigham Young, June 14, 1854, Brigham Young Office Files.
6. Wilford Woodruff, Journal, June 15, 1851, 36.
7. *Journal of Discourses*, 13:310, April 17, 1870.
8. General Church Minutes, April 30, 1860.
9. *Journal of Discourses*, 12:111, December 8, 1867.

10. *Journal of Discourses,* 3:49, October 6, 1855.
11. Burton, *City of the Saints,* 239.
12. Frederick S. Dellenbaugh to Charles Kelly, August 16, 1934, Otis Marston Collection.
13. *Journal of Discourses,* 11:281, 282, December 23, 1866.
14. John D. Lee, Diary, February 9, 11, 1849, as published in Cleland and Brooks, *A Mormon Chronicle,* 1:88, 89.
15. *Journal of Discourses,* 1:108, 109, April 8, 1853.
16. *Journal of Discourses,* 1:213, October 9, 1852.
17. *Journal of Discourses,* 3:6, September 16, 1855.
18. Brigham Young to Evan A. Williams, March 7, 1854, Brigham Young Office Files.
19. *Journal of Discourses,* 3:122, October 8, 1855.
20. *Journal of Discourses,* 8:11–12, March 5, 1860.
21. Brigham Young, Diary, July 24, 1857, as published in Cooley, *Diary of Brigham Young 1857,* 49.
22. *Journal of Discourses,* 5:78, July 26, 1857.
23. Watson, *Manuscript History of Brigham Young, 1801–1844,* 162; *Journal of Discourses,* 7:46, March 28, 1858.
24. Brigham Young to Col. A. S. Johnston or Col. E. B. Alexander, November 26, 1857, as published in Hafen and Hafen, *The Utah War,* 166-67.
25. Brigham Young to Thomas L. Kane, March 9, 1858, Brigham Young Office Files.
26. *Journal of Discourses,* 4:24, August 17, 1856.
27. Wilford Woodruff, Journal, September 14, 1856.
28. James H. Martineau, Journal, December 23, 28, 30, 1856.
29. *Journal of Discourses,* 4:219, February 8, 1857.
30. Brigham Young to Isaac Haight, March 5, 1857, Brigham Young Office Files.
31. Brigham Young to Philo Farnsworth, April 4, 1857, Brigham Young Office Files.
32. Isaiah Coombs, Journal, August 15, 1877, Isaiah Coombs Collection.
33. Hartley, *The Priesthood Reorganization of 1877,* 24.

# Chapter 25
## AMERICA'S BOGEYMAN

1. Bishop, *Mormonism Unveiled,* 381.
2. *New York Herald,* May 6, 1877.
3. *Journal of Discourses,* 1:103–4, April 8, 1853.
4. Brigham Young to Joseph A. Young, February 3, 1855, as published in Jessee, *Letters of Brigham Young,* 14.
5. Spencer and Harmer, *Brigham Young at Home,* 164.
6. Bishop, *Mormonism Unveiled,* 381.
7. *Journal of Discourses,* 13:33, April 8, 1869.
8. *Journal of Discourses,* 13:317-18, April 17, 1870.
9. *Journal of Discourses,* 6:46, November 15, 1857.

10. *Journal of Discourses,* 14:121, May 21, 1871.

11. As published in Arrington and Esplin, "Building a Commonwealth," 229.

12. *Journal of Discourses,* 14:95, April 8, 1871.

13. *Journal of Discourses,* 14:94, April 8, 1871.

14. *Journal of Discourses,* 8:11, March 5, 1860.

15. Bishop, *Mormonism Unveiled,* 381.

16. Twain, *Roughing It,* 119.

17. Elizabeth Cumming to Anne Eliza Cumming Smith, September 24, 1858, as published in Mulder and Mortensen, *Among the Mormons,* 315.

18. Brigham Young to the Church in Caldwell County, December 16, 1838, as published in Jessee, *Personal Writings of Joseph Smith,* 420.

19. Statement of Lorenzo Dow Young, as published in Arrington, *Brigham Young: American Moses,* 65.

20. Undated newspaper clipping, ca. 1882, included between pages 144–45 in Seymour B. Young, Diary.

21. *Journal of Discourses,* 5:77, July 26, 1857.

22. "More Outrages," *Los Angeles Star,* December 26, 1857.

23. "The Mormons in the Capacity of Savages," *San Joaquin Republican* (Stockton, Calif.), October 28, 1857.

24. Remy, *A Journey to Great Salt Lake City,* 1:214–15.

25. *Crescent City [California] Oracle,* May 22, 1857.

26. Report of the Committee on Indian Affairs, January 21, 1859, Records of the Committee on Indian Affairs.

27. As cited in the *Nevada Tribune,* March 29, 1877.

28. *Journal of Discourses,* 11:281–82, December 23, 1866.

29. *Journal of Discourses,* 19:63, July 24, 1877.

30. Hoffman Birney to Charles Kelly, ca. 1937, Otis Marston Collection.

31. *Journal of Discourses,* 11:281, December 23, 1866.

32. Brigham Young, Office Journal, January 27, 1857, Brigham Young Office Files.

33. Hiram McKee to Brigham Young, April 4, 1860, Brigham Young Office Files; Brigham Young to Hiram McKee, May 3, 1860, Brigham Young Office Files.

# Chapter 26
## FUN FACTS

1. Brown, *Giant of the Lord,* 133.

2. Holzapfel and Shupe, *My Servant Brigham,* 51.

3. Gates and Widtsoe, *Life Story of Brigham Young,* 333.

4. *Journal of Discourses,* 9:35–36, April 7, 1861.

5. Historian's Office, Journal, April 28, 1862.

6. Andrew Jackson Allen, Reminiscences and Journal, May 10, 1863.

7. Dictated notation of April 12, 1852, on letter of Elizabeth Green to Brigham Young, December 28, 1851, Brigham Young Office Files.

8. Brigham Young to John W. Young, February 7, 1866, and an undated and unidentified newspaper clipping accompanying a letter of John W. Young to Brigham Young, May 6, 1866, as published in Jessee, *Letters of Brigham Young,* 100, 103–4.
9. *Journal of Discourses,* 3:4, September 16, 1855; Brigham Young to William H. Hooper, April 12, 1860, Brigham Young Office Files.
10. *Journal of Discourses,* 13:300, November 13, 1870.
11. *Journal of Discourses,* 14:218–19, July 23, 1871.
12. *Journal of Discourses,* 7:228, April 7, 1860.
13. Brummit, *Brother Van,* 107.
14. *Deseret News,* September 3, 1877.

## Chapter 27
### HIS FINEST HOUR: THE 1856 RESCUE OF THE STRANDED HANDCART AND WAGON COMPANIES

1. Brigham Young to Orson Pratt, October 30, 1856, as published in *Millennial Star* 7 (February 14, 1857): 99.
2. Stenhouse, *Rocky Mountain Saints,* 539.
3. Historian's Office, Journal, October 4, 1856.
4. *Journal of Discourses,* 4:115, October 5, 1856.
5. Historian's Office, Journal, October 4, 1856.
6. Stenhouse, *Rocky Mountain Saints,* 539.
7. Jones, *Forty Years Among the Indians,* 62.
8. *Journal of Discourses,* 4:113, October 5, 1856.
9. *Deseret News,* October 15, 1856.
10. Bartholomew and Arrington, *Rescue of the 1856 Handcart Companies,* 7.
11. Lucy Meserve Smith, Autobiographical Sketch, 15.
12. John Oborn, Autobiography, in *Heart Throbs of the West,* 6:366; and John Chislett's Narrative in Stenhouse, *Rocky Mountain Saints,* 322.
13. George D. Grant to Brigham Young, November 2, 1856, as published in *Deseret News,* November 19, 1856.
14. Paul, "The Handcart Companies of 1856," 13.
15. *Journal of Discourses,* 4:62, November 2, 1857.

## Chapter 28
### HIS GREATEST DISCOURSE: NOVEMBER 30, 1856

1. Brigham Young to Edmund Ellsworth, September 29–30, 1855, LDS Church History Library.
2. *Journal of Discourses,* 4:65, November 2, 1856.
3. *Journal of Discourses,* 4:66, 67, 69, November 2, 1856, 481.
4. Wilford Woodruff, Journal, October 26, 1856, 481.
5. Wilford Woodruff, Journal, October 26, 1856, 481.

6. *Journal of Discourses*, 4:67, November 2, 1856.

7. *Journal of Discourses*, 17:114, June 26, 1874.

8. Brigham Young, Sermon, November 30, 1856, as published in *Deseret News*, December 10, 1856.

## *Chapter 29*
### THE DARK CLOUD: THE MOUNTAIN MEADOWS MASSACRE

1. Mrs. C. V. Wait, *The Mormon Prophet*, as cited in Twain, *Roughing It*, 576.

2. *New York Herald*, March 22, 1877.

3. *Virginia* [Nevada] *Enterprise*, February 16, 1877, as published in *Salt Lake Tribune*, February 21, 1877.

4. Brigham Young to William K. Belknap, May 21, 1872, Brigham Young Office Files.

5. *New York Herald*, May 7, 1877.

6. *New York Herald*, May 6, 1877.

7. *Deseret News*, March 24, 1877.

8. *Journal of Discourses*, 5:353, October 25, 1857.

9. *Journal of Discourses*, 1:266, August 14, 1853.

10. *Journal of Discourses*, 11:19, December 11, 1864.

11. D&C 64:9, 11.

12. *Journal of Discourses*, 8:33, August 5, 1860.

13. Watson, *Manuscript History of Brigham Young, 1846–1847*, 529.

14. *Journal of Discourses*, 1:32–33, March 4, 1852.

15. *Journal of Discourses*, 12:287, October 8, 1868.

16. *Journal of Discourses*, 10:316, July 17, 1864.

17. *Journal of Discourses*, 2:20, July 24, 1854.

18. *Journal of Discourses*, 4:42, August 31, 1856.

19. *Journal of Discourses*, 1:359, August 1, 1852.

20. *Journal of Discourses*, 14:97, April 8, 1871.

21. *Journal of Discourses*, 1:146, July 24, 1852.

22. D&C 136:38–39.

23. *Journal of Discourses*, 2:317, July 8, 1855.

24. Manuscript History of the Church, July 8, 1849.

25. *Journal of Discourses*, 2:32, April 6, 1853.

26. *Journal of Discourses*, 13:95, January 2, 1870.

27. Journal History, June 25, 1857.

28. Brigham Young to Silas Smith and the Brethren on the Sandwich Islands, July 4, 1857, Brigham Young Office Files.

29. *Journal of Discourses*, 1:105, May 8, 1853.

30. D&C 136:30.

31. *Journal of Discourses*, 5:168, 170, 171, August 30, 1857.

32. James H. Martineau, Journal, December 30, 1856.

33. *Journal of Discourses*, 1:198, April 6, 1852.

34. Brigham Young to Isaac C. Haight, September 10, 1857, Brigham Young Office Files.

35. *Journal of Discourses,* 8:66, June 3, 1862.

36. *Journal of Discourses,* 4:32, August 17, 1856.

37. Brigham Young to George Q. Cannon, January 7, 1857, Brigham Young Office Files.

38. *Ogden Junction,* March 26, 1877.

39. William W. Bishop to William Nelson, December 20, 1876, John D. Lee Collection; William W. Bishop to John D. Lee, February 23, 1877, John D. Lee Collection.

# Chapter 30
## TRUST AND LOYALTY: TWO STRENGTHS AND A WEAKNESS

1. *Journal of Discourses,* 1:33, March 4, 1852.

2. *Times and Seasons* 3 (May 2, 1842): 776.

3. Historian's Office, Journal, October 4, 1856.

4. Jones, *Forty Years Among the Indians,* 286.

5. Jones, *Forty Years Among the Indians,* 288, 289.

6. D&C 121:41, 44.

7. *Journal of Discourses,* 9:334, August 3, 1862.

8. *Journal of Discourses,* 8:37, April 6, 1860.

9. *Journal of Discourses,* 19:7–8, April 29, 1877.

10. *Journal of Discourses,* 13:91, January 2, 1870.

11. *Millennial Star* 27 (October 21, 1865): 659.

12. *Journal of Discourses,* 14:204, August 13, 1871.

13. Gates and Widtsoe, *Life Story of Brigham Young,* 318.

14. Joseph Smith to Emma Smith, April 4, 1839, as published in Jessee, *Personal Writings of Joseph Smith,* 465.

15. *Teachings of the Prophet Joseph Smith,* 30.

16. Twain, *Roughing It,* 573.

17. *History of the Church,* 7:242.

18. Journal History, June 25, 1857.

19. Jessee, *Papers of Joseph Smith,* 2:147.

20. Wilford Woodruff, Journal, October 19, 1856.

21. Alexander, *Brigham Young and the Investigation of the Mountain Meadows Massacre,* 26.

22. *New York Herald,* March 24, 1876.

23. *Deseret News,* October 26, 1876.

24. *Journal of Discourses,* 3:120, October 8, 1855.

25. "Testimony of James Holt Haslam," December 4, 1884, as published in Penrose, *The Mountain Meadows Massacre,* 102.

## Chapter 31
### BRIGHAM WELCOMES THE WORLD

1.  Richardson, *Beyond the Mississippi*, 364, 365.
2.  *The Galaxy* 2 (1866): 381, as cited in Arrington, *Great Basin Kingdom*, 255.
3.  Whitney, *History of Utah*, 2:240–41.
4.  *Journal of Discourses*, 12:54, May 26, 1867.
5.  Bowles, *Our New West*, 260.
6.  Brigham Young to John W. Young, February 5, 1867, as included in Jessee, *Letters of Brigham Young*, 105–6.
7.  Arrington, *Great Basin Kingdom*, 200.
8.  *Journal of Discourses*, 10:111, March 8, 1863.
9.  As quoted in Nibley, *Brigham Young: The Man and His Work*, 429.
10. *Journal of Discourses*, 4:32; August 17, 1856.
11. *Journal of Discourses*, 8:288, June 7, 1860.
12. Twain, *Roughing It*, 574.
13. Warren Hussey to Rev. Daniel S. Tuttle, March 13, 1867, as cited in Mulder and Mortensen, *Among the Mormons*, 370–71.
14. *Journal of Discourses*, 14:97, April 9, 1871.
15. *Journal of Discourses*, 15:121, August 11, 1872.
16. *Journal of Discourses*, 14:197, June 3, 1871.
17. Brigham Young to Willard Young, July 25, 1871, as published in Jessee, *Letters of Brigham Young*, 171.
18. *Journal of Discourses*, 11:280, December 23, 1866.

## Chapter 32
### FAMOUS OF HIS TIME

1.  *Frank Leslie's Illustrated Newspaper* 44 (June 30, 1877): 282, as published in Holzapfel and Shupe, *My Servant Brigham*, 15.
2.  Twain, *Roughing It*, 108.
3.  Carter, "Journal Record of Photographs Taken."
4.  Remy and Brenchley, *A Journey to Great Salt Lake City*, 1:499.
5.  Carter, "Journal Record of Photographs Taken."
6.  Brigham Young to Wilford Woodruff, June 12, 1877, Brigham Young Office Files.
7.  Remy, *A Journey to Great Salt Lake City*, 1:200, 202–3, 204.
8.  Burton, *The City of the Saints*, 237–38, 239.
9.  Burton, *The City of the Saints*, 245.
10. Boorstin, *The Image: A Guide to Pseudo Events in America*, 15.
11. "Two Hours with Brigham Young," *Millennial Star* 21 (September 17, 1859): 610–11.
12. Twain, *Roughing It*, 112–13.
13. "An After-clap of Puritanism," as published in Mulder and Mortensen, *Among the Mormons*, 382–84.

14. Murphy, *Rambles in North-Western America*, 242–43.

15. Leslie, *California: A Pleasure Trip*, 96, 97, 102.

16. Leslie, *California: A Pleasure Trip*, 103.

# Chapter 33
## BRIGHAM AS SEEN BY OTHERS

1. Stansbury, *Exploration and Survey of the Valley of the Great Salt Lake of Utah*, 133–34.

2. Hafen and Hafen, *Journals of Forty-Niners: Salt Lake to Los Angeles*, 276n.

3. Remy, *Journey to Great Salt Lake City*, 1:201.

4. "Journal Across the Plains: kept by Miss Clara E. Downes," as cited in Woods, "Surely This City is Bound to Shine," 341.

5. Burton, *City of the Saints*, 263–64.

6. Twain, *Roughing It*, 112.

7. William H. Knight, Reminiscence, as published in Walker, "Raining Pitchforks," 6.

8. Bowles, *Across the Continent*, 86–87.

9. Richardson, *Beyond the Mississippi*, 352–53.

10. Ludlow, *Heart of the Continent*, 366–67.

11. Nibley, *Brigham Young: The Man and His Work*, 468–69.

12. Kane, *Twelve Mormon Homes*, 5.

13. Sketch by S. A. Kenner in *History of the Bench and Bar of Utah*, 12; *New York Herald*, October 12, 1868, as published in Walker, "Raining Pitchforks," 5.

14. Burton, *City of the Saints*, 261.

15. William H. Knight, Reminiscence, as published in Walker, "Raining Pitchforks," 6.

16. Burton, *City of the Saints*, 288.

17. Hill, "A Sunday in Great Salt Lake City," 132.

18. Tuttle, *Reminiscences of a Missionary Bishop*, 345.

19. "Journal Across the Plains: kept by Miss Clara E. Downes," as cited in Woods, "Surely This City is Bound to Shine," 341.

20. Bowles, *Across the Continent*, 119–20.

21. Ludlow, *Heart of the Continent*, 372.

22. Remy, *A Journey to Great Salt Lake City*, 1:498, 499.

23. Munro, "Among the Mormons in the Days of Brigham Young," 219.

24. Remy, *A Journey to Great Salt Lake City*, 1:497.

25. Burton, *City of the Saints*, 245.

26. Burton, *City of the Saints*, 239.

27. Chandless, *A Visit to Salt Lake City*, 189.

28. Ludlow, *Heart of the Continent*, 368.

29. Richardson, *Beyond the Mississippi*, 353.

30. Langley, *To Utah with the Dragoons*, 107–8.

## Chapter 34
### BRIGHAM AS RENAISSANCE MAN

1. Susan Young Gates, "Brigham Young, Patriot, Pioneer, Prophet," as included in Arrington, *Brigham Young: American Moses,* 244.
2. Werner, *Brigham Young,* 454–55.
3. *Journal of Discourses,* 1:111, May 8, 1853.
4. *Millennial Star* 25 (December 12, 1863): 791.
5. Historian's Office, Journal, September 30, 1858, and March 24, 1859.
6. Brigham Young to B. Morris Young, October 6, 1874, as published in Jessee, *Letters of Brigham Young,* 251.
7. Historians Office Journal, June 14, 1861.
8. *Journal of Discourses,* 14:88–89, April 9, 1871.
9. Bowles, *Across the Continent,* 91.
10. Ludlow, *The Heart of the Continent,* 372.
11. Ludlow, *The Heart of the Continent,* 372–73.
12. Burton, *City of the Saints,* 239–40, 245.
13. Arrington, *Brigham Young: American Moses,* 324.
14. Historian's Office, Journal, February 17, 1855.
15. Brigham Young, Office Journal, February 16, 1857, Brigham Young Office Files.
16. *Journal of Discourses,* 2:284, May 27, 1855.
17. Spencer and Harmer, *Brigham Young at Home,* 23–24.
18. Ludlow, *The Heart of the Continent,* 370–71.
19. Spencer and Harmer, *Brigham Young at Home,* 167–68.
20. Arrington, *Brigham Young: American Moses,* 157–58.
21. Wilford Woodruff, Journal, March 15, 1856.
22. Anderson, "St. George Tabernacle," 27.

## Chapter 35
### THE WISDOM OF BRIGHAM YOUNG

1. *Journal of Discourses,* 13:91, January 2, 1870.
2. Brigham Young to Brigham Young Jr., January 22, 1866, as published in Jessee, *Letters of Brigham Young,* 63.
3. *Journal of Discourses,* 13:93–94, January 2, 1870.
4. As quoted in Nibley, *Brigham Young: The Man and His Work,* 366.
5. Brigham Young to Brigham Heber Young, September 30, 1867, as published in Jessee, *Letters of Brigham Young,* 130.
6. Brigham Young to B. Morris Young, September 7, 1874, as published in Jessee, *Letters of Brigham Young,* 249.
7. Brigham Young to Feramorz L. Young, February 15, 1876, as published in Jessee, *Letters of Brigham Young,* 308–9.

8. Brigham Young to Feramorz L. Young, November 24, 1875, as published in Jessee, *Letters of Brigham Young,* 305–6.

9. Brigham Young to Willard Young, November 11, 1875, as published in Jessee, *Letters of Brigham Young,* 191.

10. *Journal of Discourses,* 9:305, June 15, 1862.

11. *Journal of Discourses,* 10:251, October 6, 1853.

12. *Journal of Discourses,* 5:52, July 19, 1857.

13. *Journal of Discourses,* 5:54, July 19, 1857.

14. *Journal of Discourses,* 16:114, June 27, 1873.

15. John D. Lee, Diary, July 16, 1848, as published in Cleland and Brooks, *A Mormon Chronicle,* 1:59. Spelling standardized.

16. Brigham Young to Willard Young, February 17, 1876, as published in Jessee, *Letters of Brigham Young,* 193.

17. *Journal of Discourses,* 7:133–34, December 18, 1859.

18. *Journal of Discourses,* 14:161, June 4, 1871.

19. Circular letter, July 11, 1877, as published in Clark, *Messages of First Presidency,* 2:291–92.

20. *Journal of Discourses,* 15:37, May 26, 1872.

21. As quoted in Nibley, *Brigham Young: The Man and His Work,* 379.

22. Brigham Young to Daniel H. Wells and Brigham Young Jr., December 8, 1864, as published in Jessee, *Letters of Brigham Young,* 48–49.

23. Brigham Young to B. Morris Young, October 23, 1873, as published in Jessee, *Letters of Brigham Young,* 246.

24. Brigham Young to Joseph Don Carlos and Feramorz Little Young, July 16, 1877, as published in Jessee, *Letters of Brigham Young,* 278.

25. *Journal of Discourses,* 13:155, November 14, 1869.

26. *Journal of Discourses,* 11:252, June 17, 1866.

27. *Millennial Star* 16 (May 27, 1854): 327.

28. *Journal of Discourses,* 9:282, February 23, 1862.

29. *Journal of Discourses,* 15:136, August 24, 1872.

30. Brigham Young to Philip B. Lewis, B. F. Johnson and the Brethren on the Sandwich Islands Mission, January 30, 1855, Brigham Young Office Files.

# *Chapter 36*
## "The Object of This Existence": Brigham on Education

1. *Journal of Discourses,* 9:167, January 26, 1862.

2. *Journal of Discourses,* 8:160, September 2, 1860.

3. *Journal of Discourses,* 2:94, February 6, 1853.

4. *Journal of Discourses,* 13:310, April 17, 1870.

5. D&C 130:18–19.

6. *Teachings of the Prophet Joseph Smith,* 137.

7. *Journal of Discourses,* 5:97, August 2, 1857.

8. Watson, *Manuscript History of Brigham Young, 1801–1844,* 62.

9. *Journal of Discourses,* 1:39, July 11, 1852.

10. *Journal of Discourses,* 9:149, January 12, 1862; *Journal of Discourses,* 11:213, April 29, 1866.

11. *Journal of Discourses,* 13:147, July 11, 1869.

12. *Journal of Discourses,* 17:52, May 3, 1874.

13. *Journal of Discourses,* 14:116, May, 14, 1871.

14. *Journal of Discourses,* 10:224, instruction given April and May 1863.

15. *Journal of Discourses,* 10:224, instruction given April and May 1863; *Journal of Discourses,* 1:39, July 11, 1852.

16. *Journal of Discourses,* 2:93–94, February 6, 1853.

17. *Journal of Discourses,* 9:173, January 26, 1862.

18. Brigham Young to Feramorz Young, August 23, 1877, as published in Jessee, *Letters of Brigham Young,* 313–14.

19. *Journal of Discourses,* 8:135, July 29, 1860.

20. *Journal of Discourses,* 12:326, January 10, 1869.

21. *Journal of Discourses,* 14:210, August 13, 1871.

22. *Journal of Discourses,* 13:260, October 6, 1870.

23. *Journal of Discourses,* 12:172, March 29, 1868.

24. Chamberlain, *The University of Utah,* 5.

25. *Journal of Discourses,* 10:266, 267, October 6, 1863.

26. Brigham Young to Willard Young, October 19, 1876, as published in Jessee, *Letters of Brigham Young,* 199.

27. Maeser, *Karl G. Maeser: A Biography,* 79.

28. Brigham Young to Willard Young, November 11, 1875, as published in Jessee, *Letters of Brigham Young,* 191.

29. *Journal of Discourses,* 11:328, February 10, 1867.

30. *Journal of Discourses,* 3:204, February 17, 1856.

31. *Journal of Discourses,* 19:93, August 19, 1877.

## *Chapter 37*
### "The Earth Is the Lord's": Brigham As Steward

1. D&C 136:27.

2. Psalm 24:1.

3. *Journal of Discourses,* 8:67, June 3, 1860.

4. *Journal of Discourses,* 2:308, 1855.

5. *Journal of Discourses,* 10:320, July 3, 1864.

6. *Journal of Discourses,* 8:80, June 10, 1860.

7. *Journal of Discourses,* 9:284, February 23, 1862.

8. *Journal of Discourses,* 8:79, June 10, 1860.

9. Lasch, *The World of Nations,* 67.

10. Baillie-Grohmann, *Camps In the Rockies,* 21.

11. Twain, *Roughing It,* 176.

12. Twain, *Roughing It,* 177.
13. Ward, *The West: An Illustrated History,* 261.
14. D&C 49:19, 21.
15. *History of the Church,* 2:71–72.
16. Thomas Bullock, Journal, April 25, 1847.
17. Appleton M. Harmon, Journal, May 7, 1847, as published in Arrington, *American Moses,* 137.
18. Bancroft, *History of Utah,* 262.
19. Anderson, *Desert Saints,* 68.
20. *Millennial Star* 22 (November 3, 1860): 702.
21. *Journal of Discourses,* 8:79, June 12, 1860.
22. Historians Office Journal, October 17, 1861, 97–98.
23. Morgan, *State of Deseret,* 160.
24. General Church Minutes, April 13, 1851; spelling standardized.
25. "Regulations of City Creek Kanyon," 1853, Brigham Young, letterpress copybook, 1:237, Brigham Young Office Files.
26. Ludlow, *Heart of the Continent,* 328–29.

## *Chapter 38*
### His Enduring Monuments: Brigham As Temple Builder

1. *Journal of Discourses,* 2:31, April 6, 1853.
2. *History of the Church,* 4:470.
3. *Times and Seasons* 3 (December 15, 1841): 626.
4. Watson, *Manuscript History of Brigham Young, 1801–1844,* 116; *History of the Church,* 4:603.
5. *Times and Seasons* 6 (November 1, 1845): 1017–18.
6. *History of the Church,* 7:567.
7. *History of the Church,* 7:580.
8. Gates and Widtsoe, *Life Story of Brigham Young,* 104.
9. *Journal of Discourses,* 1:277, February 14, 1853.
10. *Journal of Discourses,* 1:133, April 6, 1853.
11. *Journal of Discourses,* 10:254, October 6, 1863.
12. *Journal of Discourses,* 10:252, 254, October 6, 1863.
13. L. John Nuttall, Diary, February 7, 1877, as cited in Holzapfel and Shupe, *My Servant Brigham,* 64.
14. George A. Smith to John Henry Smith, January 3, 1875, as cited in Nibley, *Brigham Young: The Man and His Work,* 512.
15. "Journal and Diary of Robert Gardner," in *Heart Throbs of the West,* 10:321.
16. *Journal of Discourses,* 18:303–4, January 1, 1877.
17. Wilford Woodruff, Journal, January 1, 1877, 319–20.
18. Brigham Young to Ward E. Pack, May 23, 1877, Brigham Young Office Files.

## Chapter 39
### Brigham's Final Achievement:
### The 1877 Priesthood Reorganization

1. Salt Lake Stake, Historical Record, August 11, 1877, 46.
2. *Deseret News,* September 3, 1877.
3. Brigham Young to Willard Young, May 23, 1877, as published in Jessee, *Letters of Brigham Young,* 205.
4. *Journal of Discourses,* 14:95, April 8, 1871; Collier, *The Teachings of President Brigham Young,* 3:230.
5. *Journal of Discourses,* 7:66, June 6, 1858.
6. *Journal of Discourses,* 4:299, March 29, 1857.
7. *Journal of Discourses,* 19:130, October 13, 1877.
8. Utah Stake, Historical Record, June 2, 1877.
9. Hartley, "The Priesthood Reorganization of 1877," 8.
10. Hartley, "Brigham Young and Priesthood Work," in Black and Porter, *Lion of the Lord,* 340.
11. *Journal of Discourses,* 19:11, 12, May 20, 1877.
12. Wilford Woodruff, Journal, March 21, 1877, 340.
13. Brigham Young to William C. Staines, May 11, 1877, Brigham Young Office Files.
14. Brigham Young to Wilford Woodruff, June 12, 1877, Brigham Young Office Files.
15. Hartley, "Common People: Church Activity During the Brigham Young Era," 250–70.
16. Circular of the First Presidency, July 11, 1877, as included in Clark, *Messages of the First Presidency* 2:283–95. The reference to ordaining youth to the Aaronic Priesthood is found on page 287.
17. Brigham Young to W. E. Pack, August 6, 1877, Brigham Young Office Files; *Journal of Discourses* 19:43, June 17, 1877.
18. Benjamin H. Tolman, Journal, December 1877.
19. *Deseret News Weekly,* October 24, 1877.
20. Roberts, *Comprehensive History,* 5:516–17.
21. Roberts, *Comprehensive History,* 5:508.
22. *Journal of Discourses,* 19:146, October 21, 1877.

## Chapter 40
### Brigham Editorialized and Eulogized

1. As published in *Salt Lake Tribune,* September 4, 1877.
2. As published in *Salt Lake Tribune,* September 4, 1877.
3. As published in *Salt Lake Tribune,* September 4, 1877.
4. As published in *Salt Lake Tribune,* September 4, 1877.
5. *Salt Lake Tribune,* August 30, 1877.
6. As published in *Salt Lake Tribune,* September 4, 1877.

7. As published in *Salt Lake Tribune,* September 4, 1877.
8. As published in *Salt Lake Tribune,* September 4 and 5, 1877.
9. As published in *Salt Lake Tribune,* September 2, 1877.
10. As published in *Salt Lake Tribune,* September 6, 1877.
11. As published in *Salt Lake Tribune,* September 7, 1877.
12. As published in *Salt Lake Tribune,* September 6, 1877.
13. As published in *Salt Lake Tribune,* September 4, 1877.
14. *Deseret News,* August 29 and 30, 1877.
15. *Deseret News,* September 3, 1877.
16. *Millennial Star* 39 (October 15, 1877): 680–81.
17. Brigham Young to James Gordon Bennett, April 10, 1873, Brigham Young Office Files.

# SELECTED BIBLIOGRAPHY

BOOKS AND MONOGRAPHS

Alexander, Thomas G. *Brigham Young, the Quorum of the Twelve, and the Latter-day Saint Investigation of the Mountain Meadows Massacre.* Leonard J. Arrington Mormon History Lecture Series No. 12. Logan, Utah: Utah State University Press, 2007.

Allen, James B. *The Man—Brigham Young.* Provo, Utah: Brigham Young University Press, 1968.

Allen, James B., and Glen M. Leonard. *The Story of the Latter-day Saints.* 2d ed., revised and enlarged. Salt Lake City: Deseret Book, 1992.

Allen, James B., Ronald K. Esplin, and David J. Whittaker. *Men with a Mission, The Quorum of the Twelve Apostles in the British Mission, 1837–1841.* Salt Lake City: Deseret Book, 1992.

Anderson, Nels. *Desert Saints: The Mormon Frontier in Utah.* Chicago and London: The University of Chicago Press, 1996.

Arrington, Leonard J. *Brigham Young: American Moses.* New York: Alfred A. Knopf, 1985.

———. *Great Basin Kingdom: An Economic History of the Latter-day Saints, 1830–1900.* Cambridge, Mass.: Harvard University Press, 1958.

Arrington, Leonard J., ed. *The Presidents of the Church.* Salt Lake City: Deseret Book, 1986.

Arrington, Leonard J., Susan Arrington Madsen, and Emily Madsen Jones. *Mothers of the Prophets.* Rev. ed. Salt Lake City: Bookcraft, 2001.

Arrington, Leonard J., and Davis Bitton. *The Mormon Experience: A History of the Latter-day Saints.* New York: Alfred A. Knopf, 1979.

Arrington, Leonard J., Feramorz Y. Fox, and Dean L. May. *Building the City of God: Community and Cooperation among the Mormons.* Salt Lake City: Deseret Book, 1976.

Bagley, Will, ed. *The Pioneer Camp of the Saints: The 1846 and 1847 Mormon Trail Journals of Thomas Bullock.* Spokane, Wash.: The Arthur H. Clark Company, 1997.

Baillie-Grohmann, William Adolf. *Camps in the Rockies; Being a Narrative of Life on the Frontier, and Sport in the Rocky Mountains, With an Account of the Cattle Ranches of the West.* New York: Charles Scribner's Sons, 1902.

Bancroft, Hubert Howe. *History of Utah.* San Francisco: The History Co., 1889.

Barney, Ronald O., ed. *The Mormon Vanguard Brigade of 1847: Norton Jacob's Record.* Logan, Utah: Utah State University Press, 2005.

Bishop, William W., ed. *Mormonism Unveiled: or the Life and Confessions of the Late Mormon Bishop, John D. Lee.* St. Louis: Bryan, Brand & Co., 1877.

Black, Susan Easton, and Larry C. Porter. *Lion of the Lord: Essays on the Life and Service of Brigham Young.* Salt Lake City: Deseret Book, 1995.

Boorstin, Daniel J. *The Image: A Guide to Pseudo Events in America.* New York: Atheneum, 1985.

Bowles, Samuel. *Across the Continent: A Summer's Journey to the Rocky Mountains, the Mormons and the Pacific States, with Speaker Colfax.* Springfield, Mass.: Samuel Bowles & Co.; and New York: Hurd & Houghton, 1866.

———. *Our New West. Records of Travel between the Mississippi River and the Pacific Ocean.* Hartford, Conn.: Hartford Publishing, 1869.

Brown, James S. *Giant of the Lord: A Life of a Pioneer.* Salt Lake City: Bookcraft, 1960.

Bringhurst, Newell G. *Brigham Young and the Expanding American Frontier.* Boston: Little, Brown and Company, 1986.

Brummitt, Stella W. *Brother Van.* New York: Missionary Education Movement of the United States and Canada, ca. 1919.

Burton, Richard F. *The City of the Saints, and Across the Rocky Mountains to California.* New York: Harper and Brothers, 1862.

Chamberlain, Ralph V. *The University of Utah: A History of Its First Hundred Years, 1850 to 1950.* Salt Lake City: University of Utah Press, 1960.

Chandless, William. *A Visit to Salt Lake City; Being a Journey Across the Plains and a Residence in the Mormon Settlements at Utah.* London: Smith, Elder and Co., 1857.

Clark, James R., comp. *Messages of the First Presidency of The Church of Jesus Christ of Latter-day Saints.* 6 vols. Salt Lake City: Bookcraft, 1966.

Cleland, Robert G., and Juanita Brooks, eds. *A Mormon Chronicle: The Diaries of John D. Lee, 1848–1876.* 2 vols. San Marino: Huntington Library, 1955.

*Collected Discourses, Delivered by President Wilford Woodruff, His Two Counselors, the Twelve Apostles, and Others.* Compiled and edited by Brian H. Stuy. 5 vols. Burbank, Calif. and Woodland Hills, Utah: B.H.S. Publishing, 1987–92.

Collier, Fred C. *The Teachings of President Brigham Young, 1852–1854.* Vol. 3. Collier's Publishing, 1987.

*Congressional Globe.* 46 vols. Washington, D.C., 1834–73.

Cooley, Everett L., ed. *Diary of Brigham Young, 1857.* Salt Lake City: Tanner Trust Fund, University of Utah Library, 1980.

Cornwall, Rebecca, and Leonard J. Arrington. *Rescue of the 1856 Handcart Companies.* Charles

Redd Monographs in Western History No. 11. Provo, Utah: Brigham Young University Press, 1981.

Derr, Jill Mulvay, Janath R. Cannon, and Maureen Ursenbach Beecher. *Women of Covenant: The Story of Relief Society.* Salt Lake City: Deseret Book, 1992.

*Encyclopedia of Mormonism.* Daniel H. Ludlow, ed. 4 vols. New York: Macmillan Publishing Company, 1992.

England, Eugene. *Brother Brigham.* Salt Lake City: Bookcraft, 1980.

———. *Why the Church Is as True as the Gospel: Personal Essays on Mormon Experience.* Salt Lake City: Bookcraft, 1986.

Gates, Susa Young, and Leah D. Widtsoe. *The Life Story of Brigham Young.* New York: Macmillan, 1930.

Givens, Terryl L. *People of Paradox: A History of Mormon Culture.* New York: Oxford University Press, 2007.

*Governor's Message to the Legislative Assembly of the Territory of Utah; Delivered in the Capitol, Fillmore City, Millard County, December Tenth [Eleventh] A.D. Eighteen Hundred and Fifty-five.* Fillmore City, Utah: s.n., 1855.

Hafen, Le Roy R., and Ann W. Hafen, eds. *Journals of Forty-Niners: Salt Lake to Los Angeles.* Vol. 2, Far West and the Rockies Series. Glendale, Calif.: Arthur H. Clark, 1954.

———. *The Utah Expedition: A Documentary Account of the United States Military Movement under Colonel Albert Sidney Johnston, and the Resistance by Brigham Young and the Mormon Nauvoo Legion.* Vol. 8, Far West and the Rockies Series. Glendale, California: Arthur H. Clark, 1982.

*Heart Throbs of the West.* Compiled by Kate B. Carter. 12 vols. Salt Lake City: Daughters of the Utah Pioneers, 1939–51.

Hirshon, Stanley P. *The Lion of the Lord: A Biography of Brigham Young.* New York: Alfred A. Knopf, 1969.

*History of the Bench and Bar in Utah.* Salt Lake City: Interstate Press Association Publishers, 1913.

*History of The Church of Jesus Christ of Latter-day Saints.* Introduction and notes by B. H. Roberts. 7 vols. Salt Lake City: Deseret Book, 1976.

Holmes, Oliver Wendell. *The Complete Poetical Works of Oliver Wendell Holmes.* Edited by Horace E. Scudder. Cambridge: The Riverside Press, 1923.

Holzapfel, Richard Neitzel, and R. Q. Shupe. *Brigham Young: Images of a Mormon Prophet.* Salt Lake City: Eagle Gate, 2000.

———. *My Servant Brigham: Portrait of a Prophet.* Salt Lake City: Bookcraft, 1997.

Hulbert, Archer B., ed. *Letters of an Overland Mail Agent in Utah.* Worcester, Mass.: American Antiquarian Society, 1929.

Hyde, John. *Mormonism: Its Leaders and Designs.* New York: W. P. Fetridge & Company, 1857.

Jessee, Dean C., ed. *Letters of Brigham Young to His Sons.* Salt Lake City: Deseret Book, 1974.

———. *Personal Writings of Joseph Smith.* Rev. ed. Salt Lake City: Deseret Book; and Provo: Brigham Young University Press, 2002.

———. *The Papers of Joseph Smith.* Vol. 2. Journal, 1832–1842. Salt Lake City: Deseret Book Company, 1992.

Jones, Daniel W. *Forty Years Among the Indians: A True Yet Thrilling Narrative of the Author's Experiences Among the Natives.* Salt Lake City: Bookcraft, 1960.

*Journal of Discourses.* 26 vols. Liverpool: F. D. and S. W. Richards, 1854–1886. Photo reprint. Salt Lake City: Deseret News Press, 1967.

Kane, Elizabeth Wood. *Twelve Mormon Homes Visited in Succession on Journey through Utah to Arizona.* Philadelphia: William Wood, 1874.

Kelly, Brian, and Petrea Kelly. *Latter-day History of The Church of Jesus Christ of Latter-day Saints.* American Fork, Utah: Covenant Communications, 2000.

Langley, Harold D., ed. *To Utah with the Dragoons and Glimpses of Life in Arizona and California, 1858–1859.* Salt Lake City: University of Utah Press, 1974.

Larson, Andrew Karl. *Erastus Snow: The Life of a Missionary and Pioneer for the Early Mormon Church.* Salt Lake City: University of Utah Press, 1971.

Larson, A. Karl, and Katharine Miles Larson, eds. *Diary of Charles Lowell Walker.* 2 vols. Logan, Utah: Utah State University Press, 1980.

Lasch, Christopher. *The World of Nations: Reflections on American History, Politics, and Culture.* New York: Vintage Books, 1973.

Leslie, Mrs. Frank [Miriam]. *California: A Pleasure Trip from Gotham to the Golden Gate.* New York: G. W. Carleton & Co., 1877.

Ludlow, Hugh Fitz. *The Heart of a Continent: A Record of Travel Across the Plains and in Oregon, with an Examination of the Mormon Principle.* New York: Hurd and Houghton, 1870.

Madsen, Susan Arrington. *The Lord Needed a Prophet.* 2d ed. Salt Lake City: Deseret Book, 1996.

Maeser, Reinhard. *Karl G. Maeser: A Biography.* Provo, Utah: Brigham Young University, 1928.

Morgan, Dale L. *The State of Deseret.* Logan, Utah: Utah State University Press, 1987.

Mulder, William, and A. Russell Mortensen, *Among the Mormons: Historic Accounts By Contemporary Observers.* Lincoln: University of Nebraska Press, 1973.

Murphy, J. Mortimer. *Rambles in North-Western America from the Pacific Ocean to the Rocky Mountains.* London: Chapman and Hall, 1879.

*Names of Persons and Sureties Indebted to the Perpetual Emigrating Fund Company from 1850 to 1877 Inclusive.* Salt Lake City: Star Book and Job Printing Office, 1878. Copy available in Perpetual Emigrating Fund Company, Financial Accounts, 1849–85, LDS Church History Library.

Neff, Andrew L. *History of Utah, 1847–1869.* Edited and annotated by Leland Hargrave Creer. Salt Lake City: Deseret News Press, 1940.

Nibley, Hugh. *Brother Brigham Challenges the Saints.* Edited by Don E. Norton and Shirley S. Ricks. The Collected Works of Hugh Nibley, vol. 13. Salt Lake City: Deseret Book; and Provo, Utah: Foundation for Ancient Research and Mormon Studies, 1994.

———. *Tinkling Cymbals and Sounding Brass: The Art of Telling Stories about Joseph Smith and Brigham Young.* Edited by David J. Whittaker. The Collected Works of Hugh Nibley, vol. 11. Salt Lake City: Deseret Book; and Provo, Utah: Foundation for Ancient Research and Mormon Studies, 1991.

Nibley, Preston. *Brigham Young: The Man and His Work.* Salt Lake City: Deseret Book, 1965.

————. *The Presidents of the Church.* Salt Lake City: Deseret Book, 1974.

*Our Pioneer Heritage.* Compiled by Kate B. Carter. 20 vols. Salt Lake City: Daughters of Utah Pioneers, 1958–77.

Owens, Kenneth N. *Gold Rush Saints: California Mormons and the Great Rush for Riches.* Spokane, Wash.: The Arthur H. Clark Company, 2004.

Palmer, Richard F., and Karl D. Butler. *Brigham Young: The New York Years.* Charles Redd Monographs in Western History No. 14. Provo, Utah: Brigham Young University Press, 1982.

Penrose, Charles W. *The Mountain Meadows Massacre: Who Were Guilty of the Crime, An Address by Elder Charles W. Penrose, October 26, 1884. Also a supplement containing important additional testimony subsequently received.* Salt Lake City: Geo. Q. Cannon & Sons Co., 1899.

Petersen, Charles S. *Take Up Your Mission: Mormon Colonizing Along the Little Colorado River, 1870–1900.* Provo, Utah: Brigham Young University Press, 1973.

Peterson, Paul H. *The Mormon Reformation.* Salt Lake City: Joseph Fielding Smith Institute for Latter-day Saint History, 1992.

Poll, Richard D., Thomas G. Alexander, Eugene E. Campbell, and David E. Miller. *Utah's History.* Provo, Utah: Brigham Young University Press, 1978.

Reed, Thomas Brackett, Rossiter Johnson, Justin McCarthy, and Albert Bergh. *Modern Eloquence.* 15 vols. Philadelphia: J. D. Morris, 1900–1903.

Remy, Jules. *A Journey to Great Salt Lake City With a Sketch of the History, Religion, and Customs of the Mormons.* 2 vols. London: W. Jeffs, 1861.

Richardson, Albert D. *Beyond the Mississippi: From the Great River to the Great Ocean.* Hartford, Conn.: American Publishing, 1867.

Roberts, B. H. *A Comprehensive History of The Church of Jesus Christ of Latter-day Saints.* 6 vols. Provo, Utah: Brigham Young University Press, 1965.

Rubin, Gretchen. *40 Ways to Look at Winston Churchill: A Brief Account of a Long Life.* New York: Random House Publishing Group, 2004.

Seward, Olive Risely, ed. *William H. Seward's Travels Around the World.* New York: D. Appleton and Co., 1873.

Slaughter, William W., and Michael Landon. *Trail of Hope: The Story of the Mormon Trail.* Salt Lake City: Shadow Mountain, 1997.

Smart, Donna T., ed. *Mormon Midwife: The 1846–1888 Diaries of Patty Bartlett Sessions.* Logan, Utah: Utah State University Press, 1997.

Smith, George D., ed. *An Intimate Chronicle: The Journals of William Clayton.* Salt Lake City: Signature Books, 1991.

Smith, Joseph. *Teachings of the Prophet Joseph Smith.* Compiled by Joseph Fielding Smith. Salt Lake City: Deseret Book, 1976.

Spencer, Clarissa Young, with Mable Harmer. *Brigham Young at Home.* Salt Lake City: Deseret Book, 1963.

Stansbury, Howard. *Exploration and Survey of the Valley of the Great Salt Lake of Utah, Including a Reconnoissance [sic] of a New Route Through the Rocky Mountains.* Philadelphia: Lippincott, Grambo & Co., 1852.

Stenhouse, T. B. H. *The Rocky Mountain Saints: A Full and Complete History of the Mormons.* New York: D. Appleton and Company, 1873.

Thoreau, Henry David. *Walden.* As included in Brooks Atkinson, ed., *Walden and Other Writings of Henry David Thoreau.* Modern Library Edition. New York: Random House, 1937.

Todd, John. *The Sunset Land; or, The Great Pacific Slope.* Boston: Lee and Shepard, 1870.

Tullidge, Edward W. *Life of Brigham Young; or Utah and Her Founders.* New York: n.p., 1876.

Tuttle, Daniel S. *Reminiscences of a Missionary Bishop.* New York: Thomas Whittaker, 2 and 3 Bible House, 1906.

Twain, Mark. *Roughing It.* Hartford, Conn.: American Publishing, 1872.

*The Utah Pioneers, Celebration of the Entrance of the Pioneers into Great Salt Lake Valley, Thirty-Third Anniversary, July 24, 1880, Full Account of the Proceedings.* Salt Lake City: Deseret News, 1880.

Walker, Ronald W., and Doris R. Dant. *Nearly Everything Imaginable: The Everyday Life of Utah's Mormon Pioneers.* Provo, Utah: Brigham Young University Press, 1999.

Ward, Geoffrey C. *The West: An Illustrated History.* New York: Little, Brown and Company, 1996.

Watson, Elden J., ed. *Manuscript History of Brigham Young 1801–1844.* Salt Lake City: Elden J. Watson, 1967.

———. *Manuscript History of Brigham Young 1846–1847.* Salt Lake City: Elden J. Watson, 1971.

Werner, M. R. *Brigham Young.* New York: Harcourt, Brace and Co., 1925.

West, Emerson Roy. *Profiles of the Presidents.* Salt Lake City: Deseret Book, 1974.

Whitney, Orson F. *History of Utah.* 4 vols. Salt Lake City: George Q. Cannon & Sons Co., 1892–1904.

———. *The Life of Heber C. Kimball.* Salt Lake City: Bookcraft, 1992.

Whitley, Colleen, ed. *Brigham Young's Homes.* Logan, Utah: Utah State University Press, 2002.

Widtsoe, John A., ed. *Discourses of Brigham Young.* Salt Lake City: Deseret Book, 1925.

Young, Ann Eliza. *Wife Number 19; or, The Story of a Life in Bondage, Being a Complete Exposé of Mormonism, and Revealing the Sorrows, Sacrifices and Sufferings of Women in Polygamy.* Hartford, Conn.: Dustin, Gillman, 1876.

Young, John R. *Memoirs of John R. Young, Utah Pioneer 1847, Written by Himself.* Salt Lake City: Deseret News Press, 1920.

## ARTICLES AND ADDRESSES

Anderson, Paul L. "St. George Tabernacle." *Pioneer* 53:4 (2006): 25–27.

Arrington, Leonard J. "The Six Pillars of Utah's Pioneer Economy." *Encyclia: Journal of the Utah Academy of Sciences, Arts, and Letters* 54 (Part 1, 1977): 9–24.

Arrington, Leonard J., and Ronald K. Esplin. "Building a Commonwealth: The Secular Leadership of Brigham Young." *Utah Historical Quarterly* 45 (Summer 1977): 216–32.

Bitton, Davis. "Those Licentious Days: Dancing among the Mormons," *Sunstone* 2 (Spring 1977): 16–27.

Esplin, Ronald K. "Fire in His Bones." *Ensign* (March 1993): 44–48.

Hartley, William G. "The Priesthood Reorganization of 1877: Brigham Young's Last Achievement." *BYU Studies* 20 (Fall 1979): 3–36.

Hill, Hamilton A. "A Sunday in Great Salt Lake City." *Penn Monthly* 2 (March 1871): 129–40.

Irving, Gordon. "Encouraging the Saints: Brigham Young's Annual Tours of Mormon Settlements." *Utah Historical Quarterly* 45 (Summer 1977): 233–51.

———. "The Law of Adoption: One Phase of the Development of the Mormon Concept of Salvation, 1830–1900." *BYU Studies* 14 (Spring 1974): 291–314.

Jessee, Dean C. "'A Man of God and a Good Kind Father': Brigham Young at Home." *BYU Studies* 40:2 (2001): 23–53.

———. "The Writings of Brigham Young." *The Western Historical Quarterly* 4 (July 1973): 273–94.

Johnson, Jeffery Ogden. "Determining and Defining 'Wife': The Brigham Young Households." *Dialogue: A Journal of Mormon Thought* 20:3 (Fall 1987): 57–70.

Kennedy, John F. Yale University commencement address, June 11, 1962. American Presidency Project Website.

Marshall, Charles. "Salt Lake City and the Valley Settlements." *Fraser's Magazine* (July 1871): 97–108.

Munro, Wilfred H. "Among the Mormons in the Days of Brigham Young," *Proceedings of the American Antiquarian Society* 36 (October 1926): 214–30.

Rogers, Kristen. "Steward of the Earth," *This People* (Spring 1990): 11–15.

Taylor, Philip A. M. "Early Mormon Loyalty and the Leadership of Brigham Young." *Utah Historical Quarterly* 30 (1962): 102–32.

Thatcher, Moses. "Life and Character of Brigham Young." *Contributor* 10 (June 1889): 330–37.

Walker, Ronald W. "Brigham Young on the Social Order." *BYU Studies* 28 (Summer 1988): 37–52.

———. "Brigham Young: Student of the Prophet." *Ensign* (February 1998): 50–57.

———. "It Never Was a Sacrifice." *Ensign* (January 1999): 51–57.

———. "Raining Pitchforks: Brigham Young as Preacher." *Sunstone* 8 (May–June 1983): 4–9.

Walker, Ronald W., and Ronald K. Esplin. "Brigham Himself: An Autobiographical Recollection." *Journal of Mormon History* 4 (1977): 19–34.

Woods, Fred E. "'Surely This City is Bound to Shine': Descriptions of Salt Lake City by Western-Bound Emigrants, 1849–1868." *Utah Historical Quarterly* 74 (Fall 2006): 334–48.

## NEWSPAPERS AND PERIODICALS

*Crescent City (CA) Oracle*
*Deseret News* (Salt Lake City)
*Deseret News Weekly* (Salt Lake City)

*Deseret Weekly* (Salt Lake City)
*Kanesville (IA) Frontier Guardian*
*Gleason's Pictorial Drawing Room Companion*
*Los Angeles Star*
*Millennial Star* (Manchester and London, England)
*Nevada Tribune* (Carson City)
*New York Herald*
*Ogden (UT) Junction*
*Salt Lake Tribune*
*San Joaquin Republican* (Stockton, California)
*Sangamo Journal* (Springfield, Illinois)
*Times and Seasons* (Nauvoo, Illinois)

## UNPUBLISHED MANUSCRIPTS AND ARCHIVAL RECORDS

Allen, Andrew Jackson. Reminiscences and Journal, 1857–84. LDS Church History Library.

Bullock, Thomas. Journals, 1843–49. LDS Church History Library.

Carter, Charles W. "Journal Record of Photographs Taken." LDS Church History Library.

Committee on Indian Affairs. Claims (HR 36A-D11.1). Records of the House of Representatives (RG233). National Archives.

Coombs, Isaiah. Collection, 1835–1938. LDS Church History Library.

Critchlow, Benjamin Chamberlain. Reminiscences. Carbon copy of typescript. LDS Church History Library.

Earl, Sylvester Henry. Autobiographical Sketch, 1854. Typescript. LDS Church History Library.

General Church Minutes. LDS Church History Library.

Historian's Office. Journal, 1844–97. LDS Church History Library.

Journal History of The Church of Jesus Christ of Latter-day Saints. LDS Church History Library.

Kimball, Heber C. Journal and Record. Heber C. Kimball Papers. LDS Church History Library.

Lee, John D. Collection. Huntington Library, San Marino, California.

Manuscript History of The Church of Jesus Christ of Latter-day Saints. LDS Church History Library.

Marston, Otis. Collection. Huntington Library. San Marino, California.

Martineau, James H. Journal. Copy in possession of authors.

Paul, Earl Stanley. "The Handcart Companies of 1856 and Azra Erastus Hinckley." LDS Church History Library.

Pay, Mary Goble. Autobiographical Sketch. Typescript. LDS Church History Library.

Richards, Samuel W. Journals, 1839–1909. LDS Church History Library.

Richards, Willard. Journals, 1836–53. LDS Church History Library.

Salt Lake Stake. High Council Record, 1869–72. LDS Church History Library.

Smith, Joseph. Collection, 1827–44. LDS Church History Library.

Smith, Lucy Meserve. Autobiographical Sketch, 1888–1890, typescript. LDS Church History Library.

Thatcher, Luna Young. Collection. LDS Church Archives.

Tolman, Benjamin H. Journals, 1876–94 and 1910–13. LDS Church History Library.

Utah Stake. Historical Record. LDS Church Archives.

Woodruff, Wilford. Journals and Papers, 1828–98. LDS Church History Library.

Young, Brigham. Office Files, 1832–78. LDS Church History Library.

Young, Brigham, to Edmund Ellsworth, September 29–30, 1855. LDS Church History Library.

Young, Brigham, Letters to Vilate Young [Decker], LDS Church History Library.

Young, Brigham, to Mary Ann Young, October 16, 1840, Luna Young Thatcher Collection, LDS Church History Library.

Young, Seymour B. Diary. Utah State Historical Society.

## UNPUBLISHED THESES AND PAPERS

Curtis, Kirk Moffitt. "History of the St. George Temple." Master's thesis, Brigham Young University, 1964.

Johnson, Jeffery Ogden. "Was Being a Probate Judge in Pioneer Utah a Church Calling?" Unpublished paper in possession of authors.

Monson, Samuel C. "The Deseret Alphabet." Master's thesis, Columbia University, 1948.

# Photo and Illustration Credits

Page 7: George Edward Anderson, Church History Library.

Page 12: Lithograph, Library of Congress.

Page 60: W. H. Gibbs steel engraving, Church History Library.

Page 67: T. B. H. Stenhouse, *The Rocky Mountain Saints: A Full and Complete History of the Mormons.* New York: D. Appleton and Company, 1873, 647.

Page 75: Charles B. Hall engraving, Church History Library.

Page 82: Howard Stansbury, *An Expedition to the Valley of the Great Salt Lake.* Philadelphia: Lippincott, Grambo, and Co., 1855, 84.

Page 89: Charles W. Carter, Church History Library.

Page 96: William Hepworth Dixon, *New America.* Jena (Germany): Hermann Costenoble, 1868, 102.

Page 103: Vilhelm Topsoe, *Fra Amerika.* Kjbenhavn: Gyldendalske Boghandel, F. Hegel, 1872, 364.

Page 118: Charles W. Carter, Church History Library.

Page 130: William W. Major, Museum of Church History and Art.

*Photo section following page 130:*

    Photo 1: Lucian R. Foster, copy of daguerreotype, Church History Library.

    Photo 2: Marsena Cannon, daguerreotype, Church History Library.

    Photo 3: Marsena Cannon, daguerreotype, Church History Library.

    Photo 4: Marsena Cannon, daguerreotype, Church History Library.

    Photo 5: Marsena Cannon, copy print of daguerreotype, Church History Library.

Photo 6: Ambrotype, Church History Library.

Photo 7: Copy of daguerreotype, Church History Library.

Photo 8: Charles R. Savage, copy print, Church History Library.

Photo 9: Charles R. Savage, print, Church History Library.

Photo 10: Charles R. Savage, carte de visite, Church History Library.

Photo 11: Charles R. Savage, carte de visite, Church History Library.

Photo 12: Photographer unknown, tintype, Church History Library.

Photo 13: Charles R. Savage, carte de visite, Church History Library.

Photo 14: Charles W. Carter, print from glass negative, Church History Library.

Photo 15: Edward Martin, carte de visite, Church History Library.

Photo 16: Charles R. Savage, copy print, Church History Library.

Photo 17: Charles R. Savage (dba Savage and Ottinger), carte de visite, Church History Library.

Photo 18: Charles R. Savage (dba Savage and Ottinger), albumen print, Church History Library.

Photo 19: Detail of photograph #18.

Photo 20: Charles R. Savage, carte de visite, Church History Library.

Photo 21: Charles R. Savage, from stereo view, Church History Library.

Photo 22: Charles R. Savage, from stereo view, Church History Library.

Photo 23: Illustration from *Illustrated Times*, October 28, 1871.

Photo 24: Charles W. Carter, Church History Library.

Photo 25: Charles R. Savage, Church History Library.

Photo 26: Charles R. Savage, Church History Library.

Photo 27: Charles R. Savage, from stereo view, Church History Library.

Photo 28: Photographer unknown, Church History Library.

Photo 29: Johnson Photography Studio, Church History Library.

Page 143: T. B. H. Stenhouse, *The Rocky Mountain Saints*. New York: D. Appleton and Company, 1873, 351.

Page 179: Ann Eliza Young, *Wife no. 19, or the story of a life in bondage, being a complete exposé of Mormonism*. Hartford, Conn.: Dustin, Gilman, & Co., 1876.

Page 186: Charles R. Savage, Church History Library.

Page 208: Andrew J. Russell, Church History Library.

Page 222: *Harper's Weekly*, September 3, 1859, 561.

Page 254: Church History Library.

Page 267: Engraving by R. Dudensing based on Charles R. Savage photograph, Church History Library.

# INDEX

# ABOUT THE AUTHORS

Chad M. Orton was born in Seattle, Washington, and raised in Provo, Utah. He holds a bachelor's degree and a master's degree in history from Brigham Young University. He is employed as an archivist in the Historical Department of The Church of Jesus Christ of Latter-day Saints. His previous publications include *Joseph Smith's America* and *More Faith Than Fear: The Los Angeles Stake Story*; and articles in the *Ensign, BYU Studies,* and *Pioneer.* He is married to the former Elizabeth Sainsbury and they are the parents of seven children. They reside in Provo, Utah.

William W. Slaughter received a bachelor's degree in political science and a master's degree in library science from Brigham Young University. He is a photo historian and senior reference specialist for the Historical Department of The Church of Jesus Christ of Latter-day Saints. His previous publications include *Joseph Smith's America: His Life and Times; Trail of Hope: The Story of the Mormon Trail; Life in Zion: An Intimate Look at the Latter-day Saints, 1820–1995; Camping Out in the Yellowstone, 1882; Church History Time Line;* and articles in *Pioneer, Sports Guide,* and *Utah Holiday.* He and his wife, Sheri, have two children and reside in Salt Lake City, Utah